HISTORICAL PERSPECTIVES ON BUSINESS ENTERPRISE

Mansel G. Blackford and K. Austin Kerr, Series Editors

Kotex, Kleenex, Huggies

KIMBERLY-CLARK AND THE CONSUMER
REVOLUTION IN AMERICAN BUSINESS

Thomas Heinrich   *Bob Batchelor*

THE OHIO STATE UNIVERSITY PRESS • Columbus

Library of Congress Cataloging-in-Publication Data

Heinrich, Thomas, 1963–
Kotex, Kleenex, Huggies : Kimberly-Clark and the consumer revolution in American business / Thomas Heinrich and Bob Batchelor.
p. cm.—(Historical perspectives on business enterprise series)
Includes bibliographical references and index.
ISBN 0–8142–0976–9 (cloth : alk. paper)—ISBN 0–8142–9053–1 (cd) 1. Kimberly-Clark Corporation—History. 2. Sanitary supply industry—United States—History. 3. Consumer behavior—United States—Case studies. I. Batchelor, Bob. II. Title. III. Series.
HD9995.S24K564 2004
338.7'677—dc22
2004013886

Cover design by Janna Thompson-Chordas.
Text design by Jennifer Forsythe.
Type set in Sabon.
Printed by Thomson-Shore, Inc.

The paper used in this publication meets the minimum requirements of the American National Standard for Information Sciences—Permanence of Paper for Printed Library Materials. ANSI Z39.48-1992.

9 8 7 6 5 4 3 2 1

Contents

List of Figures

List of Tables

Acknowledgments

F IELD RESEARCH for this book started on a winter morning in February 1996 when Thomas Heinrich, kindly instructed by Nurse Beth, tried to put a diaper (newborn size) on his son Fritz at George Washington University Hospital in Washington, DC. Meanwhile, by happenstance, Bob Batchelor was busy at The History Factory in Chantilly, Virginia, researching and writing the history of Kimberly-Clark, one of the world's largest makers of disposable diapers and other hygiene products.

Bob's earlier research had taken him to the original K-C archives in Neenah, Wisconsin, and a dingy warehouse outside Philadelphia, after the discovery of the presumably "lost" Scott Paper archives. Holding one of the first Kleenex boxes and seeing early prototypes of various products that have now become everyday household items, Bob realized how such items had launched consumer culture's tight hold over the nation. Sometimes the products were stumbled upon accidentally—like Kleenex and Scott Towels—but an individual or group always seized upon the development, marketing, and advertising efforts that made them successful. In this respect, Kimberly-Clark has been a pioneer and created the path other companies would follow.

Several years later, Thomas and Bob approached Kimberly-Clark, which had commissioned Bob's above-referenced study and writing of their history, with a proposal to write an independent scholarly study of K-C's corporate structure, research and development initiatives, and marketing strategy. Continuing the company's longstanding commitment to learning more about its own history, senior vice president Tina Barry kindly agreed to grant Thomas and Bob access to Kimberly-Clark's magnificent corporate archives. The authors would like to express their sincere appreciation to her, Dave Dixon, and many other Kimberly-Clark managers and employees.

The Kimberly-Clark Archives, ably catalogued and maintained by The History Factory's archival team, is one of the world's largest and most complete collections of a major consumer company's manuscripts, photographs, and material artifacts. Archivists Alexandra Briseno, Cheryl Chouiniere, Suzanne Gould, and Jacqueline Reid provided invaluable research support, patiently processing many requests for material and bringing to attention unique nuggets of information that the authors would have otherwise missed. Bruce Weindruch, the founder and CEO of The History Factory, provided critical guidance and support. His work toward preserving America's corporate heritage has been visionary.

The authors would like to express their sincere appreciation to Harry Finley, whose online "Museum of Menstruation and Women's Health" (www.mum.org) is a treasure trove of information.

Bob and Thomas had the great fortune to work with two of the nation's finest business historians, Mansel G. Blackford and K. Austin Kerr, the editors of the Historical Perspectives on Business Enterprise Series of The Ohio State University Press. The manuscript also benefited from the guidance of Malcolm Litchfield, Director of The Ohio State University Press. Last but not least, the authors would like to thank Maggie Diehl, the superb editor who put the baby to bed safely.

Any mistakes or omissions are, of course, the authors.

✦ ✦ ✦

I have profited from the scholarly advice of my friends and colleagues at Baruch College, especially Jed Abrahamian, Carol Berkin, Stanley Buder, Myrna Chase, T. J. Desch-Obi, Vince Digirolamo, Bert Hansen, Veena Oldenburg, Kathy Pence, Alfonso Quiroz, Murray Rubenstein, Tansen Sen, and Randy Trumbach. Jessica Gonzales, the very best clerical administrator anyone could wish for, did more than she will ever know to keep things on an even keel. Cynthia Whittaker deserves special thanks for her steadfast support, enthusiasm, and unwavering friendship and for gently nudging the project along. Robert Friedman's generosity, which enabled Baruch's Department of

History to establish the Friedman Chair of American History and many other invaluable programs, was crucial during the project's final stages. Early manuscript drafts were ably reviewed and critiqued by Zeb Clark, Iva Morton, and many other students in the course "History of American Business Enterprise." Special thanks go to those who apprenticed me to the historian's craft, especially Mary Frances Berry, Rudolf Boch, Thomas Childers, Holger Dähne, Mike Frisch, Mike Katz, Jürgen Kocka, Reinhardt Koselleck, Walter Licht, Philip Scranton, and Hans-Ulrich Wehler.

Many thanks to my family and friends, especially Siglinde, Gottfried Christel, Irene, Michael, Ulli, Anne, Jonas, Moritz, Lara, and Nora Heinrich; Marianne, Herrman, Heike, and Maren Toewe; Frano, Nevenka, Philip, Genevieve, Mary, and Sue Rados; John and Rose Petrinec; Annie and Wade Baker; Rose Beiler; John and Laurel Delaney; Stefanie Haake; Eva and Sven Heitsch; Markus Mohr; George and Martine Ives; Marc and Caroline Jehan; Jeff-Kerr Ritchie; Johnny, Gigi, Leyla, and Sabine McCalla; Donna Rilling; Duane and Karen Schrempp; and Cornelia Vismann.

Lorie has always been there with her love, laughter, and understanding. Luka, who is the kindest and wittiest son a father could wish for, never ceases to make his Papa proud. Fritz survived the field research all in one piece and has become a great student and athlete. Little Felix makes the world a better place with his beautiful smile.

Thomas Heinrich
New York City, 2004

✦ ✦ ✦

Working with Thomas on this book has been a great experience. He is a superb collaborator and, over the years, has been a true friend and inspiration. Our shared passion for business and labor history runs through this study of Kimberly-Clark.

Foremost, I would like to thank my parents Linda and Jon Bowen and my brother, Bill Coyle, for their support and encouragement. Without their love, this book would not have been possible. Special thanks also go to Peggy, Tom, and Megan Wilbert. My grandmother, Annabell Bergbigler, has always been an inspiration. I would also like to thank my in-laws, Jerry and Nancy Roda, David and Ann Roda, and John Roda. In addition, thanks go to Barb Woody and Jim and Annie Balzer. They have all been supportive and kind over the years.

I am constantly inspired by a group of historians who taught me how to think: Sidney R. Snyder, James A. Kehl, Richard H. Immerman, and Lawrence S. Kaplan. Their work has shown me what it means to be a scholar and a writer. A special note of thanks goes to my agent, Erin Reel, who is a wonderful friend.

I would also like to acknowledge my friends Chuck Waldron and Anne Beirne; Chris and Chrissy Burtch and the girls; Kevin and Liz Mershimer and family; Jason and Emily Pettigrew; Maria Thomas; Gene and Tina Roach; Jack and Sue Burtch; Bob Osmond and Marina Ecklund and family; Dennis and Susan Jarecke and family; Mike Menser and family; Jane and Tim Goodman and family; Peter Magnani and family; Pam Boughton; Rodd Aubrey; Jessica and Jason Schroeder and family; Leslie McCray and family; and all my friends at Readerville. These people have given more than they know.

My deepest gratitude goes to my wife Katherine. She endured the long research trips away and endless hours of writing when the original manuscript was produced, and she has remained a constant source of inspiration. Words can't fully describe my appreciation for her love and support. She makes me a better person.

Bob Batchelor
San Francisco, 2004

Introduction

THE HISTORY OF Kimberly-Clark is one of the most intriguing chapters in the annals of the paper and consumer products industries. During the interwar decades the company accomplished a coveted but rare feat in marketing by making its trademarked brand names synonymous with household items in the minds of consumers. Needing to wipe or blow one's nose, one could ask for a Kleenex and safely expect to be handed a disposable handkerchief. At drugstores, customers could ask for Kotex and receive a box of sanitary napkins. Kimberly-Clark shared the distinction of introducing new words into consumer vocabulary with companies like Johnson & Johnson, whose brand name Band-Aid relegated the term "adhesive bandage" to relative obscurity, as well as Dow Chemical (Styrofoam), Room & Haas (Plexiglas), and U.S. Gypsum (Sheetrock). Bayer Corporation had paved the way in the late nineteenth century when it invented the word "Aspirin" to market an acetylsalicylic acid–based painkiller.

While Kleenex, Band-Aid, and Plexiglas were semantic inventions whose widespread use simply gave clever marketers a competitive advantage in consumer markets, Kotex served more subtle functions. Menstruation and menstrual hygiene were ill-understood phenomena that received little attention from the medical profession until the turn of the century, when the terms started to appear in a few medical journals and books. During subsequent decades menstruation remained burdened with cultural taboos that left millions of women

1

who wanted to purchase feminine hygiene products grappling for words because they often felt self-conscious vis-à-vis the overwhelmingly male sales force who staffed most interwar drugstores. Most found even the technical and somewhat antiseptic term "sanitary napkin" too embarrassing to utter in public. Kimberly-Clark, which started to market sanitary napkins in 1919, provided a remedy with the artificial word Kotex (a combination of "cotton" and "texture") and inserted it into the consumer lexicon with a multimillion-dollar advertising campaign. To make the product available to the woman who was loathe to ask a clerk at a drugstore counter to hand her a box of Kotex from the shelf behind him, Kimberly-Clark encouraged merchants to display the product on countertops, enabling the customer to take a box and pay for it with minimal communicative action. Thus Kotex became one of the first self-service items in the history of American retailing.

Little in its Victorian background suggested that Kimberly-Clark would launch something of a consumer culture revolution. Founded in 1872 in Neenah, Wisconsin, as Kimberly, Clark and Co., it manufactured a wide range of paper products from newsprint and wrapping paper to book and magazine grades. By the turn of the century conventional but reliable investment strategies had turned Kimberly-Clark into the largest midwestern paper company. Shortly before World War I, it gained a competitive advantage by creating R&D and marketing capabilities for its magazine paper business, laying the groundwork for the success of its consumer nondurables in the interwar years. In World War I it developed a side business in surgical wound dressings for hospitals, the Army, and the Red Cross, but the market collapsed after the Armistice in November 1918. A large inventory—perhaps the only factor that could persuade businessmen of that era to even think about menstrual hygiene—precipitated the search for alternative uses of the cellulose product that led to the introduction of Kotex. Together with the less controversial Kleenex paper tissue, Kotex underwrote much of the company's financial success during the interwar years, especially during the Depression when many competitors struggled to stay afloat.

This book, the first scholarly study of the company, examines Kimberly-Clark's corporate history in the context of the paper and consumer industries and in the wider framework of U.S. economic history. The firm's attempts to establish and maintain strongholds in consumer nondurables—the defining theme of this book—were hardly unique. Major U.S. pulp and paper firms frequently searched for alternatives to newsprint, the industry's bread-and-butter product whose demand structure was highly cyclical, yielding increasingly mediocre returns after the turn of the century. Papermakers' numerous attempts to develop cellulose-based consumer nondurables, from paper dresses and shoes to the more successful paper cup, highlighted the inability of newsprint markets to sustain reliable long-term growth. Some firms became successful niche market specialists for bond and artist papers. Others lowered their exposure to newsprint through heavy investments into kraft grades for linerboard cartons, liquid packaging containers, and wrapping papers, with varying degrees of success. Many firms found it difficult to decipher secular trends in markets for consumer nondurables. International Paper, for example, invested heavily into kraft production capacities in the 1920s, only to watch demand stagnate toward the end of the decade. Brown Paper mill, St. Regis Paper, and other kraft producers barely survived the Great Depression of the 1930s. Viewed in this context, Kimberly-Clark's attempt to develop hygiene products in the 1920s ranks among the more successful diversification strategies in the pulp and paper industry, not least because it enabled the company to weather the Depression virtually without negative earnings.[1]

From the late 1940s to the 1970s the major challenge facing Kimberly-Clark was how to maintain its competitive advantage. During this period the company invested $400 million into plants, equipment, and other programs. The firm's financial performance left much to be desired, however. Sales continued to grow rapidly, but profitability declined. Kimberly-Clark was particularly affected by the swift rise of resourceful competitors in sanitary napkins and facial hygiene, where the market shares of Kotex and Kleenex declined precipitously. Kimberly-Clark's attempts to break into the tampon market were derailed by inept R&D and had to be abandoned at a major loss. Its traditional stronghold in printing papers, which had been a reliable source of growth in past decades, deteriorated in the 1960s as a result of ill-advised capital investment programs. Ending more than half a century of leadership in magazine papers, Kimberly-Clark abandoned the product in the 1970s to concentrate on rebuilding its consumer nondurables business.

If the Taurus was the car that saved Ford,[2] Huggies were the diapers that rescued Kimberly-Clark. Like the Taurus, Huggies were the result of a years-long product design, engineering, and marketing effort that incorporated the painful lessons of past failures. Introduced in a clever marketing campaign, the diaper featured refastenable tape and an hourglass shape designed to reduce leaks. As a result, Kimberly-Clark was able to wrest market leadership in disposable diapers from Procter & Gamble, which had created and dominated the market since the 1960s.

Our study both profits from and contributes to a range of scholarly debates. It explores the historical dimensions of product diversification, an issue that has received attention in recent studies of corporate strategy. Students of the subject agree that successful diversifiers link new products to extant capabilities in R&D and marketing and avoid product lines that require major new investments in these areas. The history of Kimberly-Clark confirms this analysis. Largely as a result of attempts to develop specialty magazine paper after the turn of the century, the company's basic R&D capabilities were already in place by World War I. This enabled Kimberly-Clark to launch the research effort that culminated in the introduction of Kotex in 1919. Although the firm lacked extensive marketing experience, it was more sensitive to the need to advertise consumer nondurables than most competitors, motivating it to recruit experienced vendors to handle advertising.[3]

Our account of Kimberly-Clark's more recent history contributes to the literature on the transformation of American manufacturing in the postwar decades. As early as the 1970s economists identified overdiversification as a chief villain in the story of American industrial decline, launching penetrating and often harsh critiques of postwar corporate strategy in the literature. Only painful "strategic refocusing," accelerated by corporate raiders and leveraged buyouts that left companies' unwise acquisitions of the 1960s as economic roadkill, presumably turned the tide in the 1980s. Within limits, this approach helps explain the emergence and resolution of the structural crisis that bedeviled Kimberly-Clark in the 1960s.

However, the structural crisis of American business and its resolution cannot be fully understood without a detailed analysis of product R&D and organizational capabilities. In more ways than one, the crisis was attributable to factors that had contributed to the Depression forty years earlier. "Low-tech industries" like food and tobacco with limited or nonexistent R&D capacities had largely exhausted their potential for product innovation, precipitating conglomeration as firms sought more profitable markets through acquisitions-based product diversification. By contrast, chemicals, microelectronics, and other advanced industries had not reached technological maturity, enabling many firms to maintain their economic viability by flexing their R&D muscle in the 1970s and 1980s. In "stable-tech industries," opportunities for incremental product innovation did exist, but many established firms failed to invest into the prerequisite R&D programs, contributing to the decline of the American automobile and consumer electronics industries.[4]

Our study confirms the significance of incremental product innovation in stable-tech industries during the 1970s and 1980s. Most consumer hygiene products—sanitary napkins, tampons, and disposable diapers—had been developed decades earlier, rendering market leaders like Kimberly-Clark vulnerable to price competition. Parallel efforts to improve the firm's performance through product development initially yielded disappointing results, as evidenced by the failed tampon development initiatives of the 1960s. The multimillion dollar Huggies R&D program—launched as a last-ditch effort to maintain the company's viability as a major contender in consumer hygiene products—succeeded as a result of incremental but crucial product design changes. Combined with effective consumer research and shrewd marketing, the Huggies program raised profitability to levels the company had last enjoyed in the 1920s.

Origins and Growth, 1872–1916

KIMBERLY, CLARK AND COMPANY was founded on March 26, 1872, by five Wisconsin businessmen who pooled $30,000 to build a paper mill in Neenah, a small city in the eastern part of the state. Like many other newcomers to the Gilded Age paper industry, the founders had general business experience but—unlike earlier generations of entrepreneurs—were not "practical papermakers," the nineteenth-century term for craftsmen whose knowledge of papermaking technologies and business practices was the result of lifelong trade experiences. Charles Clark, the driving force behind the establishment of the company, was part owner of a local hardware store. John A. Kimberly, scion of one of the area's most prominent families, owned a general store and operated Neenah's largest flour mill in partnership with his father. Havilah Babcock, another co-founder of the paper company, was Kimberly's business associate in both the store and the flour mill. Frank Shattuck was a salesman, as was George Whiting.[1]

Their lack of industry-specific experience notwithstanding, the founders were well aware that papermaking presented major business opportunities. Locally, Myron Haynes, a pioneer of Wisconsin papermaking, ran a mill founded in 1864. His success demonstrated that the area's natural resources, notably the Fox River, provided a hospitable environment for the industry. According to company lore, Clark decided to build a paper mill after listening to Haynes boasting about his profits. Moreover, demand for printing papers rose markedly in the course of the Gilded Age when literacy improvements turned publishing into a major business. In the Midwest the swift rise of new population centers, especially Chicago, Detroit, and Milwaukee with their sizable publishing industries, created new markets for newsprint, magazine grades, and book paper that buttressed Kimberly-Clark's growth in the late nineteenth century. The pulp and paper industry also profited from major technological innovations, including the introduction of wood-based newsprint grades and manila wrapping papers, which attracted scores of newcomers to papermaking in northeastern industry centers well as the Old Northwest, with its considerable timber resources. The 1870s and 1880s marked the formation of major new paper companies that turned pulp and paper into a major American industry.

After outlining the structures and dynamics of the late-nineteenth-century pulp and paper industry that facilitated Kimberly-Clark's rise to prominence, the present chapter examines the firm's founding, its mills, and its product strategies. From 1872 to the turn of the century Kimberly-Clark grew from a one-mill newsprint operation into one of the industry's major players, operating nine mills that produced a wide range of grades. Commitment to product development and technological innovation was one of the firm's core strengths. While its early product mix of newsprint, magazine paper, and book grades was fairly conventional, the founders encouraged experiments with new production methods, pulps, and marketing strategies that enabled the company to expand into new markets. Its early ventures into product development set important trends for the interwar period, when Kimberly-Clark developed innovative consumer nondurables that were marketed in one of the most unusual sales campaigns in the history of the American paper industry.

I.

Post–Civil War papermaking was an industry in flux. The most important changes resulted from the introduction of groundwood pulp, which fundamentally altered the business structure and industrial geography of American papermaking. Traditionally dependent on rags as the principal source of pulp, the industry clustered near East Coast urban centers where the raw material was either collected from city dwellers by rag merchants or imported. In the last antebellum decade rapidly increasing rag prices emerged as a serious problem, limiting papermakers' ability to expand production to meet the growing demands of the publishing industry. Papermakers and inventors spent considerable energies and resources to develop alternative fiber sources, including hemp, straw, jute, and wood. Wood was widely seen as the most promising, partly because timber was more readily available than hemp or jute. Inventors, however, found it difficult to develop reliable grinding mechanisms that reduced logs to fibers suitable for paper production. Major technological breakthroughs were made during the 1840s in Germany, where Heinrich Völter—working from a design conceived by Friedrich Keller—developed a wood grinder that produced finely ground chips suitable for low-quality pulp that was turned into newsprint. The first American groundwood pulp was made in 1867 in Curtisville, Massachusetts, in a Völter grinder imported by Alberto Pagenstecher and other investors.[2]

Over the next two decades, a new generation of paper entrepreneurs sought out timber-rich locales suitable for groundwood paper production on a large scale. The ventures of Alberto Pagenstecher and his associates, principally his brothers Albrecht and Rudolph, as well as the Massachusetts investor Warner Miller, illustrate these trends. Like Clark, Kimberly, and Shattuck, these men had made money outside the paper industry. Alberto Pagenstecher, for example, was an engineer who made a small fortune in the South American railroad industry. Instead of developing their own wood-grinding technology, as several "practical papermakers" had tried unsuccessfully in the 1850s, the Pagenstecher group acquired the American patent rights for the Völter process and licensed them to other papermakers in return for royalties. In 1869 the group also formed the Hudson River Pulp & Paper Company to produce wood-based newsprint. Inaugurating the industry's soon-to-be continuous search for new locales suitable for wood-based paper production, Pagenstecher and his associates built a new mill in Corinth, New York. Deep in the Adirondacks with large, easily accessible spruce stands, the company took a significant step in setting up operations in upstate New York, rather than Massachusetts, the traditional center of American papermaking, where the group had conducted its first experiments with the Völter process. The Hudson River Company was capitalized at $250,000, more than three times the average amount a papermaker invested into a startup mill in 1870. Indicative of the major changes occurring in the U.S. pulp and paper industry, these considerable sums were required to finance wood-grinding operations, large mill buildings that accommodated the Corinth mill's three paper machines, as well as fourdrinier machines, which were among the largest and most expensive pieces of manufacturing equipment used in nineteenth-century America.[3]

Other new paper companies evolved along similar lines. Vermont, New Hampshire, upstate New York, and other regions with rich timber resources that were often located far from East Coast urban centers became the new core regions of the U.S. pulp and paper industry. In upstate New York, extensive mill properties were developed by the Tilden Paper Company at Watertown and by the Glens Falls Paper Company near Corinth. Pagenstecher and his associates, who remained the industry's most influential figures until the turn of the century, ventured deep into the Old Northwest. In 1870 Alberto Pagenstecher and Warner Miller teamed up with Chicago investors to build a pulp factory in Appleton, Wisconsin, the first groundwood mill west of New York State. In 1882 the group sold the property, which included valuable water rights on the Fox River, to Clark, Kimberly, and their associates.[4]

Like attempts to use iron instead of wood in shipbuilding, efforts to replace rags with groundwood touched off controversies among industrialists. Unlike rags with their high cellulose content, groundwood contained large amounts of lignin that reduced paper quality, convincing many fine paper specialists to reject wood pulp as a papermaking material. Furthermore, wood grinding produced short fibers that made groundwood paper less tear resistant than rag-based grades. As a remedy, papermakers usually mixed groundwood pulp with rag-based pulps to improve paper quality and strength in the 1870s. This method for improving quality was followed a decade later by the introduction of sulfite pulping which dissolved large woodchips chemically, producing stronger, high-quality pulps that were frequently mixed with groundwood pulp to produce newsprint. However, sulfite cooking equipment required major investments that many papermakers were unwilling to make. As a result, many paper mills clung to tried-and-proven rag-based newsprint despite higher raw material costs. Kimberly-Clark, for example, remained committed to newsprint rag pulp until 1878, when it built a new mill in Appleton to produce groundwood-based paper. Patent issues further delayed the widespread adoption of groundwood pulp. Pagenstecher and his associates jealously guarded their Völter process rights and frequently filed infringement suits against papermakers suspected of using the process without a license. The aggressive tactics employed by Pagenstecher and his colleagues earned the group the somewhat derisive label the "Völter Combine" in trade circles. The Combine's aggressive attempts to defend its valuable source of royalties delayed the widespread adoption of groundwood pulp until the early 1880s, when the expiration of the patent triggered vast increases in the production of wood-based paper.[5]

While technological innovations contributed to the transformation of the U.S. pulp and paper industry, changing demand structures also played a significant role. Rapid urbanization created large potential markets for publishers, nearly quadrupling the circulation of weekly newspapers from 11 million copies (1870) to 43 million copies (1899). Growth was even more pronounced in the circulation of daily newspapers, which quintupled to 15 million copies during the same period. Much of this increase was concentrated on the East Coast, especially New York City, where yellow journalism practiced by William Randolph Hearst's *New York Journal* and others led to enormous increases in tabloid circulation. By the end of the 1890s Joseph Pulitzer's *New York World* alone had a daily circulation exceeding 500,000 copies.[6]

Midwestern population centers also witnessed a marked growth in newspaper publishing, notably Chicago, Milwaukee, Detroit, and Kansas City. Chicago dailies such as the *Tribune* (founded 1872) and the *Daily Express* (1875), Detroit papers like the *Evening News* (1873), as well as the *Kansas City Star* (1885) and other major midwestern publications, became major customers of the newsprint industry. Some, notably the *Chicago Tribune,* procured their newsprint from East Coast manufacturers, but many turned to midwestern suppliers. Kimberly-Clark's largest newsprint customers included Milwaukee's *Evening Wisconsin* and the *Kansas City Star.*

II.

Neenah's paper industry originated in 1866, when six local investors built a one-machine plant named the Neenah Paper mill on the Fox River, which provided both energy to drive paper machines and water for freshwater-intensive production processes. Capitalized at $40,000, the mill initially produced straw paper at mediocre returns, convincing its owners to add rag-based newsprint and book grades to its product line. The founders also hired Myron Haynes, an experienced manager who had been a key figure in the Wisconsin paper industry since the 1850s, to supervise the mill. Haynes stayed with Neenah Paper after the original founders leased the property to a new group of investors in 1868, turning it into a profitable operation by hiring experienced craftsmen from Massachusetts and Connecticut. By the early 1870s the mill produced 465 tons of newsprint, 20 tons of straw paper, and 16 tons of low-quality book grades annually.[7]

During the 1860s the paper mill was one of Neenah's few manufacturing enterprises in a local economy dominated by flour milling. Situated in the heartland of Wisconsin wheat farming, the town boasted several large flour mills that shipped their output via railroad directly to Green Bay and from there to Chicago. Flour milling did not provide a basis for long-term growth, however. As Charles Glaab's and Lawrence Larsen's study of economic development in the Fox River Valley has shown, the town was unable to compete with larger and better-financed flour mills in Minneapolis. Over the long haul the secular shift in Wisconsin agriculture from wheat to dairy farming left flour milling with an uncertain future. Local entrepreneurs, aware of these looming problems, frequently plowed their flour milling profits into manufacturing industries, notably woodenware, machine building, and paper. The Kimberly family, whose patriarch John R. Kimberly had founded Neenah's first flour mill, was only one among several prominent local families whose efforts to develop more reliable sources of long-term growth turned the Fox River Valley into one of the region's most important industrial centers.[8]

It did not take entrepreneurs long to recognize the papermaking potential of the fertile valley, with its trees that had remained almost untouched for centuries. During the 1870s local as well as extra-regional investors established five pulp and paper companies in the Fox River Valley. The Pagenstecher group, in partnership with the Chicago paper merchant house Bradner Smith & Co., built a mill in Appleton to produce groundwood pulp for other papermakers. Kimberly, Clark and Co. was founded in 1872 on the initiative of Charles Clark, who learned about the success of the Neenah Paper mill from superintendent Haynes at gatherings of local business leaders at the town's hardware store. Clark and Haynes developed a plan to start another mill but lacked the funds to finance it on their own. Haynes had no cash to invest, and Clark had only about one-fourth of the necessary money, most of it collected by his widowed mother from the Army pay he had sent home while serving as an enlisted man during the Civil War. Looking for additional sponsors, Clark turned to John A. Kimberly, the co-owner of Neenah's general store, which he founded after graduating from Lawrence College in Appleton. They were joined by Kimberly's business partner, Havilah Babcock, who, in addition to co-owning the general store, was a partner in the Reliance Flour mill along with John R. Kimberly. A portion of the startup investment was still needed, and Kimberly suggested Shattuck, a traveling salesman and Wisconsin representative for a Chicago wholesale dry goods firm. They were joined by George Whiting, a salesman for a machine company in Janesville, Wisconsin. Whiting soon left the firm and teamed up with another group of investors who established Winnebago Paper mills in Neenah, which became one of Kimberly-Clark's local competitors. Realizing the potential for papermaking in the Fox River Valley, other groups quickly pooled funds to form their own companies. A group headed by Asa Patten, a cabinetmaker and flour miller, in 1874 formed the Patten Paper Company in Appleton. Two years later, Henry Hewitt, Jr. and his associates organized the Menasha Paper Company.[9]

In summer 1872 Kimberly, Clark and Co. built its first paper mill, the Globe mill, on the former site of a flour mill. The Fox River provided power as well as comparatively clean process water for pulping, creating a major advantage for Kimberly, Clark and Co. and other Fox River Valley paper companies vis-à-vis their New England competitors. In the Northeast, paper mills frequently operated on rivers with poor water quality, forcing them to rely on expensive freshwater wells. The Fox River, by contrast, provided abundant water for an industry that was highly dependent on clean water for pulping (producing one ton of paper required as much as 189 tons of water). Other ecological advantages included local river banks, whose terrain—contrary to the image evoked by the term Fox River "Valley"—was level, enabling mill builders to avoid expensive hillside construction. The latter kept mill construction costs high in Berkshire County, Massachusetts, and in New York's Hudson River Valley. There, river banks featured steep inclines, complicating the architectural layout of paper mills whose large fourdrinier machines required level, uninterrupted floors. Like other paper mills built after mid-century, the Globe mill, measuring 210 by 88 feet, was larger and more spacious than the older paper mills in New England and New York. Instead of unified structures, old mills in the Northeast were often nothing more than architectural hodgepodges of small buildings with extensions added on over the decades without much long-term planning. The two-story Globe mill was small and crowded compared to the standards of twentieth-century, single-story paper mills, which frequently exceeded 800 feet in length. Unlike electricity, which was transmittable over longer distances without appreciable power loss, waterwheels were connected to machinery through shafts and belts whose friction losses increased rapidly with distance (the same was true for steam power). As a result, nineteenth-century mill builders placed a premium on compact plant designs that kept distances between power sources and machines at a minimum instead of accommodating an efficient sequencing of machinery to facilitate throughput. Moreover, the Globe and other paper mills built after mid-century featured brick walls, a departure from earlier wooden mills that was facilitated by insurance companies keen on reducing fire hazards. Fires were especially widespread in the pulp and paper industry because its highly flammable rag supplies created frequent blazes that could not be contained within wooden build-ings.[10]

Pulp and paper production at the Globe mill involved five major steps performed by forty workers:

1. The rag department was located on the second floor, where unskilled men, women, and children sorted and cleaned cotton rags, an operation that required little heavy machinery and could hence be performed on second-story factory floors supported by wooden beams.
2. Clean rags were transferred to the bleaching room downstairs, where they were combined with water and bleaching agents and boiled for several hours in large vats, producing a whitish pulp that required further processing before it could be turned into paper.
3. Rag pulp was refined in a Hollander beater, which combined the pulp with more water and chemicals. It then pounded the slurry for several hours to flatten the fibers by delaminating their cell walls, increasing the bond potential between fibers to produce strong paper sheets.
4. The pulp was filled into a cone-shaped Jordan machine whose rotating knives cut fibers to the required length in preparation for papermaking.
5. Machines turned pulp into paper.

In the last step the Globe mill initially produced paper in a 72-inch cylinder machine, which Kimberly, Clark and Co. bought in Connecticut. Unlike the fast fourdrinier machine, the slower but more reliable cylinder machine featured a cloth-covered cylinder that rotated partially submerged in a pulp vat, depositing a fiber web on a wire. The web was then picked up by felt belts to be transferred to press-and-dry rolls, as well as calendar rolls that imparted the desired finish.[11]

The pulp- and papermaking process as described relied heavily on craft experience, often confounding outsiders who stood in awe of men and machines that turned piles of dirty rags into neat rolls of smooth book paper and newsprint. A visitor to a Neenah paper mill reported in 1875 that he

> saw the massive machinery do its work in a way which made me feel that it must be endowed with superior intelligence, saw the pulpy masses decomposed in some strange way, hidden from our inexperienced eyes, in a shower of spray upon broad wooden belts, which, gathering and holding the fibers, passed over and under seven cylinders, coming out only to pass upon cotton belts over steam heated dryers, and emerge at last, fresh and clean and dry white paper.[12]

The Kimberly, Clark and Co. partners, none of whom had any craft experience to speak of, may have felt similarly puzzled about the art and science of papermaking. The trade was, as a matter of fact, far more art than science because most craftsmen knew surprisingly little about the chemical reactions involved in bleaching and beating or about the bonding properties of microscopic fiber surfaces invisible to the naked eye. Given the scarcity of scientific inquiry and literature, most pulp composition formulas were the result of trial-and-error guesswork. Like other newcomers to papermaking after the Civil War, the Kimberly, Clark and Co. partners compensated for their lack of craft knowledge by hiring paper mill workers who had been apprenticed in New England. Initially, the results were unsatisfactory, most likely because the skilled craftsmen refused to share their technical expertise with the managers. After trying to manage production by themselves for a few months after the Globe mill came onstream on October 22, 1872, the partners hired Myron Hayes, who left his position as superintendent of the Neenah Paper mill and became foreman of the Globe.[13]

Their background in flour milling, merchandising, and sales provided the Kimberly, Clark and Co. partners with the requisite business skills that became more important than craft experience in the late-nineteenth-century paper industry. Historian Judith McGaw's investigation of survival rates among paper companies in Berkshire County has demonstrated that commercial experience became a far better predictor of business success than craft experience in the post–Civil War paper industry. Her sophisticated quantitative analysis reveals that a paper entrepreneur with general business background was twice as likely to succeed as one who had been trained as a craftsman. Kimberly and Clark's early history confirms these findings. Leaving shop-floor management to Haynes, Clark and Kimberly concentrated on accounting, raw materials purchases, and sales (Babcock and Shattuck were not closely involved in the firm's day-to-day operations). The partners developed close business relations with rag dealers in Milwaukee and Chicago, who supplied rags at rates that enabled the mill to compete with nonlocal suppliers in the Fox River Valley newsprint and book paper markets. Clark and Kimberly also cleverly touted the image of rag-based newsprint, whose printing properties were superior to those of wood-based paper, convincing newspaper publishers in Milwaukee and Chicago to buy the better product even if its price was slightly higher at 14¢ per pound, compared to 12¢ for wood-based newsprint. Economies of scale, combined with continually favorable conditions in the midwestern rag market, enabled the firm to cut its newsprint price in half by the late 1870s, to little more than 7¢ per pound. The latter price was competitive with that charged by East Coast mills, which suffered the disadvantage of higher transportation costs.[14]

Day-to-day management was based on an arduous schedule. Clark and Kimberly spent ten to twelve hours a day in the office. They arrived in the Neenah office by 7:00 each morning and spent the first couple of hours opening the mail and writing business letters. They were assisted by an office boy, and they also occasionally drew on the legal expertise of Moses Hooper, the company's general counsel. After assuming the management of another mill in Appleton in 1878, Kimberly and Clark made the four-mile trip each morning at 8:00 by carriage or sleigh. They attended to business in Appleton until noon; then they rode back to Neenah, where they spent the rest of the afternoon discussing the day's activities. The partners left each evening at 6:00 but returned for a couple more hours each evening to prepare for the next day. The schedule was maintained for many years. In fact, it took the death of Clark at age forty-seven in 1891 to end the habit.[15]

During the 1870s the partners made substantial improvements to the Globe mill, which turned it into one of the largest paper mills in the Midwest. In 1876 they acquired Neenah's Peckham & Kruger foundry, situated next to the paper mill on waterfront real estate along the Fox River. The purchase included extensive water rights, ultimately more than doubling the mill's waterpower. The partners removed the foundry and constructed a new rag storage facility. Increased energy and raw materials were necessary because the partners planned to install a $30,000 state-of-the-art fourdrinier paper machine, which produced higher economies of speed than the cylinder machine but which also required more power, wasted more pulp, and suffered frequent technical problems. The "wet end" of the fourdrinier machine (so called because it received watered pulp) featured a large head box that deposited pulp on an endless perforated wire. The wire formed a cellulose fiber web by draining excess water, feeding the sheet into press-and-dry rolls that resembled those used in cylinder machines. In the 1870s the fourdrinier machine ran at more than twice the speed of the cylinder machine, or 135 feet per minute (by the turn of the century, speeds of 400 feet per minute were common), requiring considerable amounts of pulp as well as large, precisely controlled power inputs. Kimberly, Clark and Co.'s acquisition of waterpower rights on the Fox River provided the mill with the type of strong and reliable power source required to drive a fourdrinier machine, even though dry spells and flooding created problems later on. The firm also expanded its papermaking capacity by purchasing the Neenah Paper mill and by installing a bleaching machine as well as other production equipment.[16]

While improving their holdings in Neenah, the partners helped build a new mill complex in Appleton that became the midwestern center of groundwood pulp and paper production. They launched the new venture in cooperation with the Fox River Pulp & Paper Company, formed in 1876 by a group of Milwaukee investors headed by John T. Averill to build a groundwood pulp mill in Appleton under the auspices of a newly formed firm, the Fox River Pulp & Paper Company. At this time Appleton already had a groundwood pulp mill built earlier in the decade by the Pagenstecher group and Chicago investors, who promptly charged the Averill group with infringements on the Völter patent even before the new company had completed its mill. In an implicit admission of guilt, the Averill group agreed in 1878 to pay royalties to Pagenstecher and his associates, clearing the way for the construction of the pulp mill. Keen on developing an outlet for the mill's production, Averill approached Clark and Kimberly with a proposal under which the Neenah company would build a paper mill in Appleton. Negotiations succeeded, and in February 1878 the parties signed an agreement stipulating that "the Fox River Pulp and Paper Company shall complete the erection and equipment of a pulp mill . . . to contain twelve grindstones for the manufacture of groundwood pulp." Kimberly, Clark and Co. in turn agreed to "acquire a site and water power to equal 500 [horse power] and thereon erect, furnish, and put in complete running order . . . a complete paper mill to have twelve beating engines and three paper machines to manufacture manila wrapping papers from jute butts and groundwood pulp." [17] Both parties further agreed to transfer the pulp factory and the paper mill to a new entity, the Atlas Paper Company, which was capitalized at $250,000 and whose principal stockholders were Clark, Kimberly, Shattuck, Babcock, and Averill, as well as two investors in Fox River Pulp & Paper. The new Atlas paper mill, completed in fall 1878, featured three fourdriniers that produced the first groundwood-based manila paper made in the Midwest. (Four years after its founding, Atlas Paper acquired the groundwood pulp mill built by the Pagenstecher group and their associates in 1870.) "Here," remarked Kimberly some twenty years later, "commenced the war to demonstrate to the consumer that wood manila could take the place of jute papers." [18] Jute paper, made exclusively in Ohio, was the standard heavy-duty paper used in the late 1870s. Wood manila was more cost-efficient than jute and held its own in performance tests. After a difficult start the new product became a success in the early 1880s, and Atlas gained ground over its major competitors in Ohio, producing twenty-five tons of paper per day. [19]

Kimberly, Clark and Co. incorporated in 1880 and was renamed Kimberly & Clark Company. Planning a somewhat risky expansion strategy in Neenah, the four founders evidently saw incorporation as a means to protect their personal assets, which—under Wisconsin law governing private partnerships—could be seized to pay off creditors if the company went bankrupt. Like many other partnerships that were reorganized and incorporated by their founders in the late nineteenth century, Kimberly & Clark became a "closely held corporation" whose stock was not publicly traded. Each former partner received one hundred $1,000 shares in the new company. Its major holdings included the Globe and Neenah mills, which had received substantial upgrades in the late 1870s, reflected in Kimberly & Clark's $400,000 capitalization, a thirteen-fold increase over the capitalization of the old partnership. Kimberly became president,

Babcock vice president, Clark the secretary, and Shattuck the treasurer. Locally known as the "Big Four," they managed their business from a small brick office building on Commercial Street in Neenah.[20]

Around the same time, the Atlas Paper Company acquired the Genessee Flour mill in Appleton, located in close proximity to the manila paper mill, to expand its presence in groundwood grades. The lingering effects of the Panic of 1873 made it impossible to build a mill, however. Capitalizing on their prior experience as flour millers in Neenah, Babcock and Kimberly continued to grind flour at the Genessee mill for the next four years. In 1881 Kimberly & Clark Co. built the one-machine Vulcan paper mill next to Atlas. The Vulcan mill, adjacent to the Genessee flour mill, featured an 88-inch fourdrinier machine to manufacture nine tons of groundwood-based book and printing paper a day. The new project, though owned by Kimberly & Clark, was managed as part of the Atlas mill. Two years later the old Genessee flour mill was demolished and replaced by the Tioga mill, equipped with two machines that produced groundwood-based newsprint. Like Vulcan, it was supervised by Atlas mill managers. These additions turned Appleton into the premier midwestern centers of groundwood-based paper production.[21]

The Kimberly & Clark Co. mill complex at Neenah, which continued to produce rag-based paper, expanded with the purchase of two old flour mills, the Smith & Proctor mill and Kimberly and Babcock's Reliance mill, together with water rights in 1884. The Smith & Proctor mill was subsequently demolished and replaced with the Badger paper mill, whose 88-inch fourdrinier machine had the capacity to produce 8 tons of rag-based manila and book grades. The Reliance mill became part of the Badger factory, and locals called it "the Old Stone Mill" because its limestone walls were two feet thick. In 1885 the mill complex underwent further development when Kimberly & Clark Co. tore down the Neenah mill built twenty years earlier and replaced it with a more modern, three-story paper mill featuring one 68-inch and one 84-inch fourdrinier to produce rag-based book grades. The new mill employed one hundred workers and dwarfed the output of the original mill, which produced only around three tons a day.[22]

Haynes, who had served as superintendent of the Globe, Badger, and Neenah mills, was replaced by Peter R. Thom, who had emigrated from Scotland at the age of 13 and had served an apprenticeship with a Connecticut papermaking machinery manufacturer. After learning the craft, Thom traveled widely for that company installing equipment.

Thom joined Kimberly and Clark in 1882 as superintendent of the Vulcan and Tioga operations in Appleton. He was subsequently named the company's general superintendent and a member of its board of directors.[23]

Although determined to maintain complete financial control over Kimberly & Clark Co., the four founders were willing to admit some of their managers as stockholders in new ventures. In 1887 they formed the Telulah Paper Company to build a new mill in Appleton that featured 90-inch and 110-inch fourdriniers respectively with a combined capacity to produce twenty tons of groundwood pulp newsprint a day. Clark, Kimberly, Shattuck, and Babcock owned the vast majority of stocks in the $250,000 company but gave away smaller shares to managers of the Kimberly & Clark and Atlas Paper mills to reward them for their service.[24]

In 1887 the four Appleton mills owned and operated by Clark and his associates—the Atlas, Tioga, Vulcan, and Telulah mills—received a boost from the introduction of sulfite pulp, which improved paper quality. Most producers of wood-based grades mixed groundwood and rag pulps to increase tear resistance, but some experimented with new alternatives, including chemical wood-pulping technologies that yielded longer cellulose fibers with better bonding qualities than mechanically ground pulp. The sulfite process, developed in the mid-1870s by chemists Alexander and Richard Mitscherlich in Germany and Carl Ekman in Sweden, dissolved large wood chips in a cooking liquor containing soluble and sulfurous acid, delignifying the fibers to produce cleaner pulp. Industrial-scale production required large digesters, whose considerable costs (perhaps combined with the repugnant odor released by the chemicals involved) delayed the widespread adoption of sulfite pulping. A few mills in New England and the Mid-Atlantic states introduced sulfite pulping in the early 1880s, followed in 1887 by the Appleton mill complex, which became the first papermaking center west of Pennsylvania to adopt the new technology. The Appleton complex featured two digesters with a daily output capacity of nine tons. They were made of deoxidized bronze that resisted the corrosive effects of sulfurous acids. Their output was combined with groundwood pulp to produce higher-quality manila wrapping grades, book paper, and newsprint (the latter consisted of 80 percent groundwood pulp and 20 percent sulfite pulp), giving the Appleton mills an advantage over competitors who had remained committed to a groundwood-rag mixture because sulfite pulp was cheaper than rag-based pulp. Outside the mill, sulfite pulping created environmental problems. Harmful chemicals were dumped into the Fox River until after the turn of the century. At that time papermakers developed recycling processes for some acids, and other acids were replaced with new agents that reduced the ecological impact of sulfite pulping, including calcium, which was replaced with other soluble acids.[25]

Kimberly & Clark Co. suffered a major setback in 1888, when the Atlas mill burned to the ground. Fire was a major concern for factory owners well into the twentieth century, since most towns had neither adequate fire-fighting capabilities nor a means for detecting fire before it was too late. The Atlas plant was lit by lanterns and gas and kerosene torches, which made it vulnerable. On the night of the fire a worker went into the basement with a torch to look into the stock box under the beater. He left the torch in the basement as he went upstairs on an errand, and the wind toppled the torch onto some oily rags. The fire quickly spread and destroyed the entire mill. Fortunately, no was killed, and the Vulcan and Tioga mills were spared. The ten-year-old Atlas mill represented the core of the company's groundwood paper business, and its destruction could easily have prompted customers to buy elsewhere. However, management concentrated on getting the factory rebuilt and into production, and only five months later the reconstructed mill produced at a greater capacity than before the blaze. Paper output increased from 25 tons a day to 32 tons with three fourdrinier machines, two measuring 82 inches and one 56 inches.[26]

Kimberly & Clark Co. expanded its newsprint capacity with the construction of a large pulp and paper mill in the village of Kimberly, just three miles east of Appleton. To finance the expansion and machinery, the owners increased their stock from $400,000 to $1.5 million. In 1888 they bought the farm land and waterpower rights along the Fox River for $120,000, erected a hotel, rented out or sold sixty houses, and sold lots to new residents. Kimberly & Clark Co. turned the design of the new plant over to the renowned paper mill architect A. B. Tower of Holyoke, Massachusetts. The Kimberly mill included three machines, a 25-ton-per-day groundwood pulp mill, a 30-ton sulfite mill, and a 10-ton straw wrapping paper mill. It was the first in the Fox River Valley to use a professional architect. Over the next two years four fourdriniers (each costing $35,000) were added to produce newsprint. Reflecting this increased capacity, Kimberly & Clark Co. negotiated a long-term newsprint contract with the *Kansas City Star*.[27]

In 1891 the partners entered bond and ledger paper production with the formation of the Shattuck & Babcock Company, capitalized at $500,000. Its two-machine, 20-ton mill was built downstream from Kimberly at DePere, Wisconsin, which produced high-quality, loft-dried grades. Although they held the majority of the company's stock, the founders chose to include more junior executives in the subsidiary's ownership, including Frank Sensenbrenner, who would later become president of Kimberly-Clark. Although the Shattuck & Babcock mill made the finest expensive grade book paper in the West, the 1893 economic panic made the paper difficult to sell. The problem of marketing the product caused the firm to postpone several projects. Later, a group of businessmen representing the American Writing Paper Company of Holyoke offered cash, bonds, and preferred stock to buy the plant. The shareholders of Shattuck & Babcock thought the offer was too good to refuse, so in 1899 they sold the writing paper business to the easterners.[28]

III.

Initially, the partners derived rather modest financial benefits from their papermaking ventures. When the company incorporated in 1880, the officers earned salaries comparable to those of manufacturing enterprises of similar size. Shattuck received $4,000 annually; Babcock received $3,000; and Kimberly and Clark each received $3,000 from the corporation plus $1,000 each for managing Atlas Paper. Like owner-managers of other "closely held corporations," the four men pursued fairly conservative financial policies, often plowing profits back into the mills instead of paying dividends to themselves. Kimberly & Clark Co. declared its first dividend in March 1883, three years after its formation, yielding $3,000 for each of the four stockholders. Later that same year they voted 2 percent more, which remained the dividend into the next quarter. This dividend was the last one issued for two years. During those difficult economic times the company reinvested its meager earnings back into plant improvements. In July 1886, after regaining its financial footing and posting a profitable year, the board of directors voted a 10 percent dividend and maintained that rate the next year. These dividends netted each owner $20,000.[29]

Turning the various mills owned and operated by the Kimberly & Clark partners into productive operations presented major challenges.

TABLE 1.1

Fox River paper companies, 1892

Company	Capital	Value of Product	Output per Capital Unit
Kimberly-Clark & Co.	1,500,000	2,017,927	1.35
Shattuck & Babcock	500,000	650,000	1.30
Badger Paper Co.	493,000	598,312	1.21
Fox River Paper Co.	350,000	520,000	1.49
Gilbert Paper Co.	310,000	800,000	2.58
Atlas Paper Co.	250,000	492,371	1.97
Telulah Paper Co.	250,000	345,545	1.38
Winnebago Paper Mills	200,000	300,000	1.50
Outagamie Paper Co.	200,000	298,000	1.48
Patten Paper Co.	200,000	250,000	1.25
Kaukauna Fiber Co.	175,000	300,000	1.71
Neenah Paper Co.	150,000	152,000	1.01
Charles W. Howard	135,000	245,000	1.81
Thilmany Paper Co.	130,000	337,000	2.59

By 1892 Kimberly & Clark Co. was by far the largest paper company in the Fox River Valley; their $1.5 million capital represented more than 30 percent of all investments in the region's pulp and paper industry. Remarkably, however, Kimberly & Clark Co.—whose balance sheet included the Globe, Badger, Neenah, Tioga, and Vulcan mills—ranked near the bottom of a list of nineteen regional companies in terms of capital productivity, yielding only $1.35 in output for every dollar invested compared to $2.59 in output for every dollar invested by the Thilmany Paper Company in Kaukauna, a new firm established in 1889 (table 1.1). Although the correlation is far from perfect, these statistics indicate that smaller mills yielded higher capital productivity and that Kimberly & Clark Co.'s strategy of heavy investments into equipment and physical plants did not raise its mills' productivity rates. The picture was far brighter in terms of worker productivity. With a per capita value output of more than $4,000, Kimberly & Clark Co. ranked fifth in the list of nineteen companies. The three original Kimberly & Clark mills in Neenah, with their well-managed and coordinated workforces, produced above-average per capita output ($4,349), followed by the newsprint mill in Kimberly

($4,186) and the mill complex in Appleton ($3,638). But the fact that the Gilbert mill in Menasha and the Thilmany mill in Kaukauna produced considerably higher per-worker output ($7,273 and $5,617 respectively) demonstrated that there was room for improvement in worker productivity at all Kimberly & Clark mills.[30]

In the early 1890s the partners reorganized and streamlined production at the various mills. Newsprint production was consolidated at the new Kimberly mill, which received a third fourdrinier in 1893, increasing its aggregate daily output to 55 tons. The Appleton mill complex meanwhile exited newsprint and converted to higher-quality groundwood grades. The Vulcan and Tioga mills switched to book paper while the Atlas mill was rebuilt to manufacture fancy manila wrapping and cover grades. Likewise, the Globe mill in Neenah, whose 72-inch paper machine installed in 1872 could no longer compete with more modern newsprint mills featuring 156-inch machines, abandoned newsprint production and switched to rag-based wrapping papers. The Telulah Paper Company two-machine mill in Appleton, which had produced newsprint since its formation in 1887, was rebuilt in 1893 to produce book and bond papers.[31]

Plans to install additional new equipment and build new mills were shelved in 1893, which marked the beginning of a three-year depression that caused turmoil throughout the nation's manufacturing economy. From 1893 to 1895 fifty paper companies went bankrupt as prices plunged to record lows; newsprint prices, for example, dropped by more than 40 percent, as did book and bond paper prices. In August 1893 only fifteen of the Fox River Valley's forty-five paper machines were still running. One observer noted, "Mills are running along in a from hand to mouth style, with only one or two days' orders ahead and the prospect of a shut down continually staring them in the face."[32]

Kimberly & Clark and other Fox River Valley companies weathered the crisis by cutting wages and collaboratively scaling back production. In February 1894 the region's employers reduced wages for unskilled paper workers by 8 to 10 percent, followed several months later by similar reductions for skilled workers. In a controversial move that received nationwide attention, Fox River Valley paper executives teamed up with their brethren from the Wisconsin River and Marinette districts to form the Paper Makers' Association, which coordinated mill shutdowns throughout the region. The organization was headed by John A. Kimberly and an executive committee that included George Whiting, Kimberly, Clark and Co.'s co-founder who

TABLE 1.2

Net earnings of Kimberly-Clark, 1893–1898

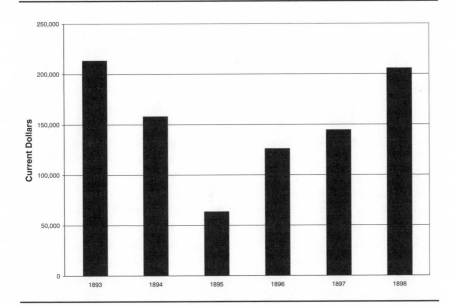

had left the partnership early on to head other paper companies. The association, like similar cartels of the early 1890s, was short-lived because it lacked enforcement mechanisms. However, in the short run it helped stabilize the Fox River Valley paper industry, which did not lose a single mill to bankruptcy or reorganization during the Depression of the 1890s. Kimberly & Clark, in fact, managed to survive the crisis virtually without negative earnings; in 1895, the worst Depression year, the company still produced almost $64,000 in profits (table 1.2).[33]

In the wake of the Panic, Kimberly & Clark Co. resurrected expansion plans dating to the years prior to 1893. After taking modest dividends, the three surviving founding partners (Clark had died in 1891) invested the bulk of the substantial 1898 profits into a new paper mill in Niagara, Wisconsin, 135 miles north of Neenah. In the Fox River Valley, the paper and lumber industries' insatiable appetite for timber had thinned out the region's spruce and hemlock stands, precipitating the search for timber-rich locales. In 1889, on the Wisconsin side of the river, a Fox River Valley papermaker established a small pulp mill employing only twelve men. Its outgoing pulp and incoming supplies had to be rafted across the Menominee River to the mill and then hauled by wagon the five miles between the dock and the North Western Railway depot in Quinnesec. In 1892 the property was acquired by the Quinnesec Falls Paper Company, a subsidiary of a Fox River Valley firm, which improved the site by building a one-machine paper mill after convincing the railroad to build a spur from Quinnesec to the mill. When Kimberly & Clark Co. arrived on the scene five years later, the area was still a tiny settlement of log cabins and no sidewalks. Abandoned tree stumps littered the main street of Quinnesec Falls, and one man served as town supervisor, general merchant, hotelkeeper, bartender, and postmaster. The Menominee River provided waterpower, the most important resource. In summer 1897 Kimberly & Clark Co. made overtures about buying the mill to the Badger Paper Company of Kaukauna. After lengthy negotiations they closed the deal on a bitterly cold day the following February after enduring a long train ride and a bobsled ride down the river to the mill. Shortly thereafter, the old mill was replaced with a larger building featuring two 156-inch fourdrinier machines with an operating speed of 400 feet per minute—among the nation's largest and fastest paper machines. The plant and the town were renamed "Niagara," although it was often referred to as Quinnesec, or simply "Q." In 1901 Kimberly & Clark Co. added two new paper machines to the Niagara mill to produce 50 tons a day of water-finish manila wrapping paper. The groundwood mill produced 60 tons daily, and the sulfite mill 50 tons daily. Niagara's output dwarfed the company's previously largest mill, the Kimberly mill, by 33 percent.[34]

Shortly after the Niagara mill turned out its first sheet of wrapping paper, tragedy struck as fire destroyed large parts of the Kimberly mill, leaving Kimberly & Clark with no newsprint capacity. At the time, Shattuck estimated the loss at more than $300,000. To respond to customers' demands and to fulfill many outstanding contracts, the firm placed emergency orders for machinists to convert Niagara's new machines from wrapping paper to newspaper. In only four weeks the Niagara mill shipped its first batch of newsprint, which remained its main product until 1916.[35]

Kimberly & Clark Co. rebuilt the Kimberly mill in 1904 to manufacture book grades, which emerged as the company's most important product line. While the Neenah, Tioga, and Vulcan mills produced low-grade book paper from a mixture of groundwood and sulfite pulps, the new two-machine Kimberly mill used sulfite pulp combined with small amounts of rag pulps, which was more expensive than groundwood-sulfite compounds but yielded higher-quality grades. Paper made from sulfite pulp gained a strong position in markets for high-quality book paper, which had heretofore been dominated by producers of rag-based grades. The latter tried to protect their position by cautioning paper merchants against manufacturers of sulfite-based book paper, claiming that the new grade was inferior in terms of brightness, printability, and tensile strength. This campaign was carried out at trade conventions and on the pages of industry periodicals.[36]

Kimberly & Clark Co. reorganized in 1906 to accommodate recent changes in ownership. Shattuck died in 1901 and Babcock in 1905, leaving John A. Kimberly as the sole survivor of the "Big Four," who owned Kimberly & Clark, Atlas Paper, and Telulah Paper in conjunction with the estates of the three other men. In late 1906 Kimberly, together with several associates, organized the Kimberly-Clark Company, which was capitalized at $2 million. A few months later, in 1907, the new company took over the property of Kimberly & Clark, Atlas Paper, and Telulah Paper. Principal stock ownership rested with John A. Kimberly and three sons of founders, Bill Clark, James C. Kimberly, and Frank Shattuck, who—with the exception of John A. Kimberly, who withdrew from active business—also served as managers and members of the board of directors. They were joined by three managers who had worked their way into ownership roles: Frank Sensenbrenner, Peter Thom, and William Ryan. James Kimberly was appointed vice president, and Sensenbrenner, who had commenced his career at Kimberly & Clark in 1889 as a bookkeeper, became general manager.[37]

The new senior managers, principally Kimberly and Sensenbrenner, changed the company's management structure, replacing the personal business practices of the founders with formal departments responsible for accounting, purchasing, materials, and sales. The founders had handled accounting until 1889, when they hired Sensenbrenner who—like many other bookkeepers in nineteenth-century paper mills—remained committed to single-entry bookkeeping. In 1908 the reorganized company hired Harry Price, an auditor who had examined Kimberly & Clark Co.'s financial records in prior years, to organize and head a separate accounting department. Price and his twelve clerks introduced double-entry bookkeeping and instituted basic cost accounting procedures for the company as well as for individual mills. The purchasing department was formed in 1908 and headed by John S. Sensenbrenner (a Frank Sensenbrenner relative) whose staff of four clerks handled procurement and storage of market pulpwood, chemicals, coal, and other materials. It soon became clear that storage management required more specialized skills, leading in 1914 to the formation of a rudimentary staff materials department headed by Edward Young, who supervised the construction and stocking of small warehouses at the company's mills. Marketing, which had previously been handled informally by John A. Kimberly and his assistant William Stuart, was formalized with the establishment of a sales organization. James Kimberly, who headed the department, opened Kimberly-Clark's first district office in Chicago in 1913, followed two years later by the New York district office, to develop close business relations with paper merchants and publishers.[38]

The technical department, organized in 1914 to handle research, development, and mill equipment problems, became by far the most important organization in the new management structure. The groundwork was laid when Kimberly and Sensenbrenner recruited professional engineers and scientists, starting in 1912 with the hiring of Frank Wheeler. Wheeler established a test laboratory at the Kimberly mill in 1913 and hired scientist H. A. Rothschild to test pulp and paper samples for composition, tear resistance, and uniformity. One year later Kimberly-Clark hired the Austrian-born research scientist Ernst Mahler, arguably one of the most important figures in the history of the company. Mahler had received his degree in chemistry from the prestigious Darmstadt Institute of Pulp and Paper Technology in Germany. In 1914 he established a research laboratory across the street from Kimberly-Clark's main office in Neenah, where he developed an innovative groundwood pulping process as well as a cellulose substance that became the base material for the Kotex sanitary napkin. Kimberly-Clark's early commitment to laboratory research stood in marked contrast to the views of most competitors, whose laboratories rarely conducted research and development. International Paper, for example, hired a paper chemist and organized a laboratory in Glens Falls, New York, in 1901. However, as with most other American paper laboratories, its activities were restricted to testing pulp and sheet samples shipped by the mills to ensure product uniformity. The Glens Falls laboratory did not conduct systematic product development until the 1940s, when Kimberly-Clark already looked back on almost three decades of active research and development.[39]

IV.

The new management organized Kimberly-Clark's exit from the newsprint market in a drawn-out process that lasted until 1916, when the Niagara mill produced its last sheet of newsprint. The decision to phase out a product that had been one of the company's mainstays since its inception in 1872 was intertwined with seismic shifts in the pulp and paper markets that reduced the profitability of newsprint production in the United States. It was hastened by the elimination of tariffs on Canadian newsprint in the Underwood Tariff Act of 1913 which transformed the entire industry.

On the surface the turn-of-the-century U.S. newsprint industry appeared prosperous. Newsprint represented more than one-fourth of the nation's aggregate paper output of 2.7 million tons in 1899, more than any other product category, and involved some of the largest American paper companies, including International Paper, Crown-Zellerbach, St. Regis Paper Company, and H. C. Craig & Co. More-over, the accelerating downward trend in newsprint prices that plagued the industry since the 1870s came to an abrupt halt in 1898, giving way to occasional increases in subsequent years. The formation of International Paper (IP) in 1898 was frequently cited at the time as a major factor that precipitated the turnaround in newsprint prices. Capitalized at $40 million, IP owned 17 northeastern mills and oper-ated 101 paper machines with 1,500 tons daily output capacity, giv-ing it control of a staggering 60 percent of the U.S. newsprint pro-duction capacity. Its board of directors included Alberto Pagenstecher and several of his associates who had pioneered groundwood pulp production in the United States thirty years earlier. Like the Pagen-stecher group during its heydays in the late 1870s, publishers quick-ly labeled IP a "Paper Combination" or "Paper Trust." They feared that the company would exploit its dominant position in the newsprint market by raising prices. Market trends in the decade after 1898 seemed to confirm this prognosis, giving a boost to a campaign led by the American Newspaper Publishers' Association to check IP's market control by lifting the tariff on Canadian newsprint.[40]

Subsequent research, including our own study of IP, revealed that the giant paper company was in no position to exercise monopoly power. Weighted down by a $5 million debt which it had accumulat-ed by 1904, IP produced mediocre net earnings and disappointing dividends as it watched its market share drop by more than half, to

26 percent by 1913. Epitomizing a trend that later plagued large segments of the U.S. newsprint industry, the gap between production costs and market prices grew dangerously narrow, largely because IP faced precipitous increases in pulpwood costs as a result of irresponsible forestry practices and rapidly shrinking timber supplies. What contemporary critics viewed as monopolistic pricing was in fact a somewhat desperate attempt to prevent newsprint prices from dropping below production costs.[41]

The development of Kimberly & Clark Co.'s newsprint business paralleled industry trends. By the end of the 1890s the company produced 55 tons of newsprint at the three-machine Kimberly mill. When large sections of the mill burned down in 1901, Kimberly & Clark transferred the contracts to the new Niagara mill. The latter manufactured newsprint for the *Evening Wisconsin* and other old Kimberly & Clark customers in the region, as well as newspapers in New Orleans and Salt Lake City, increasing its output by 43 percent from 1901 to 1906 (table 1.3). For the first two years, Kimberly & Clark bought approximately 85 percent of the mill's pulpwood supplies on the open market and procured the remainder from its own timber holdings in Wisconsin and Northern Michigan. The large

TABLE 1.3

Kimberly-Clark newsprint production at the Niagara mill, 1901–1907

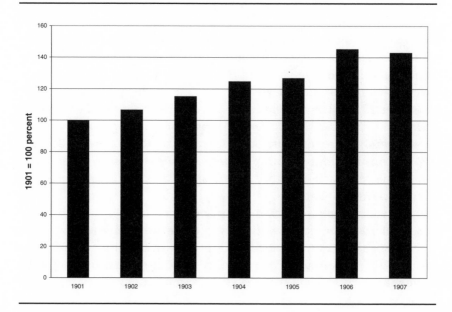

percentage of expensive market pulpwood evidently worried James Kimberly and Frank Sensenbrenner, by now the principal managers of the company. The two managers teamed up with other paper companies in the region to form the Wisconsin Wood Pulp Company. The latter circumvented pulpwood dealers, purchased timber directly from lumbermen, and supplied the affiliated mills for a nominal fee with pulpwood at cost. Mirroring broader market trends, Kimberly & Clark's newsprint prices held steady and in some years even increased slightly, particularly in 1903 and 1907, when burgeoning demand taxed production capacity to the limit (table 1.4). In 1906, Kimberly & Clark even refused to renew a contract with a Denver newspaper because, as Sensenbrenner explained, "the sizes required by it were not advantageous to our machines."[42]

Closer analysis reveals troubling trends in Kimberly-Clark's newsprint business, however. Rising costs consistently outpaced price increases in every year from 1901 to 1907 (table 1.5). The single largest factor responsible for mill costs was pulpwood, whose price grew by 55 percent over the same time period despite strenuous attempts to control the Niagara mill's pulpwood bill through the Wisconsin Wood Pulp Company. From 1905 to 1907 the difference

TABLE 1.4

Kimberly-Clark newsprint price per 100 pounds, 1878–1907

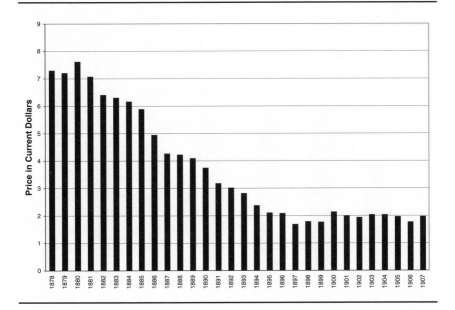

TABLE 1.5

Kimberly-Clark Niagara mill production costs and market prices, 1901–1907

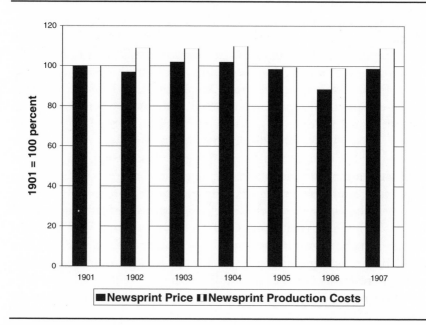

between production costs and f.o.b. mill prices shriveled to from 23.3 percent to 8.9 percent, not counting transportation costs that sometimes added 10 percent to f.o.b. mill prices—charges that were usually covered by the mill. Unnerved by this precarious situation, Kimberly-Clark's new management team switched the aging Badger mill in Neenah from newsprint to book grades in 1907, consolidating all newsprint operations at the Niagara mill.

Obtaining adequate pulpwood resources for the Niagara newsprint mill, which required 175 cords or 22,400 cubic feet of wood to sustain maximum production, became a top priority. In 1902 Kimberly & Clark Co. made its first purchase of timberland— 18,000 acres in a county west of Niagara. This purchase was followed by acquisition of the William Bonifas Lumber Company, one of the largest lumber companies in Northern Michigan. William Bonifas, who owned extensive timber lands on the so-called Garden peninsula, had supplied Kimberly-Clark with pulpwood for several years and in 1909 had formed a partnership with his three brothers. The company continued accumulating large tracts of hemlock and spruce timber in the Upper Peninsula. In 1912 Bonifas sold the company to Kimberly-Clark, which obtained a valuable pulpwood source for the Niagara mill.[43]

Kimberly-Clark's attempts to secure the viability of the Niagara newsprint mill suffered a debilitating blow in 1913 when the Underwood Tariff Act lifted the tariff on Canadian newsprint. Tariff reform was largely the result of a successful political campaign by newspaper publishers, the American Newspaper Publishers' Association, and John Norris, the business agent of *The New York Times* who became the association's full-time lobbyist. Norris and other reform advocates argued that the abrupt halt in the long-term decline in newsprint prices at the turn of the century was the result of IP's monopolistic pricing and various cartels among paper and pulp manufacturers. Eliminating the tariff could reintroduce a measure of price competition into rigidly structured markets by allowing Canadian mills to supply U.S. publishers with inexpensive newsprint, Norris and others argued. In their counteroffensive, newsprint producers predicted unsurprisingly that even mild tariff reductions would wreak irreparable damage. The complete removal of import duties had far more dramatic implications, they claimed. Canadian newsprint mills, drawing on more abundant pulpwood supplies and cheaper labor, enjoyed an $8 to $10 per-ton cost advantage over their American competitors. Eliminating the newsprint tariff, papermakers told the Wisconsin Congressional delegation in a meeting in 1909, "will bring about the ruin of the paper manufacturing industry in the States of Wisconsin, Minnesota, and Michigan."[44] Their prediction was grossly exaggerated because Kimberly-Clark, Thilmany, the Fox River Paper Company, the Park Falls Pulp & Paper Company, and other major firms in the region produced mostly non-newsprint grades. Tariff reform would have detrimental effects on non-newsprint markets, however, as Sensenbrenner pointed out to a Congressional panel in 1908: "[It would] stimulate the building of mills in Canada, and . . . take present news-paper mills off those grades and drive them to other grades," increasing competition among producers of book and magazine papers, manila grades, and writing papers.[45]

These prescient comments describe the development of the U.S. pulp and paper industry after 1913. IP and other large U.S. companies built newsprint mills in Quebec and Ontario, as did Canadian firms, precipitating the swift rise of the Canadian newsprint industry. Some U.S. producers, notably Crown-Zellerbach, responded to the Canadian challenge by improving their existing newsprint capacities south of the border. Others admitted defeat and rushed to convert their American operations to other grades, particularly tariff-protected book and magazine papers. They challenged firms that had dominated these markets in the past, creating downward price pressures that in turn unleashed a search for more profitable specialty products, including refined groundwood grades, toilet paper, linerboard, and sanitary napkins. Kimberly-Clark, whose management was keenly aware of these wider implications of the tariff revision, converted its Niagara newsprint mill to specialty groundwood paper only three years after the passage of the Underwood Tariff Act.

V.

The conversion of the Niagara mill strengthened Kimberly-Clark's position as one of the nation's leading manufacturers of book and magazine paper, by now the company's most important product. Kimberly-Clark and its predecessor firms had manufactured the product on a large scale in the 1880s and had, over the next two decades, converted the Tioga, Vulcan, Telulah, Kimberly, and Atlas mills to book and magazine paper. Using a mixture of conventional groundwood pulp and small amounts of sulfite or rag pulps, these mills produced mostly low-grade paper for publishers of cheap, mass-produced books and magazines, leaving the high-quality end of the market to manufacturers of rag-based paper. This market segmentation was reinforced by prestigious paper merchant houses like Carter Rice & Company that cautioned publishers against groundwood pulp–based book and magazine papers, which lacked the strength, brightness, and distinctive texture of rag-based grades.

Wood gained acceptance as a base material for fine papers after the turn of the century, when the Hammermill Paper Company convinced skeptical paper merchants to market sulfite pulp–based bond paper. Founded in 1898 by German emigrants in Erie, Pennsylvania, Hammermill went to great lengths to meet the needs of major wholesalers for watermarked bond paper, inventing a machine that watermarked paper at very high speeds. The company also organized annual meetings with paper merchants to discuss technical issues and plot marketing campaigns. In 1912 it introduced the industry's first mill-watermarked bond paper that was marketed in an unprecedented advertising campaign as "Hammermill Bond." The company's remarkable success in marketing fine papers made from sulfite pulp, whose quality approached that of far more expensive rag pulps, convinced other papermakers that wood-based grades could compete with rag paper in high-quality market segments, notably book paper. Hammermill's experience demonstrated that attempts to break into high-quality paper markets required a strong commitment to product development and marketing and a willingness to accommodate the needs of paper merchants.[46]

Kimberly and Sensenbrenner, keen observers of the Hammermill success story, were determined to duplicate it in the market for high-quality book and magazine paper. Their early initiatives focused on the Kimberly mill, the company's most modern mill after its reconstruction in 1904, which became a testing ground for new technologies and processes. Initially the mill produced book and magazine grades from a mixture of sulfite pulp, rag stock, and de-inked magazine paper that produced low-grade printing grades. Efforts to improve product quality to the point where wood-based paper became acceptable to paper merchants and publishers focused on pulp processing technologies. First Kimberly and Sensenbrenner hired engineers to improve the quality of sulfite pulp. In 1912 Wheeler designed and supervised the construction of an electrolytic chlorine plant at Kimberly that produced an inexpensive pulp bleaching agent, replacing dry bleaching powder which was difficult to handle and had to be shipped by rail from a chemical plant in Detroit. The new plant had a daily capacity of eight tons of chlorine that was used to bleach sulfite pulp. Kimberly and Sensenbrenner also recruited P. A. Paulson, a chemical engineer who improved the Kimberly mill's sulfite pulping processes, and installed steel revolving drums to debark large amounts of pulpwood, replacing less efficient hand-debarking equipment that sometimes left bark impurities in groundwood pulp. Furthermore, newly hired chemist Ernst Mahler developed groundwood pulps that were more suitable for high-quality paper production than conventional groundwood pulp. The latter contained large amounts of lignin that effected a brownish tinge in groundwood-based grades, rendering it unacceptable to manufacturers of high-quality papers. Searching for bleaching processes that produced higher brightness, Mahler and James Kimberly in 1914 visited Germany, widely recognized as a leading center of chemical research, where they discussed possible solutions with chemistry professors and pulp makers. Upon their return, Mahler developed a bleaching method for groundwood pulping that eliminated lignin and produced the light-blue tinge perceived as white. The process was commercialized at the Kimberly mill, which pioneered the production of refined, bleached groundwood pulp in the United States. Refined groundwood pulp, which was mixed with chlorine-bleached sulfite pulp, produced an inexpensive, high-quality grade that was particularly suitable for rotogravure printing.[47]

Combining photogravure with rotary printing, the rotogravure process transformed magazine printing. Placing a screen engraved with a photograph on a copper plate, a printer etched holes of varying depth into the plate, which was rolled up on a cylinder and covered with ink. When the cylinder was rolled over damp paper, deep holes deposited large amounts of ink, reproducing the photograph's dark fields, while shallow holes produced lighter dots. The process required high-quality paper that absorbed ink while retaining sharp borders between dots to produce a clear image. Most early rotogravure paper was made from costly sulfite pulp, limiting the use of photographs to expensive magazines. Kimberly-Clark's refined groundwood paper, which possessed the same printing qualities as sulfite-based grades but cost less, facilitated the introduction of inexpensive illustrated magazines, including magazine supplements to Sunday papers. The first customer for Roto-plate, Kimberly-Clark's trademark for the product, was *The New York Times,* which ordered it for its Sunday magazine in 1915 and remained one of the largest customers for rotogravure paper for decades.[48]

Convincing paper merchants to market high-quality wood-based grades was a more formidable challenge. Taking a leaf from Hammermill, Kimberly-Clark invited merchants to annual conventions to discuss marketing, advertising, and technical problems. The meetings usually featured an opening address on trade issues by Sensenbrenner or Kimberly, followed by Mahler or one of his assistants who explained recent improvements in pulping technology and finishing, and finally a general discussion. Remarkably, management frequently asked the assembled merchants to "vote" on new pulp mixtures, grades, colors, and finishes "proposed" by the company. These clever marketing strategies, which facilitated the introduction of Roto-plate and other refined bleached groundwood grades, distinguished Kimberly-Clark from most other paper companies that rarely asked merchants for their opinions. International Paper, for example, maintained unfriendly relations with most merchants in part because the giant paper company preferred to deal directly with publishers, circumventing the finely meshed network of jobbers and paper merchant houses. These unfriendly relationships contributed to the lackluster performance of IP's book and bond paper operations, which never rivaled those of Hammermill and Kimberly-Clark in terms of versatility, responsiveness to customer needs, and name recognition.[49]

Kimberly-Clark's attempt to turn bleached groundwood paper into a new core product was evidently successful. Detailed financial records are missing, but sales of the new product quickly overtaxed the company's ability to produce it, convincing management to expand capacity. In 1915 the chlorine plant at the Kimberly mill doubled its capacity. A year later Kimberly-Clark converted the Niagara mill from newsprint to bleached groundwood grades, including book, magazine, and catalog papers.

VI.

On the eve of World War I, Kimberly-Clark was one the nation's leading pulp and paper companies. Its core strength was not its size—IP with its capitalization of $50 million and the $30 million American Writing Company dwarfed the $4 million Neenah company—but its management's commitment to innovation, product development, and marketing. The founders' keen interest in new products and technologies became evident as early as 1878, when they pioneered groundwood-based manila grades in the midwestern paper industry, and in 1887, when Kimberly & Clark Co. became the region's first paper company to introduce sulfite pulp. Initially lacking the detailed technical knowledge of "practical papermakers," the founders invested into new technologies because they expected new products to yield solid financial returns, particularly in the case of Charles Clark, who reportedly "could smell a profit around the corner." After Clark's premature death in 1891, the surviving partners pursued somewhat more conventional product and investment strategies. However, the new generation of managers who took control after 1906 rekindled Kimberly-Clark's commitment to innovation, notably in the case of bleached groundwood pulp, which laid the groundwork for the company's new core business in high-quality book and magazine paper. When introduction of the new grade forced management to confront the difficult challenge of marketing, James Kimberly and Sensenbrenner emulated the strategies of Hammermill, the savviest innovator in the paper business. Furthermore, at a time when most paper company managers viewed laboratory work primarily as a form of product quality control, Kimberly and Sensenbrenner hired professional chemists and established a research facility with the express purpose to develop new products.

Innovation, scientific product development, and marketing played a critical role during the interwar period, when Kimberly-Clark developed consumer nondurables and launched advertising campaigns to kindle demand for the new products. As the present chapter has shown, the structural and strategic parameters for this new departure emerged before World War I. The basic product that precipitated the momentous changes of the interwar period also pre-dated the war, but only barely. In the course of their trip to Europe in 1914, when Mahler and Kimberly explored new methods to produce bleached groundwood pulp, they also queried German paper scientists about the possibility of developing a cellulose product that could serve as a substitute for cotton-based sanitary wound dressings. Mahler, in fact, developed such a product, trademarked Cellucotton, a few months after his return from Germany, at the exact time when Europe descended into unprecedented bloodshed. After the war Kimberly-Clark used Cellucotton as a base material for the Kotex sanitary napkin.

2

The Rise of Consumer Nondurables

IN 1921 EDWARD BOK, editor of *Ladies' Home Journal*, held an unpleasant business meeting with Albert Lasker, president of the Lord & Thomas advertising agency which represented a Kimberly-Clark subsidiary. Lasker and Bok argued over a proposed advertisement for Kotex sanitary napkins. Bok, known as the "supreme arbiter of the manners and morals of middle-class American womanhood,"[1] reportedly told the Chicago advertising executive that his decision not to publish the ad was "final." Lasker, however, challenged the editor to bring his secretary into the office and read the Kotex advertisement. "If she's embarrassed or repelled by it," Lasker said, "I'll accept your judgment. There'll be no further argument." Bok called in his white-haired secretary, a woman in her sixties, and handed her the copy. The two men watched in silence as the secretary started reading the ad. She stopped halfway through, looked at the editor and said, "Why, Mr. Bok, this is really a wonderful thing." After finishing reading the ad, she looked up and opined, "I certainly think we should run this in the *Journal,* Mr. Bok. Women deserve to be told about it." Bok turned to Lasker and said, "So you were right, Mr. Lasker. Now I'll show you around the plant and then have lunch. Our advertising director will be there and you two can work out the details."[2]

The episode, a textbook example of savvy salesmanship, marked a turning point in the history of Kimberly-Clark, which established a formidable presence in consumer nondurables during the 1920s. The endorsement of Bok's secretary opened the floodgates for an unprece-dented marketing campaign that broke cultural norms about men-strual hygiene and helped define new ones. The success of Kotex marketing was far from certain, however, because most retailers ini-tially refused to stock the product. Those who did frequently hid it under the counter. In response, the Kimberly-Clark subsidiary that sold sanitary napkins hired marketing professionals who helped turn the product into a success. This success encouraged the company to experiment with other consumer products, including Kleenex dispos-able handkerchiefs. Although initially viewed warily by Kimberly-Clark executives, who preferred more traditional products, the new consumer items contributed to Kimberly-Clark's stellar financial per-formance in the 1920s.

The present chapter traces the technology and business strategies that turned the company into a major player in consumer markets. It explores the invention of the base product for Kotex and Kleenex during World War I, when Kimberly-Clark converted the material into sanitary wound dressings. It also examines the development of Kotex and other consumer nondurables in the broader context of the company's postwar business strategy, which initially did not favor feminine hygiene products.[3]

Our account of Kotex and Kleenex sales strategies contributes to a revisionist interpretation of interwar consumer industries. Most previous studies have attributed the success of major new consumer items to marketing professionals like Lasker, often revered in the mar-keting literature as the "Father of American Advertising" who helped launch products such as Lucky Strike cigarettes and Pepsodent tooth-paste. Our analysis of Kotex and Kleenex marketing suggests that Kimberly-Clark profited as much from "innovation from the bottom up" as it did from the expertise of marketing professionals like Lasker. Consumers and small retailers played an active but over-looked role in the consumer culture revolution of the 1920s. Kimber-ly-Clark, Lasker, and other innovators succeeded in part because they integrated these creative impulses into their marketing strategies, facilitating the rise of consumer industries in the Roaring Twenties.[4]

I.

Cellucotton, the base material for Kotex and Kleenex, was a by-prod-uct of diversification in the pulp and paper industry after the passage of the Underwood Tariff Act in 1913. Scrambling for new business to keep their mills running, newsprint producers converted to tariff-protected book, magazine, wrapping, and toilet paper, precipitating price erosion in those markets in 1914, followed by a full-blown recession a year later. This demonstrated that a simple switch from newsprint to other conventional products offered no solution to the industry's structural crisis, leading some manufacturers to experiment with new manufacturing techniques and product lines. Kimberly-Clark, whose management had predicted as early as 1908 that lifting the newsprint tariff would result in severe price competition in other markets, developed high-quality groundwood pulp for rotogravure papers. International Paper ventured into sulfate pulp, laying the groundwork for a vast kraft paper and paperboard business that became the company's new core business during the interwar period. Philadelphia-based Scott Paper, which built its first mill in Chester, Pennsylvania, in 1910, launched a major product development effort in 1916 that improved the quality and uniformity of its toilet and tissue grades. When the United States entered World War I, Scott also developed Zorbik, a laminated cellulose substance for gas mask filters and surgical dressings that resembled Cellucotton.[5]

Kimberly-Clark developed Cellucotton as a substitute for cotton-based surgical dressings; the trademarked name for the new product combined the words "cellulose" and "cotton." The company's decision to enter the market for cotton substitutes was probably based on an analysis of cotton prices, which increased by 30 percent in the half-decade before World War I. The premier cause was the infamous boll weevil, a beetle that devastated southeastern cotton farming at the time, severely tightening supply. Cotton substitutes were available from European papermakers, but many American hospitals rejected these products for lack of cleanliness and absorbency. American cotton supplies, meanwhile, declined further as a result of floods that took large fields along the Mississippi River out of production, causing the price of market cotton to soar. These trends motivated Kimberly-Clark, Scott, and other papermakers to develop Cellucotton, Zorbik, and similar cotton substitutes.[6]

Kimberly-Clark looked back on decades of experience in developing wood-based substitutes for cotton rags in papermaking, but turning wooden logs into a cottonlike substance suitable for hospital use posed major technical challenges. Unlike printing paper which was designed to produce a given degree of brightness and ink absorbency, surgical dressings were antiseptic blood sponges that also protected wounds from postoperative infections. To gain basic technical knowledge, vice president James Kimberly and chemist Ernst Mahler traveled to Germany, where they held discussions with scientists and papermakers at the Darmstadt Institute of Pulp and Paper Technology, at other academic institutions, and at paper mills. The results were largely disappointing because Kimberly and Mahler learned that German papermakers made cotton substitutes from tree species that were unavailable in marketable quantities in the United States.[7]

Upon their return to Wisconsin, Mahler investigated the suitability of various tree species for the production of antiseptic surgical wadding. After several months he settled on spruce, citing its long, clean fiber and quick absorbency. Next Mahler and his three laboratory assistants experimented with pulping technologies. They ruled out conventional sulfite pulping because it failed to eliminate lignin and resinous substances that rendered the product unsuitable for hospital applications. After twelve months of research they developed a chemical pulping process that eliminated the impurities without damaging individual fibers, producing a pulp whose antiseptic properties resembled those of virgin cotton.[8]

Like other paper researchers, Mahler and his assistants tried to process the pulp on miniature paper machines built by the company's engineering staff. When the results proved unsatisfactory, Mahler convinced management to turn the aging, two-machine Globe mill into an experimental mill. The challenge was to produce an ultrathin web, 3,300 square feet of which weighed only three pounds, on a paper machine without breaking the filmy web. This was accomplished with a custom-made felt designed to carry the web, as well as special calender and drying rolls, all of which had to be precision-synchronized to prevent breaks in the web. After rebuilding one of the Globe mill's 80-inch cylinder machines for eight months, Mahler and his assistants produced the first acceptable Cellucotton wadding in 1915. Female employees laminated several dozen sheets and encased them in a gauze wrapper, turning the product into surgical dressings.[9]

While experimental production runs were underway, Kimberly-Clark asked several hospitals to participate in product testing. The first tests were conducted with satisfactory results at Mercy Hospital in Chicago under medical supervision. In addition to demonstrating that Cellucotton met hospitals' sanitary standards, the tests determined that wood-based surgical dressings were several times as absorbent as comparable cotton and required changing at longer intervals than cotton-based dressings, a feature prized by efficiency-minded hospital administrators. Furthermore, one pound of Cellu-cotton cost 60 percent less than a pound of cotton, creating a finan-cial incentive for hospitals to introduce the substitute. By 1917 Kim-berly-Clark had started to receive orders for Cellucotton from hospitals around the country.[10]

Somewhat ironically, America's entry into the war generated unprecedented demand for surgical dressings, but Cellucotton did not become a profit maker for Kimberly-Clark. The company decided to supply surgical dressings to the Red Cross and the War Department at cost. One motive was to avoid the impression of wartime profi-teering by a firm that employed ethnic Germans in key positions, including Frank Sensenbrenner as general manager and Mahler as chief chemist. Demand increased precipitously, thanks in part to clever sales tactics that capitalized on successful hospital testing. Shortly after the United States entered the war, Kimberly-Clark con-tacted the Surgeon General of the War Department, inviting him to review the product and test results. He promptly endorsed the prod-uct after the company announced its "patriotic" policy to forgo prof-its on sales to the government and the Red Cross. The latter, which usually shied away from sanctioning trademarked products for fear that the vendor would exploit the endorsement in advertisements, list-ed all wood-based surgical dressings as Cellucotton in its supply lists, the only instance in which the Red Cross listed a product under its trademarked name during World War I. Early in 1918 the Gas Defense Division of the Chemical Warfare Service investigated Cellu-cotton's suitability as a filter material in gas masks to protect troops from German G-76 gas. When it asked Kimberly-Clark for research support, the company complied, turning its research laboratory over to the Army, whose scientists developed special Cellucotton wadding for gas masks at the Neenah lab in collaboration with company researchers.[11]

At the end of 1917 the Army and the Red Cross ordered Cellu-cotton surgical dressings by the carload. At the time, production was still concentrated at the Globe mill, which produced nine tons in Jan-uary 1918. Volume increased rapidly to 42.5 tons in February and plateaued at 50 tons a month thereafter. To meet surging demand, Kimberly-Clark refitted the Neenah book paper mill for Cellucotton production at a cost of $65,000, more than doubling the company's aggregate capacity. The Neenah mill shipped its first carload of 15.5 tons in July 1918, reaching its full capacity of 88 tons a month in October. Turning Cellucotton into surgical dressings, still a manual operation, was organized by the Red Cross, which recruited thousands of volunteers to laminate sheets and encase them in gauze wrappers.[12]

The Armistice in November 1918 resulted in the cancellation of a partially fulfilled Army contract for 375 tons of Cellucotton, as well as a Red Cross contract for a similar amount. The Neenah mill phased out Cellucotton production almost immediately, but the Globe mill continued to run at wartime levels to supply hospitals that started to place orders at the end of 1918. Conditions deteriorated sharply in March 1919, however, when the Red Cross distributed its surplus surgical dressings to hospitals at no cost and the Army sold its excess stock to speculators who flooded the market. Kimberly-Clark scaled back production at the Globe mill to 13 tons in March, followed by an almost complete shutdown in May.[13]

The crisis of spring 1919 could have spelled the end of Kimberly-Clark's foray into cellulose-based wadding. At the time, management would not have perceived this as a strategic loss because the company's core business lay in bleached groundwood paper and other commodity printing grades. Cellucotton production involved only two aging mills whose narrow paper machines were unsuitable for most other grades. Taking a leaf from Scott Paper, which phased out Zorbik surgical dressings at the end of the war, Kimberly-Clark could have quietly abandoned Cellucotton.

II.

With the exception of Mahler and Kimberly, most Kimberly-Clark executives initially viewed Cellucotton as a diversion from more pressing business. Given the glut in the market for surgical dressings, Cellucotton would have to be converted into an alternative end product, distracting management from the daunting task of maintaining the company's long-term viability in the chaotic postwar period. From 1914 to 1919 the overall consumer price index rose 73 percent, and raw material prices in the paper industry increased more than 100 percent. Kimberly-Clark reported an average 137 percent increase in hourly wages compared to 1914. Transportation costs rose at comparable rates because wartime service had worn out the railroads' rolling stock, more than 15 percent of which was out of commission by 1919. Customers, notably book and magazine publishers, complained about a 135 percent increase in overall paper prices.[14]

Industrial relations warranted close attention because workers were determined to secure wartime wage gains. By 1919 mill worker communities across the country were rife with rumors of looming strikes to fend off employers' attempts to slash wages. Most paper companies did in fact announce wage cuts exceeding 20 percent in late April 1920, precipitating a labor conflict known as the "Great Paper War." The latter paralyzed International Paper, which became embroiled in a year-long struggle with workers that produced staggering financial losses for the company and crippled industrial relations for more than a decade. More enlightened employers escaped a similar fate by negotiating less drastic wage cuts with the International Brotherhood of Pulp, Sulfite, and Paper Mill Workers. Kimberly-Clark shunned this strategy and instead established mill councils, a euphemism for company unions. In spring 1920 council members met with management representatives in each community to conduct surveys of retail prices and negotiate wage reductions. General manager Sensenbrenner later claimed that these investigations determined a 23.3 percent fall from 1919 to 1920 (an unrealistically high figure), justifying a 19 percent wage cut that was announced by the company in May 1920 with the consent of mill council members. Combined with a company pension plan, mill safety committees, company housing, and an employee newsletter, these tactics enabled Kimberly-Clark to avoid strike-related losses throughout the interwar years.[15]

In addition to maintaining manageable industrial relations, executives and middle managers spent considerable time and effort improving customer relations with paper merchants. The latter not only complained about soaring paper prices but also worried about trade gossip that Kimberly-Clark intended to increase its direct business with publishers, effectively cutting jobbers out of paper marketing. This strategy was pursued by other paper companies, notably International Paper, which negotiated the bulk of its contracts directly with publishers, souring business relations with Carter, Rice & Company and other prestigious paper merchant houses. James Kimberly, head of the sales department, and general manager Sensenbrenner tried to reassure jobbers that the company had no such plans, but he could not resist the temptation to "encourage" merchants to order more paper. In his keynote address at the company's 1921 annual meeting with jobbers, Sensenbrenner directly addressed the

> rumor . . . that the Kimberly-Clark Company were [*sic*] gradually weaning themselves away from merchant trade and going into

the direct business exclusively. I want to emphasize, as I said before, that nothing is further from our thought than that; that during last year we determined definitely that we were going to allot a certain part of our production for the merchant trade. . . .

But, he added,

It depends, of course, upon the merchants as to whether or not we can make good on that policy. Of course, if we don't get any business from the merchants, why, we will have to look for channels of trade wherever we can find them and wherever we can place our product.[16]

Paper merchants duly increased their orders in 1922, although it remains unclear whether this was a result of Sensenbrenner's veiled threat or, more likely, a sharp upsurge in demand for market book, magazine, and school paper in that year.

Strategic production issues also loomed large in the immediate postwar years. In 1920 Kimberly-Clark sold the aging two-machine Telulah mill in Appleton to the Fox River Paper Company and invested the proceeds into the construction of a refined groundwood paper mill in Niagara Falls, New York, to increase the company's capacity to produce book and rotogravure magazine paper. The main objective of building a paper mill 700 miles east of Wisconsin was to improve the company's competitive position in East Coast markets by decreasing transportation costs f.o.b. customer warehouses, most of which were located in New York City. The Niagara Falls mill featured an electric, 196-inch fourdrinier, the world's largest paper machine at the time and only the second electric fourdrinier in the United States. Separate motors powered the belt, press dryers, and winder sections, creating major synchronization problems that took company engineers almost two years to solve. In September 1922 Sensenbrenner, Kimberly, and other executives who closely followed the engineers' attempts to synchronize the prized machine breathed a collective sigh of relief when the Niagara Falls mill went onstream with a daily capacity for 75 tons, which doubled shortly thereafter with the installation of a second fourdrinier.[17]

The aging Atlas mill in Appleton presented a different set of problems. Saddled with outdated production equipment, it was no longer viable as a wrapping paper mill, forcing Kimberly-Clark to seek other product lines to avoid shutdown. Conversion to box cover grades and colored kindergarten paper failed to sustain the mill during the post–World War I recession. After much internal debate Sensenbrenner and Kimberly received the board of directors' approval of a plan to convert the mill to wallpaper. Initially lacking the machinery needed to manufacture finished wallpaper, the Atlas mill produced basic stock for United Wallpaper Factories, Inc., one of the nation's largest wallpaper companies which applied various finishes at its plant in Jersey City, New Jersey. In 1919 Kimberly-Clark's board approved funds for specialized embossing and rolling machines that enabled the mill to produce finished wallpapers. One of the first and most popular grades produced at the Atlas mill featured a rough texture known as "oatmeal finish" or Polychrome Duplex. Atlas papermakers used the technique to produce a variety of new wallpapers that produced a three-dimensional "cloud effect of visionary depth." Machines effected the finish by coating conventional wallpaper stock with small but visible wood particles to roughen the stock's surface and produce Polychrome's soft, stylish appearance. Kimberly-Clark continued to develop its wallpaper business in close collaboration with United Wallpaper, which obtained designs, maintained an office at the Atlas mill that supervised various production steps, and handled marketing.[18]

Labor and customer relations—combined with the difficult start-up of the Niagara Falls mill, the reconfiguration of the Atlas mill, and the construction of a sulfite pulp mill in the Canadian wilderness (see below)—preoccupied management in the immediate postwar years. As a result, most executives and middle managers initially wanted to phase out Cellucotton because it lacked a viable market and required a product development initiative that would divert precious financial and managerial resources. The product that later emerged as the company's most reliable profit maker was looked upon as little more than a nuisance.

III.

Cellucotton survived as part of the Kimberly-Clark product line thanks to the initiative of Mahler and Kimberly. In February 1919 they visited Walter Luecke, a Chicago sales representative for Sears-Roebuck (which bought its catalog paper from Kimberly-Clark) to discuss a possible commercial use for Cellucotton. On March 1, 1919, after meeting general manager Sensenbrenner, Luecke was offered a job with the company and was tasked with finding outlets for Cellucotton.[19]

Luecke saw some potential in converting the product into sanitary napkins, which he later described as the only market that required "the enormous volume needed to keep their factory busy."[20] The idea had been proposed to Kimberly-Clark by the American Fund for the French Wounded, which received letters from Army nurses claiming that they used Cellucotton surgical dressings as makeshift sanitary napkins. Luecke quickly became an outspoken advocate of the idea, urging Kimberly-Clark officials to go into the sanitary napkin business. Although Kimberly and Mahler agreed, Luecke was initially unable to find other supporters. Somewhat desperate, he then contacted two jobbers, offering them exclusive rights to Cellucotton for sanitary napkin manufacturing, provided that they agreed to use the entire Cellucotton product Kimberly-Clark could deliver. Both firms turned him down, claiming that the quantity was too great for them to commit to buying it, and arguing that sanitary napkins were too personal and could never be advertised.[21]

In summer 1919 the indefatigable Luecke continued to make the case for sanitary napkins in discussions with directors Sensenbrenner, William Bonifas, and Frank Shattuck, but he was unable to "get them to commit themselves definitely," he later recalled.[22] Upon consultation with Mahler and Kimberly, they reluctantly approved Luecke's plan to resume Cellucotton production and convert the product into sanitary napkins in early September. Luecke, tasked with finding an advertising agency, recruited the Charles F. W. Nichols Company to handle marketing, including the development of a trademarked name. In one of his first meetings with A. B. Taylor, the Nichols agent who was in charge of the sanitary napkin project, Luecke discussed possible names. At a meeting in early September 1919, someone remarked that the filler used in the product featured a cottonlike texture. "Right there a name was coined," Luecke later recalled, "namely, cottex, meaning cotton texture. We decided, however, that the name cottex would be mispronounced by some customers, so we simplified the pronunciation as well as the spelling and from that moment on, our sanitary napkin was known [as] 'Kotex.'"[23]

Several days later Kimberly-Clark produced a few dozen Kotex samples for shipment to retail stores. One of the first boxes was sent to Woolworth, the New York retail giant, on September 23, 1919. Woolworth responded cautiously:

We do not know whether this all paper [*sic*] Fibre Napkin would be a good seller, and whether it would give satisfaction. We are, however, willing to try it out, and are issuing a list to stores under our Chicago District calling their particular attention to this, and asking them to give it a trial, and if it proves to be good we are willing to put it in all of our stores."[24]

Woolworth's Chicago store sold the first box of Kotex in October.[25]

The first episode in the history of Kotex encapsulated the complicated cultural and gender issues involved in marketing feminine hygiene products. First, Kimberly-Clark sold the first sanitary napkins under its own name, contrary to its intention of keeping the product at arm's length from the company. This policy, motivated by fears that Kimberly-Clark's reputation would suffer if the company came to be associated with a culturally sensitive item, was already evident in Luecke's earliest discussions with Taylor, when he insisted that the name Kimberly-Clark was "in no way to be even suggested, all or in part, in the selection of a trade name."[26] In line with this policy Kimberly-Clark established a new subsidiary, the Cellucotton Products Company, whose name intentionally did not hint at its affiliation with Kimberly-Clark. The fact that Kimberly-Clark initially did sell Kotex under its own name suggests that the company was so anxious to dispose of its bulging Cellucotton inventory as to break its carefully-thought-out marketing rules. Second, the boxes that were for sale at Woolworth did not carry the content description "sanitary napkin." Store clerks likely informed customers orally about the nature of the product, a potentially embarrassing situation because most clerks were men who were unaccustomed to discussing feminine hygiene issues. Vice versa, a female customer was unlikely to ask a male clerk for sanitary napkins. The multimillion-dollar Kotex marketing campaigns of the 1920s were designed to prevent precisely this type of encounter by establishing brand-name recognition through advertising, enabling customers to ask clerks for sanitary napkins by demanding the neutral-sounding Kotex—and without having to utter the dreaded term.

Commercial menstrual products had been available since the late 1880s, when some women replaced homemade pads (usually cotton batting wrapped in cheesecloth) with cotton-based sanitary napkins. By the end of the nineteenth century a variety of brands were available from Sears, Roebuck; Montgomery Ward; and other mail-order houses, as well as from a few local pharmacies and drugstores. Ads appeared in *Harper's Bazaar* and *Delineator*. As historians Jane Farrell-Beck and Laura Kidd have documented, however, menstrual product marketing dropped off after the turn of the century, perhaps because product quality fell precipitously (no single manufacturer remained in the sanitary napkin business for more than a few years). The vast majority of women continued to use homemade pads, but menstrual hygiene practices improved because nurses, whose professional training increasingly emphasized sterile wound treatment, helped disseminate information about proper pad use to obstetrical patients. Commercial sales remained abysmal, however, because the dozen or so manufacturers who produced sanitary napkins after World War I were unable or unwilling to meet the formidable challenges of marketing their products. [27]

In late fall 1919 Luecke got a taste of the cultural obstacles facing the new product. Dealers refused to display Kotex and did not put it in their show windows. Most kept it out of sight behind counters or in back rooms. Letters flooded Kimberly-Clark from individuals and organizations objecting to the sale of the product. Luecke pressed on, however, and in November 1919 he started a sales campaign in New York City, taking a sales crew of six agents with him. Since Kotex advertising campaigns were not launched until later, Luecke and his men had to buttress their initial sales pitches with copies of proposed trade ads, which they showed to pharmacists, department store purchase agents, and jobbers. "After much forceful selling talk," they obtained a few orders.[28]

IV.

In 1920 Kimberly-Clark established the Cellucotton Products Company (CPC) as a wholly owned subsidiary capitalized at $400,000. Reflecting the continued disagreements among members of Kimberly-Clark's board over the wisdom of entering the sanitary napkin field, director Harry Price voted against the move, making it one of the board's few strategic decisions that lacked unanimity. The CPC board of directors consisted mostly of Kimberly-Clark executives: James Kimberly, Frank Sensenbrenner, Ernst Mahler, Frank Shattuck, Harry Price, and William Bonifas. They were by joined by two advertising professionals, Walter Luecke and A. B. Taylor. Mahler, the inventor of

Cellucotton, was elected president, but day-to-day management was handled by Luecke, who served as general manager. The company changed its name several times over the course of the 1920s, but in 1927 it settled on International Cellucotton Products Company.[29]

Luecke's first order of business as general manager was to obtain a registered trademark for Kotex. Having used the brand name informally in correspondence with retailers and jobbers since September 1919, Luecke asked Wallace Meyer, the Nichols agent now in charge of Kotex marketing, to have the name researched by a Chicago law firm. The latter determined the existence of a Cotex Company, a New York–based furniture factory that sold Cotex upholstery products, but counseled Meyer that possible objections by the Cotex company to CPC's trademark application would likely be rejected by the U.S. Patent Office. Meyer advised Luecke in August 1920 to apply for the trademark, adding, "'Kotex' is a wonderful name—easy, quick, inoffensive and already distinguishable."[30] The trademark was issued on September 21, 1920.[31]

Kimberly-Clark tested the waters for Kotex marketing through direct sales, but the results were disappointing. Luecke sent samples to women whose addresses he took from the phone book, enclosing a letter that asked recipients to contact the company if they wished to obtain regular Kotex deliveries by mail. He did not receive a single response. He then tried sending the letter and sample separately, "but it did not bring any replies either, which shows that the direct selling method using the company's name did not work out," as Luecke told Sensenbrenner in April 1920. Touting his own horn a bit, he added, "[T]he only method of marketing this product is through the regular jobbing and retail channels. It will therefore be necessary that we immediately call on each and all of the jobbers and retailers in the country and that we also decide on our advertising campaign which, as has been agreed, is essential to get the volume business on this article."[32]

In 1920 Luecke and Meyer developed a marketing campaign aimed at retailers. They placed Kotex advertisements with a wide variety of specialized trade journals and magazines, including *The American Druggist, Pharmaceutical Record, Retail Druggist, Western Druggist, Pacific Drug Review, Drug Topics, The Corset and Underwear Review, Dry Goods Merchants Trade Journal, Dry Goods Economist, Dry Goods Reporter,* and *The Modern Hospital Journal.* The ads contained a brief history of Cellucotton and its conversion into Kotex. "Large hospitals in the United States now use Cellucotton where a soft, rapidly-absorbing, moisture-retaining dressing is required, such as in obstetrical cases," read the one of the first ads, published in November 1920 in the *Dry Goods Economist.* "This proves its superiority as a product to be used in the manufacture of a sanitary napkin."[33] Ads also contained basic technical information highlighting Cellucotton's advantages over cotton: five times the absorption capacity, three times as rapid absorption, freedom from chafing because Cellucotton did not dry hard as cotton, and ease of disposal through disintegration in water. The ads also encouraged retailers to display Kotex in shop windows and on counters. The results were mixed, as many retailers continued to ignore the product. During a long and frustrating sales trip to Syracuse, New York, Taylor reported to Luecke about his difficulties to get drugstore owners to "talk Kotex." Indicative of continued opposition against Kotex among retailers, one drugstore manager told Taylor that he wouldn't "handle [sanitary] napkins of any kind." [34] An Erie, Pennsylvania, dealer was "interested but not at present."[35] Taylor summed up his frustrations in February 1921, when he told Luecke, "My sales for this month are ABSOLUTELY ROTTEN, as you will learn at the end of the month. I have suffered more abuse at the hands of the trade than ever before in my life." But, he added, "[M]y enthusiasm for Kotex is not waning one bit." He planned to go on another sales trip to New England, "to beat every buyer I call upon and I'll be damned if any are going to beat or procrastinate with me."[36]

Consumer advertising of Kotex started in 1921. Written by Meyer, the first ad draft was developed two years before and played on three major themes: patriotism, war, and science (figure 2.1). Entitled "To Save Men's Lives Science Discovered Kotex," the copy omitted all direct references to Kimberly-Clark, whose management had stiffened its opposition to associating the company's name with the product.[37] The text read, "Our boys were falling wounded on the battlefields of France. Army doctors were calling for an unlimited supply of antiseptic surgical dressings that could be more absorbent than cotton. The government said, 'Can you give us such a surgical dressing?' We could and we did."[38] This account omitted the fact that Kimberly-Clark had initially sold Cellucotton surgical dressings to hospitals before 1917. It suggested instead that the product owed its existence to a company that heeded the nation's call to arms. Under the heading "A War Emergency," the draft continued with a fully fictionalized account of the product's origins: "Men working in feverish haste built a great plant . . . near the forest district of the North. And

a wonderful surgical dressing was produced."[39] The fact that Cellucotton was produced not at a brand-new plant hacked out of the
wilderness but at the fifty-year old Globe mill apparently interfered
with the proposed ad's message that Cellucotton and Kotex were
modern, scientific products. "Many a sorely wounded soldier has reason to thank American scientific inventive genius for this great practical discovery."[40] The proposed artwork reinforced the theme, depicting two uniformed men recuperating from war wounds under a tree,
with two other soldiers—evidently recovered from their injuries—

FIGURE 2.1 Draft for Kotex print advertisement, 1921

standing in the background. Remarkably, the only woman depicted in the artwork was a nurse assisting one of the soldiers. Meyer, sensitive to the need to appeal to female audiences, viewed this as a significant flaw, citing it as his principal reason for rejecting the artwork. Moreover, unlike later ads, the draft did not explain that Army nurses had pioneered the use of wound dressings as sanitary napkins, leaving unexploited a major opportunity to gear the ad toward female audiences.[41] Turning to a more upbeat theme, the draft copy portrayed Kotex as something of a "peace dividend," declaring, "Now that the war is over we are devoting this great factory to peace time usefulness."[42] The draft text also ventured to predict that "before long Kotex will be available in restrooms, dry goods, department and drug stores all over the country"—a somewhat optimistic guess in light of Kimberly-Clark's continuing difficulties with retailers. Elaborating a wound metaphor of menstruation, the draft noted that "Kotex are also excellent for dressing bad cuts, burns or bruises." This statement insinuated a correlation between the menstrual cycle and injuries, evoking a problematic image of menstruation that has been criticized in much of the recent literature.[43]

To Meyer's credit, he substantially edited the draft before the first Kotex ads appeared in magazines. He eliminated the fictionalized account of Cellucotton's origins in World War I and the recommendation to use Kotex pads as wound dressings. The artwork, drawn by the Nichols agency's illustrator John Taucke, resembled that of the first draft, depicting a nurse and a woman assisting a man in a wheelchair; but on Meyer's insistence Taucke added a young woman sitting on the grass (figure 2.2). This eliminated the draft's visual predominance of men, unequivocally aiming the new ad at its intended target audience. In more subtle language than the first draft, the text elaborated the themes of war and science but scaled back company patriotism, proclaiming, "Kotex enters universal service from a romantic background. For, although a woman's article, it started as Cellucotton—a wonderful sanitary absorbent which science perfected for use of our men and allied soldiers wounded in France." The copy did not elaborate why "romantic" was an appropriate adjective to describe conditions on the Western Front. Unlike the first draft, the new copy did explain the inclusion of a nurse in the artwork, mentioning "letters from nurses in France, regarding a new use for this wonderful absorbent." Remarkably, however, the text still left readers speculating what "a new use" for the product actually meant, avoiding the term "sanitary napkin" throughout (the term made its debut in a

FIGURE 2.2 Kotex print advertisement, 1921

Kotex ad in November 1921). Medical advice, nurses, and medical symbolism became standard features of Kotex ads throughout the interwar period to imply that sanitary napkins were quasi-medical products.

To drive home that message, designer Albert Ross included a white St. George's cross on a blue background in the Kotex box design, shown in all ads. The purpose was to establish Kotex as a medical product by using the symbol of the Red Cross. The International Red Cross had adopted a red St. George's cross on a white background as the organization's symbol of neutrality and mercy at its founding convention in Geneva in 1863, reversing the color composition of the Swiss national flag. Keen to prevent its commercial use, the American Red Cross asked the United States Congress to protect the symbol in its charter and supplemental legislation, including the U.S. Criminal Code. It did not, however, prevent marketers of medical items from using the St. George's cross (usually in colors other than red) in advertisements to enhance product credibility by suggesting some type of Red Cross endorsement or to insinuate a product's medical purpose. Ross followed this trend by choosing the cross as the Kotex symbol.[44]

Throughout 1921 Meyer and his team experimented with new marketing messages. Artwork unveiled in May marked a departure from World War I themes and concomitantly eliminated men, who disappeared from sanitary napkin advertisements until World War II. The May ad instead depicted two women in a study. One donned the bobbed hairdo that came in vogue in the early 1920s and held a sheet of paper[45] (likely meant to represent Kotex information); a similarly coiffured woman wearing a stylishly loose dress was standing in front of her. The purpose was to show two New Women of the 1920s in a private conversation of feminine hygiene. More practical issues were addressed in an advertisement released in November 1921 depicting a mistress and her maid. Entitled "Simplify the Laundry Problem," it was the first Kotex consumer advertisement that included the term "sanitary pads" and informed women that the product required no cleaning after use because it was "cheap enough to throw away, and easy to dispose of." The latter claim, repeated in most Kotex ads of the 1920s, was dubious at best. Disposal required taking the filling out of the gauze, soaking it thoroughly, and flushing it down the toilet, with a similar procedure applied to the wrapper. Women who failed to follow this procedure usually had to call a plumber. Be this as it may, after Lasker had broken the ice in his famous meeting with the editor of *Ladies' Home Journal,* the first consumer ads appeared in a variety of popular women's magazines, principally *LHJ, Cosmopolitan, Vogue,* and *Good Housekeeping.*[46]

CPC's advertising expenses totaled $173,000 in the first year and were projected to exceed $200,000 in 1922, raising questions among board members whether further investments were justifiable in light of disappointing sales. James Kimberly, who had supported Kotex from the beginning, later recalled saying at a meeting of the board of directors, "We knew this wasn't a penny-ante game when we got into it. The pot is big and we've got to put more into it. I say, let's not drop out." Sensenbrenner, who turned from a skeptic to a Kotex convert, agreed. "This reminds me of a poker game" in which "it costs another million dollars to call the previous raise," he remarked. "Since we have so much money invested, I am perfectly agreeable to spending this additional money."[47] CPC's board of directors approved the necessary investments into consumer advertising.[48]

Sensenbrenner's characterization of the investment as a high-stakes gamble was correct in light of the fact that Kotex sales remained slow. Like a Geneva, Illinois, merchant, who told CPC bluntly that he did "not care to handle this kind of an article," most retailers refused to display the product openly.[49] CPC frankly acknowledged that with some retailers it was "evident from the looks of their store that they will not be able to sell an article such as ours."[50] CPC tried to mobilize consumers by telling them that "nearly every store that caters to women can supply you with Kotex," implying that customers should exert pressure on retailers to make the product available. The results were disappointing, demonstrating the limits of consumer advertising.

The decisive breakthrough came with the introduction of self-service in 1922, when CPC recommended that retailers place stacks of Kotex boxes on their counters. Druggists and department stores customarily displayed their wares on shelves behind the counter, creating the now-familiar situation that was uncomfortable to both customer and sales clerk. Self-service had been pioneered in groceries several years earlier, most famously by Clarence Saunders's Piggly Wiggly store in Memphis, Tennessee, in 1916; but most retailers remained committed to traditional store service. CPC's attempt to turn Kotex into a self-service item introduced many retailers to the new sales concept. A series of CPC trade ads instructed retailers, "Keep a supply of Kotex packages on a prominent counter."[51] Unlike sanitary napkin containers sold from behind the counter, the countertop boxes contained no labels or text except the name Kotex and the familiar white cross. Accompanying artwork suggested that this sales technique was particularly suitable for high-income groups whose members could presumably be trusted to pay for the product after taking a box from the stack. A coin box placed next to the stack where customers could deposit their 65¢ for a box of Kotex completely eliminated the need for communicative action. CPC later added package holders with instructions to "[w]rap the day's supply of Kotex packages in plain paper. Use the attractive metal wrapped package holder we supply. . . . Mark the goods plainly with the price, so that the customer can help herself, pay the clerk, without questions or conversations."[52]

The origin of the idea remains a matter of dispute. Lasker, never prone to diminishing his contributions to American marketing, claimed credit thirty years later in an article for *Advertising Age,* writing, "We developed for Kotex the simple idea of putting wrapped packages on the dealer's counter."[53] His claim was disputed twelve years later by Meyer who credited an ingenious Wisconsin druggist. According to Meyer:

> The idea was first reported by a [Nichols agency] copywriter, O. T. Frash, while in Watertown, Wisconsin, on a field trip. He saw it in an Apothecary Shop owned by a German-American druggist who found that women would buy many more packages if they were wrapped in plain white paper and tied with blue string, then piled on the counter in a pyramid surmounted by a small neat card reading, "Kotex—Take a box—65 cents."[54]

According to Meyer, Frash returned to Chicago and convinced the Nichols agency to apply the idea to Kotex marketing. This account appears credible in part because it provides a level of specificity lacking in Lasker's version. Unlike Lasker, Meyer made no attempt to claim credit for himself; furthermore, he recounted the story in an unpublished letter to the Wisconsin State Historical Society in an attempt to "set the historical record straight." If Meyer's account can be believed, self-service originated not as the brilliant invention of professional marketers but as an "innovation from the bottom up" that was incorporated into Kotex marketing by Nichols salesmen. It precipitated major increases in Kotex sales and was quickly adopted by other sanitary napkin marketers.

Technologically, Kotex production shifted from manual to machine folding in the early 1920s. The first pads, measuring 9 by 3½ inches and consisting of 40 plies of wadding wrapped in gauze, were made by hand at the Neenah mill by unskilled workers. Manual labor persisted until 1924, when CPC introduced a machine invented by company engineer William Bauer that automated production. The Bauer machine cut wadding and gauze from continuous strips and dropped wadding plies on the gauze, whose sides were folded over to form the pad. The machine then cut the folded gauze to leave a flap at both ends for fastening. In the early 1920s Kimberly-Clark installed eight Bauer machines at the Neenah mill, each with a capacity to fold thirty pads a minute. The machine was sufficiently flexible to produce pads of varying thickness, facilitating the switch from 40 plies in the first pad to 37 plies in a follow-up design introduced in 1924. That same year CPC introduced the Super Kotex whose 74 plies featured higher absorbency. Later changes reduced the pad's width from 3½ inches to 3⅜ in 1925 and 3¼ a year later.[55]

In 1924 Kimberly-Clark expanded its Kotex-related production capacity with the start-up of a wadding mill in Niagara Falls, New York, adjacent to its vast rotogravure paper mill. The new mill was built in 1922 as a joint venture between Kimberly-Clark and the Thilmany Pulp and Paper Company of Kaukauna, Wisconsin, to produce light wrapping paper. Strong Kotex sales, however, convinced Kimberly-Clark in 1924 to buy out Thilmany for $100,000, convert the mill to Cellucotton and Kotex, and upgrade it with a $500,000 investment. Its main production equipment consisted of two Yankee paper machines. A variation of the cylinder machine, the Yankee machine dried the cellulose web on a single steam-heated cylinder featuring a polished surface, unlike the fourdrinier machine that dried the web in press rolls. The Yankee process produced a variety of special finishes, including machine-glazed paper and machine-creped tissue, enabling Kimberly-Clark to convert the two machines from wrapping grades to Cellucotton with a few minor adjustments. Beginning in August 1924 the Yankee machines produced Kotex Cellucotton on a 24-hour-a-day production schedule. Their output was converted into Kotex in an adjoining building by workers tending eight Bauer cutting machines, each with a capacity to fold thirty-one sanitary napkins per minute.[56]

Automated equipment also made its presence felt at the point of sale with the introduction of Kotex vending machines. Pioneered by marketers of candy and chewing gum, coin vending machines gained popularity for higher-priced items in the 1920s, when William Rowe developed one for cigarettes, later followed by Coca-Cola and by food marketers for other products. The Kotex machine was based on a patent by George Weiss, a Chicago engineer, who agreed to license the patent to CPC for a 75¢ royalty for every machine. Introduced in women's restrooms in 1922, it enabled CPC to expand sales far beyond traditional outlets, into restaurants, hotels, railroad cars, and offices (figure 2.3). The technology could have solved the company's familiar marketing problems in one fell swoop by rendering store visits superfluous, but the company decided not to antagonize retailers whose patronage it had carefully nurtured. Instead of conventional Kotex boxes that contained twelve sanitary napkins, the vending machine dispensed single pads at 10¢ each, almost double the per-unit price of boxed pads. Although vending machines produced lucrative new business, Kotex sales remained primarily anchored in retail

FIGURE 2.3 Kotex vending machine

stores. Smaller manufacturers copied the strategy for their own products, including Neps pads, which were available from coin vending machines in the late 1920s.[57]

Unsurprisingly, competitors quickly sought to capitalize on CPC's success. In 1923 Bloomingdale Brothers, the J.C. Penney department store, and other, smaller competitors flooded the market with sanitary napkins priced 40 percent less than Kotex. Although Kimberly-Clark and CPC found it difficult to challenge the new products with patent litigation, they successfully struck out against trademark infringements. One Earl Wilson, for example, who sold "Protex" sanitary napkins in blue boxes emblazoned with the Geneva cross, was promptly sued by CPC in the Federal District Court for the Northern District of Illinois for trademark infringement and unfair competition. In a consent decree dated December 1, 1923, the defendant agreed to refrain from "using the word 'Pro-tex' or any other word terminating in the suffix 'otex' or 'tex' or 'tecs' or 'tec' or any other word simulating the plaintiff's trade-mark KOTEX as a trade-mark for catamenial bandages or sanitary napkins . . . or in connection with the advertising, offering for sale, or sale thereof." Wilson also agreed to cease using "packaging, marketing, labeling, or dressing said bandages in any manner likely to cause the public to be confused, misled, or deceived."[58] CPC brought a similar trademark infringement suit against Bloomingdale's, which also signed a consent decree in 1923. Attempts to protect the trademark through a ban on imported Kotex imitations were rejected by the Federal Trade Commission.[59]

CPC and Kimberly-Clark responded to the introduction of cheaper sanitary napkins by improving Kotex, developing a variety of new pads, and changing the thrust of marketing campaigns. In 1924 a Kimberly-Clark research team developed the thick Super Kotex and added a deodorant based on boric acid and zinc phenyl sulfate. These changes precipitated a proliferation of advertising, reflected in the growth of CPC's advertising budget from less than $400,000 in 1923 to more than $1million two years later (table 2.1). To elaborate the medical themes of earlier marketing campaigns, CPC hired Ellen Buckland, a registered nurse, who endorsed the product in advertisements and letters that were inserted into Kotex boxes. George Williamson, billed a "consulting physician," wrote a CPC booklet entitled "Hygiene of Menstruation," the first piece of Kotex marketing material that included the term "menstruation." In addition to a short description of the menstrual cycle and basic feminine hygiene procedures, the booklet contained lengthy discussions of diseases that could presumably be detected through proper pad use, including womb cancer and fibroid tumors. Reinforcing the message of recent trademark litigation, Williamson cautioned customers, "A large number of difficulties may be the result of unclean, improperly made pads that do not readily take up the discharges."[60] Buckland made similar claims, asserting that "60% of many ills, according to many leading medical authorities, are traced to the use of unsafe and unsanitary makeshift methods."[61] In the final analysis this marketing material conveyed the message that women needed "protection from themselves" which remained pervasive in twentieth-century menstrual product advertising, as historian Shelley Park has pointed out.[62]

TABLE 2.1

Kotex advertising expenses, 1921–1929

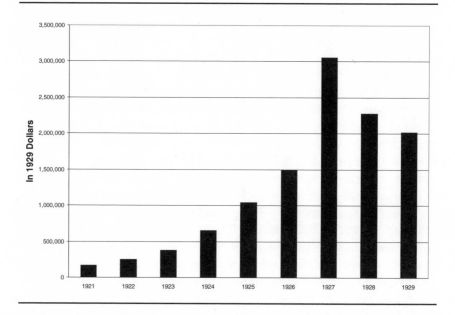

The advertising campaigns of the mid-1920s turned Kotex into a virtual synonym for sanitary napkin, a consumer survey commissioned by the company determined. Investigators reported that "Kotex is so common a term now that it has almost become disassociated in the minds of . . . women from the actual circumstances involved." At a J.C. Penney department store that sold sanitary napkins under a store brand name at 19¢ a box, customers asked "for a 19¢ box of your Kotex." Not all comments were positive: "I tried Kotex, several kinds of it, but they are all the same—hard and uncomfortable," one customer opined.[63]

Kotex was the most expensive sanitary pad available, costing almost twice as much as other brands. Partly to recover its enormous advertising costs, CPC increased per-unit retail prices by 8 percent, from 5¢ (1921) to 5.41¢ (1924) at current prices (table 2.2). At Mahler's initiative the CPC board brought the rapid increase in sales costs to a halt in 1928, allowing the company to cut per-unit retail prices from 5.41¢ to 3.75¢ in order to fend off smaller competitors. CPC estimated that it controlled 70 percent of the sanitary napkin market of the late 1920s, a credible figure because the company

TABLE 2.2
Kotex per-unit price in cents, 1921–1929

Year	Per-Unit Price in Cents	Per-Unit Price in 1929 Cents
1921	5	4.78
1922	5	5.09
1923	5	5
1924	5.41	5.41
1925	5.41	5.29
1926	5.41	5.23
1927	5.41	5.32
1928	3.75	3.75
1929	3.75	3.75

included it in a report to the Federal Trade Commission, an unlikely venue for exaggerated claims of market dominance.[64]

CPC soon faced a formidable new competitor, Johnson & Johnson, which entered the sanitary napkin market in 1926. Founded forty years earlier in New Brunswick, New Jersey, the company initially produced cotton-based surgical dressings and in 1891 built a bacteriological research facility that was one of the nation's first corporate laboratories. Five years later Johnson & Johnson introduced "Lister's Towels," probably the first commercial sanitary napkin in history, but it quickly abandoned the product because of marketing problems. In 1921 it entered the market for consumer nondurables with Band-Aid adhesive bandages and Johnson & Johnson baby cream while maintaining its position as the nation's leading manufacturer of cotton-based surgical dressings. In 1926 the company established a permanent presence in sanitary napkins with the introduction of the cotton-based Modess and Nupak pads. An advertising campaign, whose stylish artwork made Kotex ads look pedestrian, helped launch the products. Further indicating that CPC was confronted with its first serious competitor, Johnson & Johnson commissioned Lillian Gilbreth to conduct the first scientific survey of the sanitary napkin market and to recommend product development and marketing strategies. Gilbreth, a proponent of scientific management who became the first female member of the American Society of Mechanical Engineers in

1926, wrote a 137-page, no-nonsense report that was based on a survey of menstrual hygiene practices among college students.[65]

The report contained a thorough analysis of Kotex pads, setting the benchmark for all other sanitary napkins. As could be expected, most of the 1,037 students surveyed used Kotex, citing availability as the primary reason. CPC's relentless efforts to convince retailers across the country to display the product and use innovative sales techniques evidently had paid off. Furthermore, Kotex earned high marks for name recognition, indicating that the millions invested into consumer advertising was money well spent. The name was so recognizable, in fact, that it survived some mispronunciations intact, as evidenced by the experience of a young German woman who "asked for kodaks in a shop and was promptly supplied with a box of Kotex."[66] On the other hand, many respondents were critical of Kotex disposal methods. Some who did not follow the disposal instructions included in the box reported mortifying experiences with overflowing toilets. The report also indicated that disposal problems cost CPC valuable corporate business. The head nurse of Metropolitan Life Insurance Company, for example, struck CPC from the vendor list because office clerks flushed unopened pads down the toilet, resulting in higher plumber bills for the company. Gilbreth's respondents also complained that Kotex pads were too long and bulky and that fillers required adjustments.[67]

The report included withering reviews of other pads. Gilbreth deemed Flush Down Ideal "too clumsy and obvious" with an "unattractive" label that told "a lie. No gauze will flush." The Safety Ideal box included "ugly phrasing, false wording, a lie." "Mi Ladi Dainti" was "absolutely the opposite of the name. . . . It is too long, is spelled foolishly, and has no point." To buy Gimbro Nap, "one would probably have to repeat [the brand name] a number of times to the clerk and finally ask in exasperation for a sanitary napkin." The size of Johnson & Johnson's Nupak was "all right while in use, but too large for carrying or packing." Its cotton-based filler was "very good and it would be very soft and comfortable, but it is entirely too large and bulky. . . . [Some] of the thickness should be taken out of the center and more towards the ends."[68]

The report precipitated major changes in pad design. Gilbreth recommended that Johnson & Johnson reduce overall pad size, shorten front tabs, thicken fillers at the center, round filler corners and sides, and develop a softer gauze. She also suggested that Johnson & Johnson hire a female manager or researcher to support product design.

FIGURE 2.4 Kotex advertisement, 1929

Johnson & Johnson's managers and staff researchers apparently stud-
ied the Gilbreth report carefully, because most of its suggestions were
incorporated in the redesigned Modess pad. CPC took up the challenge. General manager Luecke, keenly aware that Johnson & Johnson intended to compete on the basis of product quality, urged the
board to approve funds for a major product development effort in
1928. CPC product designers quickly introduced rounded corners,
softer gauze, and thinner filling which enabled Kotex to keep pace
with its largest competitor. In 1929 Kimberly-Clark established the
Kotex Research Laboratory as part of its Neenah-based research

department which developed further product improvements in the 1930s. Unwittingly heeding Gilbreth's advice to Johnson & Johnson, Kimberly-Clark put the Kotex Research Department under a Mrs. Heitmeyer, the first woman employed in a Kimberly-Clark management position.[69]

The redesigned Kotex was marketed in an innovative advertising campaign that included an ad released in 1929 (figure 2.4). The ad is remarkable for two reasons. First, it addressed concerns documented in the Gilbreth report that sanitary napkins were visible under garments, particularly thin silk dresses that gained popularity in the mid-1920s. "Many a smart costume has failed its effect, many a perfect evening has been ruined because of certain outstanding flaws in grooming," it stated. Following the first rule of marketing that ads should never state a problem without offering a solution, the text continued: "Women who have been aware of awkward bulkiness in sanitary protection now welcome the Improved Kotex, which is so rounded and tapered at the ends that it fits with an entirely new security. Now there is no break in the lines of a costume, no need for unhappy self-consciousness." Playing on the cultural imperative that women should keep their menstrual cycle private, the product enhanced consumers' ability to conceal evidence of their feminine hygiene practices.

Second, and more important, the ad featured fashion model Lee Miller, the first real person to appear in an advertisement for feminine hygiene products.[70] Her appearance raised a number of complicated issues, not least for Miller herself, who was initially mortified finding herself depicted in Kotex ads. (She soon changed her mind, however, because the photographer, who had made her pictures available to the Kotex marketers without her knowledge, made amends by introducing her to surrealist Man Ray, facilitating her career as an avant-garde model and photographer in Paris.[71]) Virtually all artwork included in early feminine hygiene product ads depicted fictional characters in drawings, even though rotogravure papers which reduced the cost of reproducing photographs in magazines were widely available. Print advertisers' reluctance to use photographs was widespread because many viewed the medium as ill-suited for visual idealization, deemed a critical element in early-twentieth-century marketing, as historian Elspeth Brown has shown. The use of fictional characters in advertising posed particular problems for feminine hygiene marketers because it inherently contradicted ad claims that customers could shop for sanitary napkins without feeling embarrassed. Unintentionally, the use of fictional ad characters actually reinforced the normative assumption that real people should not discuss menstrual hygiene in public. The Kotex ads featuring Miller, although highly controversial when initially released, resolved that contradiction, reestablishing CPC's lead in sanitary napkin marketing vis-à-vis arch rival Johnson & Johnson on the eve of the Great Depression.[72]

Kotex and Cellucotton paid handsome financial returns. In 1923 Kimberly-Clark awarded a $10,000 bonus to inventor Mahler, followed by an identical bonus a year later. He also received 2 percent of all CPC profits not exceeding $25,000 annually. In 1926 Mahler asked the company's board of directors to sell him one hundred CPC stock at $400 each from Kimberly-Clark's holdings. The request was granted, but Bill Clark and Harry Price refused to vote, "having expressed their opinions as being opposed to this sale, on the ground that the Cellucotton Products Co. stock should be held as far as possible by Kimberly-Clark Co., and not by individual stockholders of Kimberly-Clark Co."[73] Kimberly-Clark established a stock deposit committee composed of directors Frank Sensenbrenner, William Babcock, Mahler, and others, who voted on behalf of the parent company in CPC stockholder meetings. Lasker and Charles S. Pearce joined the CPC board in 1927. In 1928 CPC reported a respectable $780,000 or 8.1 percent after-tax net profit, followed in 1929 by a remarkable $1.85 million, 14.7 percent, more than three-quarters of which went to Kimberly-Clark in the form of dividends.[74]

V.

New materials developed during the interwar period often found an astonishing range of applications. The best-known example is perhaps nylon, developed by DuPont as a silk substitute for women's hosiery that was later used for parachutes, tents, ropes, and tires. Cellucotton, a similarly versatile material, was converted by Kimberly-Clark researchers into Kleenex tissues, barber strips, refrigerator lining, and packing material. Although less controversial than Kotex, some of these products profited from CPC's experience in marketing sanitary napkins and solidified Kimberly-Clark's presence in consumer nondurables and other product lines.

The origins of Kleenex dated to 1917, when company and Army researchers at the Neenah mill experimented with ultrathin Cellucotton samples to produce filter lining for gas masks. The experiments produced viable lining that was manufactured in considerable quantities on two creped wadding machines at the Neenah mill, but Kimberly-Clark abandoned the product shortly after the Armistice when its market collapsed. The Army's research files gathered dust until 1923, when one of Mahler's laboratory assistants proposed to convert ultrathin Cellucotton into cleansing tissue to remove lipstick, rouge, and other cosmetics.[75]

Cosmetics was one of the fastest-growing industries of the 1920s. Prior to World War I, usage had been largely confined to prostitutes and professional actors, but cultural changes created vast new markets during the interwar period that also boosted demand for makeup removal tissue. Some historians and feminist scholars, piqued by the timing of the "cosmetics revolution" in the wake of the passage of the Nineteenth Amendment, have speculated that cosmetics "re-feminized" women whose enfranchisement and growing presence in the professions raised fears of the "masculine woman." In applying makeup, historian Vincent Vinikas has written, "women could both acknowledge recent alterations in gender identity and mute the more threatening ambiguities that accompanied the emergence of the New Woman."[76] This intriguing interpretation suffers from a lack of evidentiary support, but the fact remains that by 1930, American women applied on average 6 tons of rouge, 24 tons of foundation cream, and 144 tons of cleansing cream a day.[77]

To remove cosmetics, many women used general-purpose cotton towels, a practice quickly deemed as unsanitary by manufacturers and advertisers that were eager to sell cosmetics removal tissue. One of the first to do so was Elizabeth Arden, the beauty salon that established a thriving side-business in cleansing tissue during the early 1920s. Perhaps inspired by Arden's success, CPC approved a proposal to turn Cellucotton into cleansing tissue in fall 1923. General manager Luecke met with Lasker to discuss brand names and marketing strategies. They determined that the product would be marketed by CPC as a disposable cold cream remover and settled on the trademark Kleenex. Taking a leaf from the medical references in Kotex advertising, the Kleenex marketers suggested that the "sanitary cold cream remover" was a more healthful product than cotton towels. CPC in fact trademarked Kleenex in 1925 as a brand name for "[a]bsorbent pads or sheets (not medicated) for surgical or curative purposes or in relation to the health [sic]."[78]

Kleenex marketing initially evolved from Kotex campaigns but quickly developed its own dynamics. CPC released its first ads in 1924 in magazines with an aggregate circulation of 16.2 million that also advertised Kotex. Kleenex was for sale in department stores, pharmacies, and drugstores in 65¢ boxes, each containing 200 sheets measuring 5 by 6 inches, but it was not displayed in countertop stacks for self-service because the product was not burdened with cultural taboos. Initial sales were somewhat disappointing (they actually declined in the second year) but grew when CPC introduced a larger 9-inch-by-10-inch sheet in 1926 (table 2.3). Lasker later claimed credit for the idea, recalling:

> I personally asked half a dozen women who I knew spent a lot of money on cosmetics to use [the 5-inch-by-6-inch Kleenex], and these half dozen all said, "it may be all right, but I can't use it, it is too small; it ought to be the size that is now being put out in paper by Elizabeth Arden and the Dennison Company. . . . So I went to the Cellucotton people and told them, and they changed the size to 9 × 10."[79]

TABLE 2.3
Kleenex net sales, 1926–1929

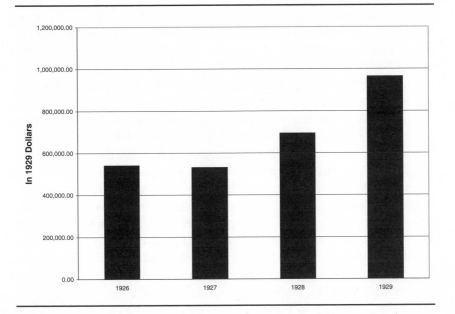

The first boxes featured the widely known CPC blue color, another reference to Kotex, but were replaced in 1926 with boxes featuring gray stripes combined with lavender and Persian orange colors to distinguish the tissue product. In 1928 CPC introduced a pop-up box that left a new tissue available when one was pulled for use, making the product more consumer friendly. Kleenex was primarily marketed as a cold cream remover until 1930, when surveys determined that consumers preferred using it to wipe their noses. Consumer-induced product innovation turned Kleenex into one of the most profitable consumer nondurables of the 1930s.[80]

In the 1920s Kimberly-Clark introduced Sanek barber strips, another Cellucotton-based product. The strips, which evolved from sanitary surgical dressings, were initially distributed by the Lewis Manufacturing Company, a Kimberly-Clark contractor that helped organize the sales of wound dressings to hospitals. When the Lewis Company proved unable to develop even rudimentary sales, Kimberly-Clark took direct control of the product and assigned it to company salesman Neill Graham, who developed the trademarked brand name Sanek for the *sanitary neck* strip. Sales, initially concentrated in New York and Chicago, were handled by Graham and Biederman, who marketed the product to barber and beautician suppliers. They also lobbied for state sanitary regulations requiring the use of paper strips to prevent hair cloth from touching a patron's hair. Marketing involved advertisements in the *Beautician* and other trade journals, as well as the introduction of a glass jar with an aluminum cover as a user-friendly container. As a result of these efforts, Sanek production at the Neenah mill increased from 5 tons in 1924 to 100 tons two years later. Advertising was minuscule compared to advertising of Kotex and Kleenex, with only $12,400 budgeted for 1928.[81]

Graham and Biederman also marketed Kimpak packaging material, the first Cellucotton product whose brand name suggested a Kimberly-Clark connection. The company developed the material in response to an initiative by the Simmons Company, a major producer of high-quality furniture. A Simmons representative, looking for packaging material for the company's new line of steel-polished, wood-grain furniture which often suffered severe shipping damage, saw Cellucotton wadding at a hospital supply exhibit. Simmons inquired in 1923 whether Kimberly-Clark could convert Cellucotton into packaging material, prompting research that produced unbleached wadding. Named Kimpak in 1926, the product was marketed by Graham and Biederman to furniture companies and later gained acceptance as a packaging material for other fragile items. Kimpak underwent further development in 1929, when a refrigerator company approached Kimberly-Clark with a request to turn the product into insulation panels. Researchers at Kimberly-Clark's laboratory in Neenah developed a pulp additive that improved Cellucotton's moisture resistance, laying the groundwork for a thriving business in refrigerator lining and building materials in the 1930s.[82]

VI.

Consumer nondurables emerged as a lucrative side business for Kimberly-Clark, but printing papers remained its core business. Capitalizing on prewar technological gains, the company refined and trademarked some of its most successful product lines for the booming magazine, book, and catalog paper markets of the 1920s. Annual magazine circulation increased by more than 56 percent over the course of the decade, reaching 202 million copies in 1929. The primary cause was the proliferation of general popular magazines, notably *Time* (founded in 1923), and the strong growth among magazines targeted at specific audiences, including women (*Ladies' Home Journal* and *Delineator*) and upper-class readers (*Saturday Evening Post* and *American Golfer*).

Kimberly-Clark produced the bulk of its printing paper at the Niagara Falls (New York), Niagara (Wisconsin), and Kimberly (Wisconsin) mills. The Kimberly mill, a key facility in the Kimberly-Clark mill system of the interwar period, added a laboratory in 1925 where company researchers developed a variety of specialty papers. Most were first produced on a commercial scale on one of the Kimberly mill's four paper machines. The first specialty grades in this category included the trademarked American Law Book paper, which combined a high-quality finish with durability for books that had to endure more frequent usage than most others: Bibles and legal reference texts. Furthermore, company researchers at the Kimberly mill developed a high-gloss grade that featured a deckle edge, the ragged sheet edge usually seen in handmade papers. To commercialize the grade, engineers installed a full deckle super calendar machine at the Kimberly mill in 1926. More conventional grades included catalog paper for National Bellas Hess, one of the nation's largest mail-order companies that awarded most of its paper contracts to Kimberly-Clark. Kimberly-Clark also increased its sales of rotogravure paper through a $120,000 advertising campaign handled by the Nichols agency.[83]

The company marketed its new grades under trademarked names. It did so to meet the demands of jobbers who argued that trademarks improved the marketability of specialty paper, citing the example of the Hammermill Paper Company, which had pioneered the practice before the war. One paper merchant recommended in 1921 that Sensenbrenner and Kimberly emulate the practice, claiming "Hammermill today are [sic] enjoying a much better profit on their papers by virtue of the fact that they have put through for several years a very strong campaign for advertising."[84] Kimberly-Clark duly developed colorful trademarks for most of its specialty grades, including Featherplate, Primoplate, and Rotindia.

Shortly before the onset of the Great Depression, Kimberly-Clark resurrected its newsprint business with the start-up of the Spruce Falls mill in Kapuskasing, Ontario. The move was part of a broader trend in the North American paper industry of the 1920s, when U.S. producers built newsprint mills in Canada. Sensenbrenner and other paper executives had speculated as early as 1908 that the removal of the newsprint tariff would encourage companies to invest north of the border, but few would have predicted that Canadian newsprint would assume the vast size it did in the 1920s. International Paper (IP), for example, built the world's largest paper mill in Three Rivers, Quebec; their eight electric fourdrinier machines boasted an aggregate annual capacity of 240,000 tons. In the late 1920s IP built two more mills in Gatineau, Quebec, and Dalhousie, New Brunswick, and acquired an existing one in Corner Brook, Newfoundland, raising its aggregate annual capacity to a staggering 800,000 tons. Abitibi, Canada Power & Paper, and other Canadian companies launched similarly ambitious mill construction programs, quickly raising the specter of a market glut. The latter, in fact, started to materialize as early as 1926, when outsized supply precipitated price erosion in newsprint markets.[85]

Kimberly-Clark's Canadian venture started in 1920, when it incorporated the Spruce Falls Company, Ltd. This new subsidiary secured extensive timber and water rights near Kapuskasing in Northern Ontario, a tiny settlement that had been founded as a prisoner-of-war camp several years earlier at a crossing of the Canadian National Railroad and the Kapuskasing River. The Spruce Falls Company built a sulfite pulp mill with a daily capacity of 115 tons, indicating that the venture's initial purpose was to secure pulp supplies for

Kimberly-Clark's book and magazine paper mills, not newsprint production. In 1923, however, Sensenbrenner approached Adolph Ochs of *The New York Times,* with a proposal to turn the Kapuskasing mill into a newsprint operation to supply *The Times* as well as other newspapers. *The Times*'s business relations with Kimberly-Clark dated back to 1915, when the paper company started to supply rotogravure grades for the newspaper's Sunday magazine. Sensenbrenner, Ochs, and members of the Ochs family discussed the proposal until January 1926, when they incorporated the Spruce Falls Power & Paper Company. Its board of directors consisted of Sensenbrenner, James Kimberly, Mahler, Ochs, Arthur Hays Sulzberger (who succeeded Ochs, his father-in-law, as publisher of *The Times* in 1935), and Julius Ochs Adler (another Ochs son-in-law who later became an Army general). Sensenbrenner was elected president, and John H. Black, a Kimberly-Clark manager who had risen through the ranks at the Globe mill, served as general manager. Kimberly-Clark held 51 percent of the stock, and *The Times* 49 percent.[86]

The Spruce Falls Power & Paper Company quickly grew into a major business. It acquired the holdings of the extant Kimberly-Clark subsidiary, added a newsprint mill with 650 tons daily capacity, constructed a power plant, and built a fifty-mile railroad track to transport pulpwood harvested north of Kapuskasing to the mill. The $16 million construction program (supported by CPC, which purchased $1 million in 5.5 percent bonds) amounted to one of the most ambitious building projects in Kimberly-Clark's history. For three years workers hacked the mill site out of the wilderness, endured sixty-below-zero temperatures, and cut through river ice fourteen feet thick. The mill came onstream in early summer 1928, and the first issue of *The New York Times* printed on Spruce Falls paper was published on July 13, 1928.[87]

Tumbling newsprint prices quickly convinced the board of directors and general manager Black to scale back their ambitions for the Spruce Falls mill. They shelved plans to supply other newspapers because market newsprint prices approached production costs during the Depression, leaving *The Times* as their sole customer. The sulfite plant produced pulp for the newsprint mill as well as for the Kimberly-Clark mill in Niagara Falls, New York, but rarely for the open market. Simultaneously, *The Times* provided the newsprint mill with a secure outlet for its 234,000 tons annual capacity, sparing Spruce Falls some of the financial problems that gripped other newsprint mills in the 1930s, when their markets collapsed.

VII.

In 1928 Kimberly-Clark was reorganized from a closely held company owned by a handful of shareholders into a publicly traded corporation that was listed on the Chicago and New York stock exchanges. Instigated by Sensenbrenner and Kimberly, the move was intended primarily to raise money for the massive Spruce Falls mill construction program and the acquisition of the Lakeview mill in Neenah, a replacement for the obsolete Neenah mill. The Kimberly-Clark Corporation, incorporated in Delaware to take advantage of that state's hospitable statutory environment for holding companies, acquired the assets of Kimberly-Clark Company, including six wholly owned paper mills, six research facilities, and the subsidiaries CPC and Bonifas Lumber Company, as well as the company's 51 percent share in the Spruce Falls newsprint mill. These holdings, combined with extensive timberlands in Michigan and waterpower rights at the various mill sites, were valued at $29.3 million. The $30 million capital stock consisted of 499,800 common stock, with a book value of $40 each, and 100,000 preferred shares. The preferred shares, valued at $100 each, resembled bonds because they carried a fixed dividend and lacked the voting rights of common stock. No common dividends could be issued before the company had paid its 6 percent preferred dividends from after-tax profits. The Kimberly-Clark Corporation also issued $6 million in 25-year, 5-percent mortgage bonds to finance various plant improvement and acquisition programs. The fourteen-member board of directors included representatives of major investors, notably John Hancock of Lehman Brothers, who were joined by seven veteran Kimberly-Clark stockholders and executives. The latter served as senior managers of the new company, principally Sensenbrenner as president and Mahler, William Bonifas, John Sensenbrenner, and Frank Shattuck as vice presidents. This personnel structure largely preserved Kimberly-Clark's traditional unity of ownership and management, enabling the company to avoid wrenching disagreements between executives and boards of directors that became commonplace in the 1930s, when many boards—including that of International Paper (IP)—solved conflicts over financial strategy by firing senior managers.[88]

Kimberly-Clark was one of the most profitable pulp and paper companies of the late 1920s. The sterling performance of its printing papers and consumer nondurables produced a 12.8 percent net profit in 1928. A year later Sensenbrenner reported that net earnings were "substantially more than [what] was forecast"—a whopping 19.3 percent on $22.3 million net sales, the best result in the industry. Scott Paper, the distant second, reported 11.5 percent. IP, the world's largest pulp and paper company, announced an anemic 2 percent net profit; and Union Bag & Paper Company reported a 7.1 percent net loss.[89]

Kimberly-Clark, Scott, Hammermill, and successful companies like them differed from the industry's underperformers in terms of marketing, product strategy, and commitment to research and development. IP largely ignored the consumer revolution of the 1920s and instead invested enormous sums into hydroelectric power plants and Canadian newsprint mills, which failed to produce the anticipated returns. Scott meanwhile, already one of the nation's leading toilet paper companies, expanded its presence in consumer nondurables with ScotTowels, marketed in a clever advertising campaign that included a motion picture. The latter conceptualized the paper towel as a cartoon character named "Thirsty Fibre," a tall, slender, fuzzy man, "in topper and tails," with a walking stick in one outstretched hand and with long striding legs leading him to an oasis where he quenched his insatiable thirst. The campaign helped Scott develop a thriving paper towel business that underwrote much of the company's financial success in the 1920s and the Great Depression.[90]

3

The Great Depression

KIMBERLY-CLARK recorded growth for almost a year after the stock market crash of 1929. Until mid-1930 the "depression had little or no effect on our sales and earnings" which were "the largest in the company's history," company president Frank Sensenbrenner told stockholders in his financial report. After June 1930 there was a "material falling off in the sales and earnings," but at the end of the year the company still boasted more than $3 million in after-tax profits and distributed $1.2 million in common dividends.[1] The year 1931 brought a 44 percent reduction in net earnings, but dividends remained at the previous year's level.[2]

These statistics confirm the conventional portrait of the Great Depression as a slow downward slide, rather than an abrupt tumble in the immediate aftermath of the stock market crash. In some industries the descent started years before the crash as a result of sector-specific problems. In textiles, obsolete New England cotton mills faced stiff competition from new southern mills and rayon producers. Coal mines, which lost ground to oil refineries in energy markets, performed poorly throughout the decade. Merchant shipbuilding never fully recovered from the sell-off of government surplus tonnage in the early 1920s; the sell-off flooded steamship markets, precipitating a wave of shipyard closures at mid-decade. Pulp and paper performed generally well, but the 1920s hardly roared in troubled subsectors, notably newsprint, where overbuilding in Canada produced price erosion after mid-decade. Kraft paper producers experienced sharply lower earnings in 1928 as a result of market saturation. Structural instabilities weakened these and other "sick industries" long before the crash, which exacerbated but did not trigger the secular downturn of the 1930s. Faced with deteriorating macroeconomic conditions after 1929, firms in these sectors tried to safeguard their market shares through price competition, which contributed to a deflationary cycle, staggering losses, and a wave of bankruptcies in the early 1930s.[3]

More versatile industries clustered at the opposite end of the economic spectrum. Producers of consumer durables such as automobiles, refrigerators, and radios introduced a steady stream of new products that yielded above-average returns in the 1920s. The most prominent example is General Motors, which pulled ahead of Ford with a wide model range, technological innovations, clever advertising, and installment plans that lured customers away from its stodgy competitor. Similar dynamics boosted consumer nondurables, including canned food, rayon textiles, specialty tissue paper, and sanitary napkins.[4]

As economic historians have pointed out, firms in these dynamic sectors faced a set of strategic choices at the onset of the Great Depression. Like companies in other industries, they could engage in price competition, grind competitors to dust with steep discounts, and try to keep the concomitant financial losses within manageable limits. But manufacturers of new consumer products faced an alternative that was unavailable to firms in technologically mature industries. Instead of joining potentially destructive price wars, they could develop innovative technologies and refine existing ones through investments into research programs to improve their competitive position with more marketable products.[5]

Its proponents readily admit that this scenario does not describe the actual behavior of most firms in the 1930s. Indeed, they argue counterfactually, if a sufficient number of firms *had* weathered the downturn with new products, the Great Depression would not have lasted as long as it did; nor would it have been as severe as it actually was. In reality, cotton, coal mining, steel rail, and other mature industries simply lacked the technological potential for strategic product innovation, leaving few alternatives to price wars except cartelization, attempted with mixed results through codes of fair competition under the National Recovery Act. New consumer products industries of the interwar period, however, enjoyed some potential for economically viable product development, as evidenced by the successful commercialization of nylon, car radios, and tampons which produced healthy financial returns for DuPont, Motorola, and Tampax Sales Corporation respectively. As economic historian Michael Bernstein has argued, conventional analyses of the Depression that diagnose a terminal failure of internally generated accumulation cannot account for these intriguing episodes in the economic history of the 1930s. Bernstein therefore distinguishes between maturing industries that rapidly approached the limits of product development in the interwar period and more dynamic sectors that took advantage of opportunities for economically viable innovation. This analytical framework puts Depression-era business decisions in an intriguing new perspective that looks beyond the crisis management aspects of corporate strategy. If possibilities for profitable competition based on product innovation did exist, how did some firms manage to ferret out these opportunities while most others became embroiled in price wars?

The case of Kimberly-Clark and its subsidiaries offers interesting insights into these problems because management engaged in price wars but also tried to compete through product development and better marketing. As the present chapter demonstrates, consumer nondurables held considerable potential, particularly in hygiene products, where firms had barely scratched the surface of new markets. Kimberly-Clark exploited this opportunity with the successful commercialization of the Kleenex disposable handkerchief. Menstrual hygiene technology held similar promise, but in their worst strategic miscalculation of the 1930s, Kimberly-Clark executives decided to embark on a debilitating price war with Johnson & Johnson that was belatedly settled by the National Recovery Administration. Attempts to compete through product refinement and innovation yielded far better results, as evidenced by a variety of research, development, and marketing programs that buttressed Kimberly-Clark's balance sheet.

Given a precipitous fall of disposable incomes in the 1930s, this strategy could be carried only so far. Consumer spending declined by 19 percent from 1929 to 1933 as a result of unemployment, a decrease in real wages, and ironclad consumer credit agreements that forced households to devote considerable resources to paying off long-term debts, as historian Martha Olney and others have argued. As is well known, the New Deal did little to alleviate the problem through Keynesian economics; according to business historian Thomas McGaw, "Deficits five to ten times as large as those actually recorded would have been required to restore prosperity."[6] In light of these statistics, it is quite remarkable that some firms—including General Motors's Cadillac division, Campbell, Tampax, and Kimberly-Clark—managed to weather the Depression through successful consumer product innovation.[7]

As comparisons with other pulp and paper companies in this chapter indicate, Kimberly-Clark remained one of the most financially sound, technologically versatile, and well-managed firms in the industry. Maintaining profitability even when the price war with Johnson & Johnson inflicted punishing financial blows, the company survived the Depression without net losses. Along with Scott Paper, Kimberly-Clark belonged to an elite group of firms that detected business opportunities in markets where most competitors saw problems and obstacles. In another marked contrast to the industry mainstream, however, Kimberly-Clark instituted a fairly conservative system of industrial relations that became an Achilles' heel in the postwar era.

I.

Financial statistics provide a useful bird's-eye view of Kimberly-Clark's general performance. Inflation-adjusted net sales stagnated at $18 million in 1930, falling 9 percent in 1931 and another 20 percent in 1932, when they plateaued for two years (table 3.1). They returned to pre-Depression levels as early as 1935 and showed strong increases for two years until the Roosevelt Recession, whose lingering effects on sales could be felt until 1939. Inflation-adjusted after-tax earnings, perhaps a more telling financial indicator, showed a slightly different trend (table 3.2). After a remarkably strong performance until 1931, profits became anemic the following year and—unlike sales—remained below pre-Depression levels until World War II. They dipped below the 4 percent mark in 1933 and 1934 but recovered the following year. The year 1935 marked the beginning of continuous growth, which—in contrast to the net sales trend—was uninterrupted by the Roosevelt Recession.

Kimberly-Clark derived approximately half of its sizable 1930 and 1931 net earnings from profitable Kotex and Kleenex sales, which were handled by the International Cellucotton Products Company (ICPC). Kotex sanitary napkins continued to sell at 45¢ a dozen, the same price as in 1928. Advertising also continued along the lines of precrash trajectories, supplemented by a new consumer ad campaign called "Only Kotex Feels Like Kotex" that cautioned consumers

TABLE 3.1
Kimberly-Clark net sales, 1929–1939

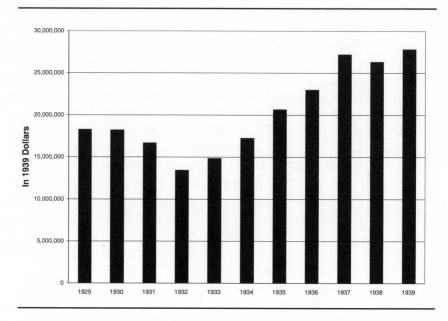

TABLE 3.2
Kimberly-Clark earnings, 1929–1939

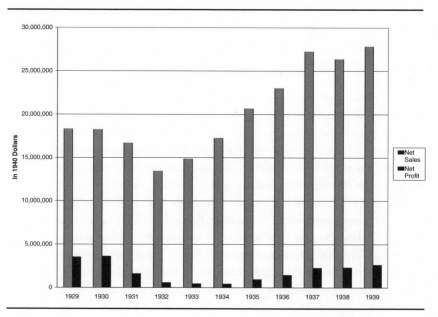

FIGURE 3.1 Kotex advertisement, 1931

against "dangerous" imitations (figure 3.1). Avoiding product changes and maintaining precrash retail prices during the first Depression years, Kimberly-Clark and ICPC cashed in on the Kotex innovations of the late 1920s. Less than a decade after the launch of the first Kotex marketing campaigns, sanitary napkins were apparently considered basic necessities by Depression-plagued consumers who curtailed their car purchases as early as 1930 but continued to buy sanitary napkins. Once considered an unmarketable product, Kotex was now billed a "business builder" for retailers in ads that claimed, "It is seldom that a woman comes in to buy a box of Kotex that she doesn't buy two or three other items. It's a 45-cent item that produces $1 sales." Kotex sales grew by more than 8 percent annually in the early 1930s, creating a market that seemed Depression-proof.[8]

Kleenex underwent significant changes in 1930. Initially leveraged as a cold cream remover, the tissue found widespread use as a handkerchief by consumers who believed that disposable tissues could help prevent the spread of colds. Later developments confirmed that demand for such a product was enormous and that market dominance belonged to the company that capitalized as quickly as possible on the innovative impulse "from the bottom up." In light of Kimberly-Clark's record of responsiveness to consumer and retailer needs, it was perhaps not by coincidence that ICPC grabbed the prize only a few months after it started to receive letters from consumers who told management how they used Kleenex. In 1930 general manager Walter Luecke and advertising professional Albert Lasker—seasoned veterans of Kotex marketing—convinced their fellow board members to conduct a consumer study to investigate consumer preferences. Conducted in Peoria, Illinois, the study determined that 61 percent of consumers "thought of Kleenex as a handkerchief, [while] 39 percent thought of it as a cleansing tissue," one manager later recalled.[9]

Shortly after the completion of the Peoria survey, ICPC repositioned Kleenex as a disposable handkerchief through a $548,000 advertising campaign aimed at consumers as well as drugstores and department stores. The name designation changed from "Kleenex Cleansing Tissues" to "Kleenex Disposable Handkerchiefs." Largely as a result of a $1.1 million advertising campaign in 1931, Kleenex captured the lion's share of the market, with informal surveys indicating that 78 percent of users preferred Kleenex (Ponds disposable handkerchiefs ranked a distant second at 14 percent). The same year, ICPC started producing private brands for large retailers, including "Klenzo" tissues for United Drugs, followed a few years later by "Perfection" for Walgreen Company, "Hazel" for the National Tea Company, and "Wards" for Montgomery Ward. Kleenex sales meanwhile skyrocketed, more than doubling only two years after the product had been repositioned (table 3.3). Capitalizing on the results of the Peoria survey which indicated that consumers liked Kleenex because it was presumably more sanitary than the cotton handkerchief, advertising positioned the product as "[t]he handkerchief for health—to prevent self-infection [!], reduce the spread of colds."[10] From 1932 to 1934 ICPC—embroiled in its sanitary napkin price war

TABLE 3.3
Kleenex sales, 1926–1940

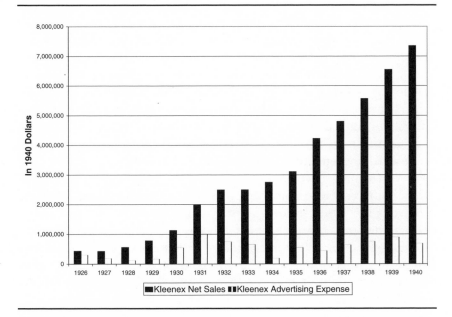

with Johnson & Johnson—drastically reduced its advertising budget, contributing to a slowdown in Kleenex sales.[11]

In 1935 Albert Lasker, the Chicago advertising executive who sat on ICPC's board of directors, rekindled Kleenex marketing by proposing a broadcast promotion. After a lengthy debate that centered on the cost of radio advertising, the board approved Lasker's proposal, launching the first radio marketing campaign in the history of the company which had hitherto relied on print advertising. ICPC joined a group of elite corporations like DuPont, Ford Motor Company, and General Motors which used broadcast promotions to improve their general image or leverage specific products. One of the first Kleenex promotions was aired during broadcasts of the NBC soap opera "The Story of Mary Marlin." In November 1935 ICPC promised a free Kleenex package to anyone who wrote to NBC's Chicago station WMAQ to keep the show on the air. The promise elicited 67,300 replies from listeners—the "largest amount of mail ever received by a single NBC station from a single offer," ICPC claimed.[12] Encouraged by the results, ICPC a year later offered $10,000 in cash prizes for listener suggestions of a name for "Mary

Marlin's" baby and for the "best ways to use Kleenex for babies."[13] The promotion produced 168,207 responses and helped boost Kleenex sales 13 percent in 1937. Two years later ICPC sponsored the new CBS radio show "Her Honor, Nancy James." In April a $30,000 promotion broadcast during the show asked listeners to answer the question "Why I like Kleenex," offering 1,000 battery radios as prizes. The promotion resulted in almost 130,000 responses, convincing ICPC to conduct similar campaigns to find out how consumers used Kleenex. In 1939 the company offered a $5 prize for every letter published and received approximately 150,000 "Kleenex True Confessions" over the next two years.[14]

Toward the end of the decade, ICPC broadened the scope of Kleenex retailing beyond department stores and drugstores with a campaign intended to convince grocers to sell the product. Taking a leaf from the Kotex trade campaigns of the 1920s, it launched a nationwide retail contest entitled "Kleenex Time in America" which offered retailers $10,000 in cash prizes for the best Kleenex window and store displays and a $1.50 check for every submission. ICPC received more than 56,000 entries for store displays and 49,000 for window displays, giving Kleenex a secure foothold in grocery stores, which had become important retail outlets in smaller towns. By 1940 Kleenex net sales exceeded $7 million, compared to little more than $1 million a decade earlier. ICPC's Depression-era marketing campaigns made Kleenex a virtual synonym for disposable handkerchiefs in the American consumer lexicon, where it has remained firmly entrenched until the present day.[15]

II.

The repositioning of Kleenex, arguably one of the greatest feats in the history of consumer marketing, started in 1930. Only one year later the ICPC management committed one of the worst blunders by joining a price war in sanitary napkin markets, with disastrous consequences for the company, its parent company Kimberly-Clark, and other firms in the industry.

Kotex remained the most expensive sanitary napkin on the market until 1931. A reduction effected in 1928 had reduced per-unit retail prices to 3.75¢ from 5.41¢ in the previous year. ICPC and Kimberly-Clark had meanwhile substantially improved product design during the late 1920s to keep abreast of Johnson & Johnson. Fueling the

TABLE 3.4

Net earnings of International Cellucotton Products Company, 1929–1939

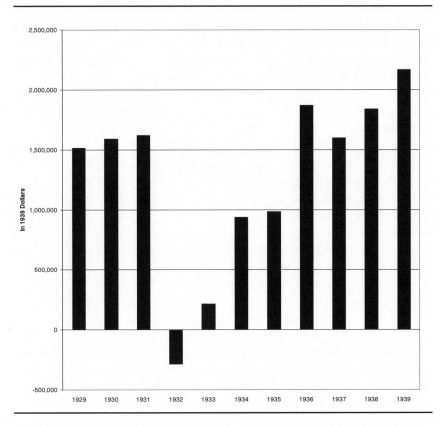

deflationary cycle of the early Depression years, several competitors cut their prices by more than half, raising eyebrows at ICPC and Kimberly-Clark, whose directors and managers grew concerned about Kotex's market share. Lasker articulated these feelings at an ICPC board meeting in May 1931, stating, "[T]he extremely low prices offered by competitive makers of private brand sanitary napkins make it very important that the . . . company seriously consider reducing the advertised price of Kotex [boxes] from 45¢ to 35¢."[16] The board apparently needed little convincing, because it approved Lasker's proposal without further discussion, adopting a 2.91¢ per-unit retail price for 1932.[17]

The price cut had an immediate and disastrous effect on ICPC's net earnings, which fell by $2 million, producing the company's only net loss of the interwar period (table 3.4). The impact of the 1932 price cut on Kimberly-Clark was cushioned by a vote of ICPC's board to issue $368,000 in common dividends out of surplus, a substantial share of which went to the parent company. Urged by Sensenbrenner, James Kimberly, Mahler, and other Kimberly-Clark executives who sat on ICPC's board, the decision to issue dividends from surplus was decidedly ill advised, however. ICPC's accumulated surplus, which was invested in outside stocks and bonds, performed poorly during the early 1930s as a result of the stock market crisis, requiring a $210,000 write-off in 1931. The 1932 dividend reduced the depleted surplus by 43 percent, leaving a paltry $857,000 for emergencies. Despite the dividend, the sanitary napkin price war had a profound impact on Kimberly-Clark's net earnings because the parent company had grown accustomed to a substantial flow of ICPC common dividends, which had amounted to $1.2 million as recently as 1931. Although Kimberly-Clark executives managed to squeeze at least some proceeds out of the troubled subsidiary, Kimberly-Clark's net earnings tumbled 66 percent from 1931 to 1932. Kimberly-Clark suspended its own common stock dividends in October 1932.[18]

Unfortunately for everyone involved, Mahler, Sensenbrenner, Lasker, and other members of ICPC's board notched up the price war in 1933. ICPC sales and advertising director Walter Luecke, skeptical of the move from the start, explained in a somewhat contradictory memorandum written a few years after the fact:

> We then decided that in order to keep . . . smaller manufacturers, who were springing up very rapidly, out of the field, we would have to sell Kotex at so low a price that these smaller competitors could not exist. So it was voted, against my own wishes and convictions, to put on a sale of Kotex at a price of 2 boxes for 25¢ retail. This was a reduction of the regular price then in force of 25¢ a box. Johnson and Johnson, our principal competitor, started this price war and in spite of my own efforts to convince Johnson and Johnson, as well as my own people, not to cut the price so low, the sale was launched. We sold a 6-months output of our factory in less than 6 weeks. A tremendous loss was taken by both Johnson & Johnson and ourselves.[19]

While the first part of Luecke's memorandum indicates that ICPC started the price war as an offensive move against smaller competitors, the fourth sentence blamed Johnson & Johnson, making ICPC's price reduction appear defensive. Be this as it may, Kotex sold for little more than 1¢ per unit in 1933, almost 66 percent less than in the previous year. Fortunately for ICPC, Kleenex by now produced sufficient earnings to offset the steep losses in Kotex sales, enabling the company to report a $200,000 net profit in 1933. To prevent further financial hemorrhaging, however, the board suspended common dividends, depriving Kimberly-Clark of an important source of profits. As a result, Kimberly-Clark's 1933 balance sheet showed only $444,000 in net earnings in current dollars, a 24 percent decrease compared to the previous year. Combined with a $35,000 loss reported by the William Bonifas Lumber Company, a wholly owned subsidiary of Kimberly-Clark, ICPC's move forced the parent company to suspend its common stock dividends for all of 1933.[20]

Sanitary napkin producers ended their price war at the behest of the National Recovery Administration (NRA) in fall 1933. Luecke represented ICPC—with more than 40 percent of the market share still the most important player—in a series of meetings that established uniform codes for packaging and advertising before turning to the all-important question of price stabilization. Chastened by the results of the unsustainable price war, ICPC's board authorized Luecke to agree to a 67 percent price increase at the NRA negotiations; the increase was supported by Johnson & Johnson and was adopted as a base figure for 1934 retail prices. For the remainder of the decade, per-unit prices stabilized around 1.6¢. Luecke, thoroughly exhausted from the quagmire, resigned as ICPC sales manager and member of the board in 1935.[21]

To restore the profitability of the battered sanitary pad, management decided to improve production efficiency by transferring Kotex operations from the aging Neenah mill to the Lakeview mill a few blocks down the street. Built by Sears, Roebuck to produce catalog paper, the Lakeview mill had been acquired by Kimberly-Clark in 1929 for more than $1 million and had initially produced a variety of specialty grades. Shortly after the price war the mill was converted to Cellucotton production, but its output was initially converted to Kotex and Kleenex at the Neenah mill. The transfer of operation accelerated in 1936 with the completion of converting facilities at the Lakeview mill which received much of the production equipment previously housed at the Neenah mill. At a cost of almost $1.7 million, Lakeview subsequently added three creped wadding machines and expanded the Kotex and Kleenex production facilities.[22]

Combined with growing and increasingly profitable Kleenex sales, the stabilized Kotex prices enabled ICPC to raise its net earnings back to almost $1 million in 1934 and 1935. A trickle of ICPC common dividends started flowing Kimberly-Clark's way in 1934, but net earnings stood at only $438,000 in current dollars, making it once again advisable for Kimberly-Clark to suspend common dividends. The financial tide finally turned in 1935, when ICPC issued almost $600,000 in dividends, contributing to Kimberly-Clark's $950,000 net earnings for the year. The parent company reported continually increasing net profits for the remainder of the Great Depression.[23]

III.

Looking beyond price wars as a means to sustain its Kotex business, ICPC tried to open up new markets throughout the 1930s. Early in the decade it launched one of the first sanitary napkin marketing campaigns that targeted adolescent girls with a pamphlet called *Marjorie May's 12th Birthday,* first released in the United States in 1932 (figure 3.2).[24] Distributed as an insert in Kotex boxes, by mail, and through retailers, the booklet contained a fictional conversation between a mother and her daughter. It began, "'Mother, dear, you are the best in the whole world,' said Marjorie May after her birthday guests had gone home." Over the next several pages Marjorie and her mother discuss the quiet demeanor of one of Marjorie's party guests, which mother attributes to "Nature . . . beginning with her a new process of development." Mother then recalls how she discussed the need for cleanliness years ago, when she told Marjorie that it is "just as important for you to be clean *inside* as it is to be clean *outside.*" Mother gets to the heart of the matter several paragraphs later:

> In sending you this *new* physical development, Nature finds it necessary to employ a means of relieving the body of [an] unused substance . . . One of these days, at any hour of the morning or even in the middle of the night, you find coming from you a slightly bloodstained fluid. When you see it, do not be afraid or worried, for this is the first indication that the new development has started.

This somewhat nebulous explanation set the stage for the key paragraph of the booklet:

FIGURE 3.2 *Marjorie May's 12th Birthday* cover page

When this happens, you are to take from your dresser one of these Kotex pads and wear it with this elastic girdle, known as a Kotex sanitary belt. You must tell me the first day this happens, so I can see that you have a box of these little pads for your own exclusive use.

Marjorie—admonished to change pads frequently, bathe regularly, and engage in normal physical activity—thanks her mother profusely. "You are wonderful to have told me about this new experience I am soon to have. I shall feel quite a young lady when the new development comes, because it will mean that I have grown up."

ICPC advertised *Marjorie May's 12th Birthday* in Kotex ads of the early 1930s, which often contained a sidebar with a mail-in coupon for the booklet. Headlined "To ease the task of enlightenment," the sidebar told "parents and guardians, in a spirit of constructive helpfulness":

Some five million mothers will face the most difficult task of motherhood. Thousands of these mothers will sit down in quiet rooms—and from that intimacy so characteristic of today's mother and daughter, there will result that understanding so vital to the daughter of today—the wife and mother of tomorrow . . . There will be thousands of mothers, courageous, intimate in all things but this. There will be thousands too timid to meet this problem—and it will pass—but with what possible unhappiness . . . what heartbreaking experience. To free this task of enlightenment from the slightest embarrassment—the . . . Company has had prepared an intimate little chat between mother and daughter. . . . In this book, the subject has been covered completely . . . in simple, understandable form. It is accompanied by a simple plan affording the child complete privacy.

Like modern-day marketing materials that praise breast-feeding before pitching infant formula, the ad first went out of its way to idealize mothers who had the courage for face-to-face interaction, but then it suggested that there was an easier way: corporate-sponsored enlightenment.

Taken at face value, the *Marjorie May's 12th Birthday* campaign was a classic case of what Jürgen Habermas has called the "colonization of life-worlds"—a hostile invasion of the intimate sphere between parent and daughter by a corporate agent of instrumental rationality. Tendered "in a spirit of constructive helpfulness," the primary purpose of *Marjorie May's 12th Birthday* was to ensure that adolescent girls developed brand name loyalty. To accomplish their objective, marketers leveraged the booklet as a substitute for interpersonal communication. Although plausible, this interpretation fails to account for the fact that mothers often failed to discuss menstrual hygiene in words that were intelligible to their daughters—more often than not, there *was* no life-world to invade. A series of oral history interviews conducted by historian Corrine Krause with ethnic women in Pittsburgh that explored pre- and interwar menstrual hygiene reveals that mothers rarely discussed menstruation-related issues. In the words of one interviewee, "We didn't learn about [menstruation] at home. We just had to learn it from each other."[25] Viewed from this angle, corporate advice literature punctured a wall of silence, not a fragile sphere of intersubjective intimacy. That said, *Marjorie May's 12th Birthday* and similar booklets certainly helped gear mother-daughter talks toward bland commercial themes. "In the twentieth century," historian Joan Brumberg writes, "intimate maternal conversations with daughters were more often than not about the use of a particular technology or product, rather than about sexuality or reproduction."[26]

For ICPC the booklet became an important marketing tool because it established brand name recognition for Kotex among ado-

FIGURE 3.3 Phantom Kotex advertisement, 1932

lescent girls—tomorrow's customers—who comprised a crucial but hitherto largely untapped market for sanitary napkins. Moreover, schools ordered thousands of copies of *Marjorie May's 12th Birthday*, opening up another new marketing venue for the company. Based on her review of the Krause interviews, Brumberg concludes, "[T]hese programs were extremely effective. Beginning in the 1930s, but especially in the 1940s, almost all the daughters of Slovak, Italian, and Jewish families [in Pittsburgh] were given corporately-sponsored pamphlets . . . either at school or by their mothers."[27] Quickly capitalizing on these accomplishments, ICPC commissioned a series of ads specifically aimed at adolescent girls and introduced Junior Kotex in July 1933.[28]

To further improve Kotex's marketability, ICPC and Kimberly-Clark developed new pad designs. In 1931 the Kotex division of

Kimberly-Clark's technical department in Neenah developed the Phantom Kotex, whose flat, pressed ends reduced its visibility under close-fitting garments. Launched in 1932 the Phantom Kotex advertisements featured women dressed in evening gowns wearing pads held in place by the Kotex sanitary belt, promising that "the combination makes for complete ease and inconspicuous protection" (figure 3.3). In a 36-month research and development effort, the Kotex division in Neenah also developed a combination pad featuring fourteen regular plies and eight high-absorbency plies, also called "equalizer strips." After having the product field tested by more than 300 women, ICPC commercialized it in 1933 as the Patented Equalizer that was thinner than regular Kotex but purportedly offered 20 to 30 percent higher absorbency.

IV.

In addition to refining Kotex, researchers developed a variety of other products, including Kimsul insulating material, washable wallpapers, new printing grades, and tampons. The development of Kimsul was based on close collaboration among scientists, engineers, and production personnel, one of the core strengths of Kimberly-Clark's research programs. Kimsul evolved from insulator lining developed in 1929 at the behest of a refrigerator company. In 1930 Kimberly-Clark supplied refrigerator lining to the Masonite Company, a Mississippi-based manufacturer of hardboard for home construction which marketed the insulator for a year or so. This early venture into construction material failed in 1931 because refrigerator lining was too expensive for home construction, precipitating a search for more economical alternatives. Laboratory researchers in Neenah experimented with a variety of new sizing materials for the Cellucotton insulator and in 1933 settled on emulsified asphalt. To make "black wadding" suitable for building construction, the material had to be fireproofed, a major research challenge because Kimberly-Clark had never developed fireproof products. "A conference was called in which the problem was outlined to the chemists concerned," according to one contemporary account. "The chemists went to the Research Library at [the Kimberly mill] and read what has been written in scientific journals about fireproofing."[29] After several months of laboratory research, the chemists developed a reliable fireproofing agent, but they encountered a variety of technical problems applying it to Cellucotton.

"Into the mill the chemists went," the account continued. "They tried to mix the fireproofing agent with the [Cellucotton] beater furnish. When that didn't work, they tried to put it on from the press felt, and then they tried printing directly on the product itself. And in all these trials the engineers concerned and the operators who would be called upon to run the material in quantity were present to contribute what they knew about machines and about operating problems. Finally a spray was tried, and the result was a success."[30] Full-scale production began fall 1933 at the Neenah mill, whose capacity was largely devoted to Kimsul when Kotex and Kleenex were transferred to the Lakeview mill. Despite a sharp decline in new home construction, Kimsul sustained the Neenah mill, which doubled its capacity in the late 1930s.[31]

Kimberly-Clark's wallpaper operations also profited from research-intensive product development in the 1930s. Produced at the Atlas mill in Appleton in collaboration with United Wallpaper Factories, the bulk of Kimberly-Clark's wallpaper output consisted of Polychrome Duplex and other oatmeal finishes for living rooms and bedrooms. When demand fell off in the early 1930s, Kimberly-Clark physicists teamed up with United Wallpaper chemists and engineers to develop washable wallpaper for bathrooms, an inexpensive alternative to ceramic tiles. Earlier attempts to develop varnish-coated washable wallpapers were largely unsuccessful because moisture variations caused wallpaper to swell and shrink, leaving microscopic cracks in the varnish glaze that eroded its moisture-proofing properties. Moreover, consumers frequently rejected glazed wallpapers because they looked cheap. Kimberly-Clark and United Wallpaper developed a nonvarnish wallpaper stock that derived its water resistance from new types of inks that were applied to the paper base with special printing rolls. The ink converted "the printed surface of the paper into a non-glossy, water resistant product which is ready to hang," a Kimberly-Clark physicist explained. "The surface of this new wipeable [sic] paper is integrally water resistant and does not depend on a lacquer or varnish coating. To satisfy the buyer who associates gloss with water resistance, methods have been devised which will give the paper this quality."[32] Marketed by United Wallpaper, washable wall coverings quickly became popular as tile substitutes in bathrooms and kitchens, ensuring the continued profitability of Kimberly-Clark's wallpaper business in the 1930s.

During the interwar period Kimberly-Clark still defined itself primarily as a manufacturer of printing papers. When demand fell by almost 25 percent in the early Depression years, accompanied by a similar drop in prices, Kimberly-Clark researchers launched several product development programs in collaboration with the large printing paper mills in Kimberly and Niagara (Wisconsin) and Niagara Falls (New York). These research efforts, which culminated in the introduction of the Kleerfect and Hyfect grades, tried to solve a technical problem familiar to printers around the country. In magazines and books printed on conventional groundwood paper, one observer explained, "The underside of the sheet revealed the telltale marks of the wire screen over which it had passed in the first stages of manufacture" on the fourdrinier machine.[33] In the early 1930s Kimberly-Clark researchers developed a groundwood production process that eliminated the wire screen marks through machine coating. At a cost of more than $500,000, engineers rebuilt five fourdrinier machines at the Kimberly mill, where Kleerfect and Hyfect were first produced on a commercial scale in 1933. Kimberly-Clark marketed the new grades in a carefully calibrated advertising campaign in 1932, six months before the Kimberly machines churned out the first sheets, assuring printers and paper jobbers that Kleerfect and Hyfect would be available at the same price as conventional printing grades. Kleerfect made a successful debut at the height of the Depression, Sensenbrenner reported in March 1933, requiring "additional equipment to be installed during the next few months to meet the growing demand."[34] Over the next two years Kimberly-Clark's board approved $2.4 million in Kleerfect- and Hyfect-related investments into the Kimberly, Niagara, and Niagara Falls mills. In a somewhat unusual move for a paper company, Kimberly-Clark in 1935 published a lavishly illustrated publication entitled *Discoveries and Inventions Thru the Ages that Have Made Today's Fine Printing Possible* on Kleerfect paper to demonstrate its printing properties to paper jobbers and printers.[35]

V.

The mid-1930s marked the beginning of a product contest between sanitary napkins and tampons that has lasted until the present day. To fend off the challenge to Kotex, Kimberly-Clark could have tried to capitalize on widespread consumer fears that tampons were unhealthy and dangerous because they ostensibly served as vaginal plugs or could cause accidental deflowering. However, the company decided to jump on the tampon bandwagon as early as 1934, only two years after a physician had patented Tampax, which eventually became a market leader. Kimberly-Clark and ICPC launched a carefully crafted research and development program that produced the Fibs tampon. To avoid competition with Kotex, however, most managers and executives conceptualized the tampon as a mere supplement to sanitary napkins, rendering the company's entry into the tampon market problematic from the start. Consumer surveys of the late 1930s determined that women liked Fibs because of its small size but complained about its lack of absorbency.

The first commercial tampon was invented by Earle Haas, a general practitioner who developed Tampax in 1932. Working in the back of his garage, Haas sewed 5-inch cotton strips together with cord, leaving a string that could be used to extract the tampon from the vagina without touching the cotton. Using a device resembling a set of pliers, he compressed the sown cotton strip into a small roll to form the tampon. He encased it in a set of paper cylinders that enabled women to insert the tampon without having to touch it. Haas named his invention Tampax, a combination of "tampon" and "vaginal pack." Unable to garner interest among sanitary napkin producers, including Johnson & Johnson, Haas sold his rights to the Denver businesswoman Gertrude Tenderich in 1933. After selling the tampon privately for a year or so, Tenderich and several Denver investors incorporated the Tampax Sales Corporation to market the product nationwide in 1934. By that year several small manufacturers sold a variety of other tampons, including Wix, manufactured by the Minneapolis-based Wix Company.[36]

Kimberly-Clark's venture into tampons originated in early 1934, when members of the technical department in Neenah started to tinker with various designs. ICPC board member Charles Pearce, who took a keen interest in these efforts, observed in June 1934 that the tampon market held considerable potential and that "we do not want to be the last ones to get in on the business."[37] At Pearce's suggestion the Kimberly-Clark and ICPC boards quickly approved funds for further study and full-scale development. In internal communications the tampon was initially referred to as the Kotex Tampax, which did not lend itself to commercialization because Haas had trademarked Tampax in 1932. After considering a variety of possible trademarks, including Koads and Kopaks, ICPC sales managers and advertising agents settled on the somewhat unfortunate choice Fibs, meant to indicate "fibers."[38] Astute consumers later pointed out to baffled marketers that the brand name evoked entirely unintended connotations, however. "'Fib' is a polite word for 'lie,'" one woman remarked. "'Fibs' suggests something nasty, secretive, unclean. . . . [If] I wanted to buy tampons at a store, I would not buy 'Fibs' just because of the awful name."[39] A nurse seconded this view: "The name 'fibs' is to my mind an extremely poor choice."[40]

Members of the technical and manufacturing departments developed the basic Fibs tampon in coordination with the Michigan-based Grand Rapids Fiber Cord Company. The key design contributions came from Charles Fourness, an engineer and manager in Kimberly-Clark's manufacturing division in Neenah, who rolled up short strings of Cellucotton surgical dressing, lined the cylinder with cotton fiber, and encased the device in braided yarn to prevent excessive expansion and chafing. Referring to the device as a fiber cord "pledget," Fourness coated the tip with starch to effect firmness and smoothness for easy insertion. Taking a leaf from Haas's Tampax design, engineers of the Grand Rapids Fiber Cord Company developed a string that was embedded into the Fibs pledget, enabling users to remove the tampon without touching the cylinder.[41]

After completion of the basic Fibs design, the Neenah technical department conducted a laboratory review of available tampons in fall 1934, compiling a report for distribution among ICPC sales managers and Kimberly-Clark production personnel. Tests determined that all tampons suffered from two major problems. First, the devices were out of shape after use, indicating to researchers that the tampons were unable to withstand vaginal pressures. Second, they "had clots on the ends, showing that they act as plugs. This occurred with all types of tampons, even the small Fibs."[42] To learn more about other possible shortcomings, the researchers advocated an informal field study.

Lord & Thomas, Lasker's advertising agency that had handled most of Kimberly-Clark's and ICPC's marketing campaigns since 1921, volunteered to distribute tampons among its New York office staff and ask for comments. After trying several brands, staff member Nadja Buckley compiled a detailed statement that alerted ICPC to Fibs' inferior absorbency. Keenly aware of marketing issues, she cautioned that "the [Fibs] tampon will not be very successful protection for the beginning of the period [when discharge tends to be heavier]. I believe the end [of the period, when discharge becomes lighter] will really prove our best sales talk."[43] Buckley's statement was welcome news to ICPC and Kimberly-Clark because it raised the possibility of marketing Fibs as a complement to Kotex sanitary napkins.

Kimberly-Clark meanwhile conducted an extensive field test

among Neenah mill shop-floor workers in October 1934, adminis-tered by female members of the technical department and mill nurs-es. Most women surveyed found the Wix tampon uncomfortable because it was difficult to insert and remove. Tampax generally received high marks, but many women expressed initial bewilder-ment. "I am sure that on my own volition I would never even con-sider using an insert with such a wicked appearance, that is, so painfully stiff and so incredibly long," one worker reported. "After much consideration, though, I am beginning to appreciate the unusu-al features of this strange appliance," she continued, agreeing with other test participants that the applicator was Tampax's most con-venient feature.[44] Other women felt less comfortable. One reported that she became "very frightened when I removed the tampax [sic] for I felt as if I was pulling all of my organs out of place."[45] Fibs were rejected by some participants who cited problems inserting the tam-pon, but most—perhaps trying to please management—reported positive experiences, particularly praising its comparatively small size. "As far as appearance goes this one is the least forbidding because of being smaller in size," one respondent opined. "After struggling with the other three kinds [Tampax, Wix, and Holly-Pax], I would say that this one is possibl[y] the least objectionable."[46] Its small size, presumably Fibs' most appealing feature, inherently lim-ited absorbency.

Based on the mill survey results, ICPC and Kimberly-Clark refined the Fibs design in January 1935 and commissioned another field test before releasing the product for full-scale production. Focusing on review comments that indicated insertability problems, the product designers dipped the tip of the tampon into a starch-glycerin solution to "facilitate digital insertion." The key managers involved in the pro-ject—Fourness in manufacturing, ICPC sales manager Morton Hague, and veteran Kotex advertising manager Lawrence Meyer—meanwhile discussed the redesigned Fibs with consulting physician Lloyd Arnold. Arnold was a tampon skeptic who claimed that his own Fibs field study with 225 participants demonstrated that only 15 percent of respondents experienced full protection, indicating that Fibs lacked sufficient absorbency. A subsequent consumer test with 93 participants administered in April 1935 contradicted Arnold's findings, convincing ICPC and Kimberly-Clark to authorize full-scale production without changes. The April survey was biased, however, because instructions suggested that participants use Fibs for the "end of the period."[47] Moreover, the survey did not instruct participants to compare Fibs to other tampons. One respondent who did make the comparison pointed out that she found "Tampax very satisfactory— more absorbent than Fibs."[48]

Mill engineers designed and built several tampon machines that were installed in the Neenah mill in early summer 1935. The main production equipment consisted of power-driven braiders, a so-called impregnating machine, drying rolls, a cutting machine, and several converting devices. Two braiding machines, operating at a speed of 8.4 feet per minute each, encased thin Cellucotton strips in a quilt, which was soaked in a starch-glycerin solution on the impregnating machine and then dried on a reel. A cutting machine sliced the quilted strips into pieces slightly more than two inches in length at a rate of 20 feet per minute. After a power-driven pointing device contoured the tip, the tampon was sown together in a stitching machine, looped, inspected, and machine packaged.[49]

The Fibs tampon was released in summer 1935. In July ICPC advertising manager Meyer told three female sales representatives who sold Kotex door-to-door that "we are definitely coming out with a tampon under the name of 'Fibs' which will pack 12 to a carton, probably to retail at 25¢." He also authorized them to distribute free samples to "any woman who expresses an interest in tampons."[50] Immediate consumer responses were discouraging. The sales representatives reported to Meyer in late August 1935 that customers questioned whether Fibs were as absorbent as other tampons. Meyer wrote an urgent telegram to James Kimberly in Neenah on August 28, requesting detailed laboratory information. The answer arrived several hours later. "The absolute capacity of some of the larger tampons would be greater than our Fibs because there is so much more material in them," it read. "However our wadding absorbs so much more quickly that in actual use Fibs are just as efficient as the larger tampons because a larger percentage of the wadding in Fibs is used."[51] When Fibs was finally released on September 21, 1935, Meyer acknowledged its limitations. "As indicated on the carton, Fibs are recommended 'for the waning days of the period,'" he told his sales staff. "They are not a substitute for a sanitary napkin. They offer invisible protection at a time when requirements are light, *usually* the last few days, but *sometimes* at the very beginning of a period."[52] Meyer's advertising campaigns, which marketed Fibs as "The Kotex Tampon," reiterated this confusing message, exacerbating the problem with a poor choice of words. Asserting that Fibs "really solves the problem of days when less protection is needed," the ad failed to

FIGURE 3.4 Fibs advertisement, 1935

specify what that problem was, violating one of the ground rules of successful advertising (figure 3.4).

Kimberly-Clark executives tried to ignore the Fibs absorbency problem for over a year, focusing their attention instead on Tampax's allegedly misleading marketing campaign. James Kimberly stated in December 1937, "Tampax has taken most of the tampon market by a considerable amount of advertising and a lot of extravagant claims. Our lab results show that 'Fibs' perform better than Tampax." In any event, he added, "Tampon products will not be satisfactory for the entire menstrual period—a pad is needed as a back-up."[53] In an implicit admission that something *was* amiss, however, researchers tried to improve absorbency and reduce the bacteria count through a Fibs redesign in 1938. The new design evidently failed to solve the absorbency problem, because a report issued the following year indicated that Fibs still compared unfavorably to other tampons in this category.[54]

The reasons for Kimberly-Clark's failure to secure a foothold in the tampon market were numerous. Committed to the company's core business in sanitary napkins, managers and executives were unable to conceptualize tampons as independent products. A combination of technological misperceptions and Kotex marketing traditions may have played a role as well. After touting the superiority of Cellucotton's absorbency compared to cotton's for more than two decades, executives and managers had probably convinced themselves that they could produce a smaller tampon than competitors, without a proportional loss in absorbency. Reducing the size of menstrual hygiene products had been a guiding principle of Kotex's development since the late 1920s, culminating in the introduction of Phantom Kotex in 1932. These trends converged in the development of the Fibs tampon, whose small size accounted for its inferior product quality.

At the time, management could claim that the ill-fated tampon cost the company nothing more than $100,000 in research and development expenses. As a result of consumer bias against insertable devices, tampons captured less than five percent of the feminine hygiene products market of the 1930s. But Kimberly-Clark's own field studies indicated that young respondents felt somewhat less intimidated by tampons than older survey participants. A 42-year-old business manager, for example, believed that tampons "undoubtedly will please the young moderns. Older women, hampered by old fashioned training and ideas will hesitate to use them. I don't know why, but I would not feel safe."[55] A 22-year-old housekeeper, by contrast, was "anxious to try [tampons] again,"[56] and a 26-year-old bookkeeper liked them for "evenings when I go out."[57] This raised troubling questions about the continued market dominance of sanitary napkins in later decades.

VI.

The price war of the early 1930s and the Fibs debacle notwithstanding, Kimberly-Clark remained one of the nation's best-performing paper companies. Maintaining a positive balance sheet, turning Kleenex into one of the fastest-growing consumer nondurables of the decade, launching a Kotex redevelopment program, and experimenting with tampons were no small feats in an industry that suffered above-average financial losses.

A financial survey of the nation's seven leading pulp and paper companies from 1930 to 1936 confirms this hypothesis (tables 3.5A and 3.5B). Kimberly-Clark's aggregate $8.83 million profit over the period was higher than that of any other company. At the other end of the spectrum International Paper—whose average annual sales of more than $90 million and assets exceeding $300 million made it the world's largest paper company—reported an aggregate loss of $13 million from 1930 to 1936, accumulated over five consecutive years. Kimberly-Clark and Scott Paper were the only firms in the group that remained profitable. In 1934, its worst year, Kimberly-Clark still reported a 2.6 percent profit. St. Regis Paper Company, by contrast, reported the most horrendous performance in this category, with negative earnings exceeding 17.6 percent in 1932, followed by a 21.6 percent loss a year later. In these two years, arguably the darkest period in American economic history, the industry wrote its earnings statements mostly in red ink, but Kimberly-Clark still managed to eke out 4.8 and 3.2 percent in profits respectively. Its ability to skirt the economic free fall of the worst Depression years stands out as the firm's most notable achievement. When the tide finally turned in 1935, most competitors emerged as debt-ridden firms with devalued assets, spending the next several years patching up their finances and reorganizing their battered corporate structures. Kimberly-Clark and Scott, meanwhile, entered the period of slow recovery in the second half of the 1930s in relative financial health, enabling them to invest money into new products and assets instead of servicing colossal debts.

A comparison with IP highlights some of the strategic underpinnings of Kimberly-Clark's above-average financial performance during the Depression. In the 1920s IP transferred its newsprint operations to Canada to take advantage of lower pulpwood and labor costs, but the sheer scale of its $60 million investments contributed to market gluts in the late 1920s. Unlike Kimberly-Clark's Canadian newsprint mill in Spruce Falls, Ontario, which could count on the fairly dependable demand of *The New York Times* through much of the 1930s, IP had no reliable long-term customers, forcing it to bid on annual newsprint contracts in fierce competition with increasingly desperate Canadian mills. When newsprint prices tumbled as a result

TABLE 3.5A

Net earnings of Kimberly-Clark, IP, Mead Corporation, and Union Bag, 1930–1936

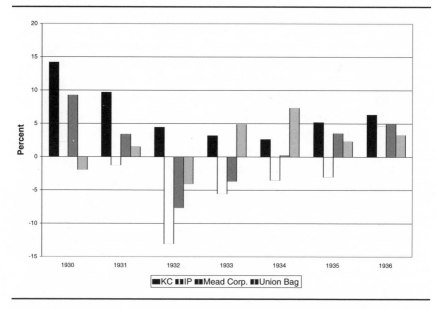

TABLE 3.5B

Net earnings of Kimberly-Clark, Container Corporation, Scott Paper, and St. Regis, 1930–1936

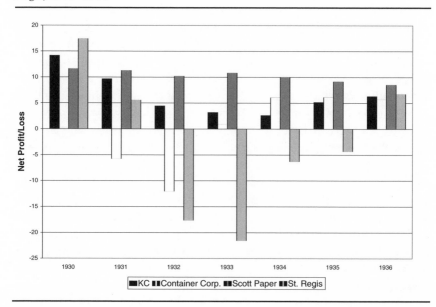

in the early 1930s, IP's Canadian newsprint subsidiary started to produce newsprint at a loss of $7.50 per ton, yielding aggregate losses of $22.8 million over the course of the 1930s.[58]

IP meanwhile converted its aging American newsprint mills to other grades. Unlike Kimberly-Clark, however, IP shunned technologically challenging products like rotogravure grades or wallpapers that required new expertise and new investments into product-specific mill equipment. Older IP mills instead converted to conventional book and bond papers. Kimberly-Clark's and Hammermill's experiences in this sector demonstrated that production and marketing of specialty papers required close coordination with jobbers and printers. But IP kept jobbers at arm's length, learned little about marketing strategies for book and bond papers, and—unlike Kimberly-Clark—rarely dispatched engineers to help printers solve problems. Moreover, like most other mass producers of printing papers, IP avoided investment-intensive research and development programs, particularly in the Depression. In the early 1930s, when Kimberly-Clark researchers were busy developing Kleerfect and Hyfect, IP fired more than half of its research staff at the Glens Falls, New York, laboratory, leaving the company's printing paper mills to their own devices. This lack of innovative capacity contributed to the demise of most book and bond paper mills in the IP system during the 1930s.[59]

The near collapse of IP's newsprint subsidiary, combined with the decline of its book and bond paper business, produced one of the industry's worst financial records. Average net losses amounted to 2.79 percent of net sales from 1930 to 1936, compared to Kimberly-Clark's 6.5 percent in net earnings. IP turned the corner after mid-decade, when it scaled back unprofitable newsprint operations and expanded its consumer nondurable business in kraft paper products through its subsidiary Southern Kraft Corporation (SKC). Created during the 1920s, SKC operated six large paper mills in the southern states; these mills initially produced unbleached wrapping papers for brown shopping bags and related items. When demand for the products slumped in the early Depression, Richard Cullen and other SKC executives decided to retool several mills for unbleached kraft grades. The latter were converted by subsidiaries into a variety of new consumer nondurables, including milk cartons, paper plates, file folders, and high-grade linerboard cartons. Impressed with SKC's ability to develop profitable new product lines, IP's board fired company president Archibald Graustein in 1936 and replaced him with Cullen, who orchestrated several large-scale refinancing and reorganization programs over the next several years. In 1937, to pry loose $2.3 million for long-overdue preferred dividends, Cullen had to convince wary shareholders to approve a recapitalization plan that reduced IP's stock value by $30 million. The same year, his colleague Sensenbrenner, whose company had not once defaulted on its preferred obligations during the Depression, announced close to $1 million in common dividends to Kimberly-Clark stockholders.[60]

A look at Scott Paper confirms the correlation between consumer nondurable product lines and strong financial performance in the Depression-era paper industry. Scott Paper was the industry's star performer, with average net earnings of 10.2 percent on net sales from 1930 to 1936, 36 percent higher than Kimberly-Clark's respectable record. Scott had carved out a dominant position in the market for paper towels and toilet paper with clever marketing strategies and substantial investments into its Chester, Pennsylvania, mill, widely regarded as one of the nation's best-equipped tissue paper mills. In the early 1930s Scott invested $1.4 million into a carefully calibrated research and plant equipment program that was designed both to improve the softness of its Waldorf toilet grade by more than 30 percent and to develop "ScotTowels for Kitchen Use," a new product that was based on its existing line of industrial grade paper towels. Almost doubling its advertising budget at the height of the Depression to $365,000, Scott conducted successful marketing campaigns for the new ScotTowel and other products that helped boost net dollar sales by 18 percent in 1934. The increase enabled Scott to compensate for an 8 percent decline in per-unit price of tissue paper in that year, yielding 9.7 percent growth in net earnings compared to 1933. Although the company invested $3.8 million into a two-year reconstruction of the Chester plant, common dividends grew uninterruptedly from $230,000 (1931) to $1.2 million (1939) in current dollars.[61]

VII.

Although a detailed history of industrial relations at Kimberly-Clark lies beyond the purview of the present study, the topic warrants some attention because labor-management conflicts affected the firm during the postwar decades. The roots of Kimberly-Clark's uneasy relations with national trade unions, which precipitated a series of strikes in the 1960s and 1970s, lay in the interwar period, when the company tried everything possible to keep national unions out of its mills.

Kimberly-Clark had long been committed to the concept of welfare capitalism, which many employers viewed as "an alternative to Taylorized bureaucracy and to market contractualism," as historian Sanford Jacoby has pointed out.[62] Beginning in the late nineteenth century, the firm had rented out or sold family homes to its employees in Kimberly and Niagara, Wisconsin, and elsewhere at low prices. In 1910 it had instituted the Kimberly-Clark Mutual Benefits Association which paid out almost $800,000 in benefits over the next eighteen years. In the 1920s company president Sensenbrenner personally financed the construction of a hospital at the Spruce Falls newsprint mill in Kapuskasing, Ontario. In the early 1930s the company increased its payroll by 70 percent to more than 4,000 production workers while instituting the six-hour workday. In the 1930s management cited these policies to buttress its claim that national unions were superfluous because Kimberly-Clark workers enjoyed better working conditions and a higher standard of living than most paper workers.[63]

Kimberly-Clark workers were organized in mill councils, instituted in 1920 to fend off the International Brotherhood of Pulp and Sulphite Mill Workers (IBPSMW) and other national unions. The mill councils—a euphemism for company unions—were composed of workers and management representatives who consistently toed the company line on wages, work hours, and benefits in the 1920s. Their chief task was to develop uniform job descriptions and classifications for all mill occupations in order to support management efforts to systematize production, particularly for Cellucotton, Kotex, Kleenex, and other new consumer items. Although these efforts contradicted the notion of welfare capitalism as an alternative to bureaucratization, Taylorism, and overly formal labor-management relations, the ideology of corporate welfare apparently remained intact. When IBPSMW organizers tried to recruit workers shortly after the passage of the National Industrial Recovery Act (NIRA), "anti-union workers explained to Brotherhood representatives that they enjoyed higher rates of pay and better working conditions and benefits under the company union than did organized pulp and paper workers in the region."[64]

Kimberly-Clark—eager to keep the unions out, but also determined to participate in National Recovery Administration (NRA) code negotiations to stabilize the troubled sanitary napkin business—revamped the mill councils in June 1933 to comply with NIRA Section 7(a). A committee consisting of twenty-one managers and the same number of workers developed a plan to expand council authority beyond wage and work-hour issues; the plan was adopted in a referendum held at all Kimberly-Clark mills during the summer. "The new plan is thorough-going," Sensenbrenner claimed. "It has 'teeth.'" To comply with Section 7(a), employees elected mill council members in secret ballots. The seven mill councils were authorized to consider and resolve disputes over "working conditions, hours, pay, supervision, health, safety, hiring, transfer, promotion, demotion, release, insurance, education, housing, recreation, community relations, and similar matters."[65] Every three months local mill councils sent representatives to a five-day general council meeting at company headquarters in Neenah to deal with companywide issues. In November 1933 the councils started a thirty-month occupational analysis and classification program that established "Standard Instructions," including detailed job specifications, pay scales for hourly rated jobs, and grievance mechanisms. Ratified by the general council in 1936, the standard instructions remained the basis for capital-labor relations at Kimberly-Clark for more than two decades. Sensenbrenner claimed that the program "resulted in some of the straightest thinking we have ever done on administrative problems. Standard instructions which are cooperatively developed provide more workable policies than management alone could devise."[66] Crediting the NIRA with creating a "new spirit of openness," management portrayed its labor provisions in glowing terms: *We feel that paragraph 7-A of the NIRA has done a powerful lot* [sic] *to build a sound basis of relations between management and employees of Kimberly-Clark Corporation.*"[67] Mill council members, in testimony before an NRA code committee, raised eyebrows throughout the paper industry by suggesting a minimum hourly wage of 50¢ and Kimberly-Clark's six-hour workday as industrywide standards. IBPSMW president John Burke, a skilled union strategist, promptly portrayed the Kimberly-Clark proposal as too ambitious, convincing several paper companies to enter collective bargaining agreements with the "reasonable" IBPSMW.[68]

The Wagner Act marked a watershed in industrial relations across the country. Shortly after passage of the act in 1935, Kimberly-Clark management still claimed that "the new law does not outlaw the Kimberly-Clark Council Plan." However, management later admitted that the system was legally untenable under the provisions of the National Labor Relations Act, owing to extensive management involvement in mill council affairs. Although the company dissolved the councils in August 1937, company unionism survived. To pre-empt national unions which dispatched labor organizers to the Fox River Valley in summer 1937, management hurriedly recognized the Employees' Independent Union (EIU), formed in August 1937 by for-mer mill council members. (Similar company unions were founded by employees of three other Wisconsin paper companies but failed to gain NLRB accreditation.) At its first meeting with the union, man-agement signed off on a closed-shop system proposed by EIU repre-sentatives—a transparent attempt to keep national unions out of the mills for good. By September 1 the company union had enrolled 3,215 of 3,532 eligible employees. Continuing at breakneck speed to create a *fait accompli,* management and EIU representatives signed a contract on September 22 that sanctioned existing labor policies, including the standard instructions, wage schedules, the basic six-hour workday, and a 36-hour workweek.[69]

As could be expected, national unions responded with hardball tactics of their own. The IBPSMW and the International Brotherhood of Paper Makers filed a complaint with the NLRB, citing various vio-lations of the Wagner Act, including company payments to EIU rep-resentatives. The NLRB, agreeing with the unions that these practices were illegal, instructed Kimberly-Clark to renounce the September 22 contract, dissolve the EIU, and admit national trade unions to all future elections. A red-faced Frank Shattuck stated publicly:

> Certain technical provisions of the Wagner Act were unintention-ally violated. The former mill council plan, for instance, had not been entirely abandoned during the early stages of organization of the union. Under the council plan the company paid wages to employees while engaged in council business other than joint bar-gaining meetings with management.[70]

Moreover, the company had reimbursed council members for travel and hotel expenses and had paid the salary of a full-time secretary. "Such practices," Shattuck acknowledged, "are named as unfair under the Wagner Act and, inasmuch as there was an overlapping between the outgoing council pan and the incoming independent union, the management is charged with unfair labor practices and the independent union is labeled as company dominated."[71]

While acknowledging the NLRB findings, Shattuck remained con-vinced that Kimberly-Clark employees were still committed to com-pany unionism. "So far as we know," he told a business associate, "the employees' attitudes have not changed since the Independent Union went out of existence in October." Subsequent events confirmed this view. EIU activists organized local independent unions at the Kimberly, Atlas, Lakeview, and Niagara Falls mills. Management supported the movement with an advertising campaign in local newspapers entitled "Kimberly-Clark Industrial Relations Talks" that portrayed national trade unions as unwelcome "outsiders."[72] The campaign carried over into 1938, when Kimberly-Clark mills held Wagner Act elections. Shortly before the vote an editorial published in the company's employee newsletter *Cooperation* claimed that the NLRB ruling of the previous year had been a union-inspired act of willful destruction that threatened democracy itself. "Constitutional representative government worked more genuinely in Kimberly-Clark under the old Council Plan than it works in most of our political subdivisions. . . . Odd, isn't it, that our national government, through one of its bureaus . . . should drive from existence so wholesome an influence in our national life."[73] Hinting at dark machinations involving liberal members of Congress, the NLRB, the Roosevelt administration, and above all organized labor, management portrayed national trade unions as agents of an increasingly antidemocratic state. Partly as a result of such rhetoric, most employees rejected the IBPSMW, the International Brotherhood of Paper Makers (IBPM), the International Association of Machinists (IAM), and other national unions that competed in the elections, casting their lot instead with the local independent unions. The independents, unlike the EIU, meticulously avoided management involvement in internal affairs, including company funding of clerical services. Chastened by the events of fall 1937, management did not recognize the company unions until they had received NLRB certification. In 1939 management and company union representatives signed their first collective bargaining contracts. The contracts ratified both the standard instructions and a small wage increase that management had granted voluntarily in 1937; however, they also reinstated the eight-hour workday.

Management's attempt to keep national unions at bay in the late 1930s was largely successful. Except a handful of trades that were represented by the IAM, the IBPSMW, and the IBPM, most of Kimberly-Clark's 4,300 hourly workers opted for company unions. As a result, the corporate welfare system instituted after World War I and modified in 1933 remained in place well into the postwar era. Most other paper companies, by contrast, recognized and negotiated with national unions shortly after the passage of the Wagner Act. IP, for example, long the industry's bastion of strident anti-unionism, signed its first contract with the IBPSMW and the IBPM in November 1937, supplemented a year later by a multi-mill contracting system that enabled IP to maintain relatively trouble-free industrial relations until the 1980s.

Kimberly-Clark's system of industrial relations was far more than an anachronism, however. As late as the 1950s company unions represented more than 400,000 American workers in some of the nation's largest corporations, including DuPont and TRW. Operating with the parameters of Section 7(a) and later the Wagner Act, many company union representatives viewed themselves as independent collective bargaining agents. Some even took positions that exceeded demands raised by trade union leaders, as evidenced by the proposal of Kimberly-Clark council representatives at the NRA code hearings to adopt the company's six-hour workday as an industry standard. Furthermore, many managers believed that their labor policies met modern collective bargaining standards. Charles Eubank, for example, a Kimberly-Clark industrial relations specialist, remarked at a labor conference in Chicago:

> Some of you probably are thinking that I'm either kidding myself or trying to kid you when I refer to a genuinely legislative employee representation plan through which major decisions are really made, and binding contracts really negotiated. Your argument probably is that the management representatives, with their inside information and ability to talk, are able to sell gold bricks or are powerful enough to make the workers feel compelled to agree. . . . But your argument does not apply to an employee representation plan which honestly tries to satisfy today's requirements by settling major issues. The man who says that elected representatives today are unwilling or unable to aggressively and effectively present their case simply does not know what he is talking about.[74]

Managers who reiterated these claims in subsequent years neglected to mention that company union objections to management decisions were usually based on the standard instructions first adopted in 1936, a pivotal link between "old" and "new" labor relations that ensured management hegemony. Be this as it may, management was convinced that company unionism contradicted neither the letter nor the spirit of the Wagner Act.

This attitude left management ill-prepared to negotiate with national trade unions, which remained its *bête noire* well into the postwar era. Cola Parker, for example, had joined Kimberly-Clark in 1937 as a senior executive, succeeded Sensenbrenner as company president in 1942, and later served as president of the National Association of Manufacturers. Parker regularly referred to national trade union activists as "bosses" who allegedly engaged in "union goonism." When Kimberly-Clark employees started to join national trade unions in large numbers during the early 1960s, management was stunned and outraged at these acts of "betrayal." Unaccustomed to collective bargaining procedures that had become routine in large parts of the industry since the late 1930s, Kimberly-Clark became embroiled in a series of labor conflicts that hurt the company at a time when it struggled to maintain its financial viability.

VIII.

Kimberly-Clark emerged from the Great Depression as one of the nation's most resourceful pulp and paper companies. Despite a steep plunge in profitability and suspension of common stock dividends from 1932 to 1935, it largely maintained its financial viability without increasing its $8 million long-term debts. In 1939 its surplus amounted to $9.2 million—slightly less than that of International Paper, whose assets and sales exceeded Kimberly-Clark's by a factor of four. Its 150-member research department, whose average annual budget in the late 1930s exceeded $400,000, was the largest and most versatile in the industry. Cellucotton-based consumer nondurables employed more than half of its workforce, a larger share than that of any other paper company except Scott. Failures like Fibs notwithstanding, Kimberly-Clark, Scott, and Hammermill probably knew more about consumer marketing than the rest of the industry combined.

Industry analysts took note, commending Kimberly-Clark for sensible product and financial strategies under extraordinarily difficult circumstances. In 1938 Thomas Foristall, an analyst for *The Wall Street Journal,* noted in his widely read "Inquiring Investor" column: "Although considerable fluctuation is experienced in its returns, Kimberly-Clark Corp. enjoys a far greater measure of stability than the average unit engaged in the inherently erratic paper manufacturing industry. . . . Benefiting from [an] integrated operating status and from relatively stable demand for products, the company has been able under the worst trade conditions to record 'black ink' results."[75]

4

In the Mainstream:
EXPANSION AND CRISIS, 1940s–1971

THE POSTWAR DECADES marked a period of massive expansion and growth. A mill construction and acquisition program launched after World War II expanded the geographical scope of manufacturing operations, adding plants in Tennessee, Alabama, California, and Connecticut. International acquisitions provided the company with a growing presence in Western European, Central American, and South African markets. Diversification added a slew of new products, from cigarette paper to nonwoven fabrics. Kotex and Kleenex marketing campaigns included promotional films on feminine hygiene and cold prevention that were shown to millions of viewers across the country. Sales grew twenty-fold from 1945 to 1971, reaching close to $1 billion in the latter year. In the early 1960s Kimberly-Clark became Wisconsin's largest corporation, joined the ranks of Fortune 500 companies, and was the nation's fourth largest pulp and paper company (table 4.1).

The veneer of a classic postwar success story masked strategic problems, however. Kimberly-Clark's market share shrank precipitously and across the board. Insufficient product development weakened the company's position in core markets, including sanitary napkins and facial tissue, rendering it vulnerable to resourceful competitors. Attempts to stage a decisive breakthrough in tampon markets were as unsuccessful during the postwar era as they had been in the interwar years. Financial results worsened in the late 1960s. "God, they're behind the times," one industry analyst summed up

111

TABLE 4.1

Eight largest U.S. pulp and paper companies, 1962

Company	Sales	Assets
International Paper	$1,095,671,662	$1,009,398,253
Crown-Zellerbach	589,101,779	615,959,105
St. Regis	579,017,961	585,731,035
Kimberly-Clark	151,238,667	443,678,485
Mead Corporation	435,116,370	315,231,807
Champion	357,689,940	253,844,773
Scott Paper	354,449,607	365,985,893
West Virginia Pulp & Paper	276,605,000	275,012,000

Wall Street's view of Kimberly-Clark in the early 1970s. "The big guys will come in and clean their clock."[1]

The notion that Kimberly-Clark missed the boat by following outdated corporate strategies is misleading, however. Many Fortune 500 companies lost shares in their core markets during the 1960s, and many tried to solve the widespread problem of declining return on investment by branching out into new product lines, adding subsidiaries, and entering new markets. Product diversification, acquisitions, and multinational expansion were corporate America's buzzwords in the 1960s. Far from missing the boat, Kimberly-Clark pursued what analysts widely regarded as safe and sound corporate strategy. The real problem was that mainstream strategy was neither safe nor sound. Costly acquisitions and product diversification programs often diverted precious resources from companies' extant core businesses, rendering them vulnerable to domestic and foreign competition, which in turn resulted in further declines in market shares. In more ways than one, Kimberly-Clark's postwar history encapsulated troubling trends in American business that precipitated the economic crisis of the 1970s.[2]

Economic historians have partially attributed this crisis to managers' inability to learn lessons from the Great Depression. As in the interwar period, many companies in mature industries—sidetracked by the acquisition bonanza of the 1960s—failed to develop profitable new product lines from existing ones, hastening a prolonged downturn. This was especially true for companies like U.S. Steel, International Paper, and Ford Motor Company, whose precipitous declines in the 1970s echoed their Depression-era experiences. While managers in these companies were often blind to past mistakes, Kimberly-Clark executives were largely unable to draw lessons from their predecessors' successes. Bucking industrywide trends as early as World War I, the company had marshaled extant R&D capabilities to develop innovative consumer nondurables and had maintained market leadership through continuous improvements in core product lines throughout much of the interwar period. Postwar managers saw considerable opportunities in consumer markets; but, unlike their interwar counterparts, they banked on acquisitions-based product diversification and multinational expansion while neglecting strategic R&D investments into core product lines. As a result, Kimberly-Clark staged no strategic breakthroughs in product development as it had during the interwar period with Kotex and Kleenex, or as it did in later decades with Huggies diapers.

I.

Kimberly-Clark entered the postwar years under new senior management. Longtime executive Frank Sensenbrenner, who had been one of the company's key figures since the turn of the century and who had served as president since 1928, retired in 1942, to be succeeded by Cola Parker. A graduate of the University of Chicago law school, Parker had been a senior partner in the New York law firm Wise, Whitney & Parker, who had served as legal counsel to leading paper companies in the 1930s, including Kimberly-Clark. After heading the book manufacturers' group in the National Recovery Administration, Parker had joined the company as vice president in 1937.[3]

During his tenure as president, Parker played a key role in formulating the company's postwar expansion strategy, the early stages of which centered on a massive mill construction and reconfiguration program launched in 1945. At the time, Kimberly-Clark scaled down wartime production—insulating material for the Army, mimeograph paper for the Navy, and packaging material for aircraft manufacturers—to take advantage of surging civilian demand for paper products. Wartime limitations on civilian items such as catalog paper, feminine hygiene products, and wallpaper had created pent-up demand which was released in the closing months of 1945. A year later the Office of Price Administration lifted ceiling rates for most paper products, enabling manufacturers to offset wage increases with higher prices.

Reflecting industrywide trends, Kimberly-Clark's inflation-adjusted sales shot up more than 30 percent from 1945 to 1947, with solid increases projected for at least a decade.[4]

Responding to the need for greater capacity, Parker and his lieutenants proposed a $67.5 million plant construction and reconfiguration program. The ambitious project— financed through a $14.2 million stock issue, $29.9 million in reinvestments, and $23.5 million in debt—enabled Kimberly-Clark to expand output of key product lines. From 1945 to 1949 book paper output increased 37 percent, pulp 57 percent, and Cellucotton 68 percent. Equally important, Parker's initiative created production linkages between Kimberly-Clark mills, particularly in pulp manufacture and Cellucotton production.[5]

Additional Cellucotton production and conversion capacity received top priority because the Lakeview mill in Neenah was unable to fill orders for Kotex and Kleenex and lacked sufficient space for major new additions. The centerpiece of the Cellucotton expansion program was a 600,000-square-foot plant in Memphis, Tennessee, acquired by Kimberly-Clark in 1946. Originally built during the war for B-25 bomber production, the Memphis plant featured a single-story layout, in contrast to the multistory designs of the company's older Wisconsin mills, where transfers of materials from one floor to the next created production bottlenecks. Taking advantage of the building's architecture, mill engineers devised a mechanized material handling system that enhanced throughput and improved sanitation by reducing "touch labor." The Memphis mill also featured four paper machines equipped with rolls 13 feet wide, a 40 percent gain over the narrower Lakeview machines. The mill enjoyed considerable location advantages, including low-cost labor and proximity to rapidly growing markets in the Southeast.[6]

The Memphis plant received the bulk of its pulp supplies from a newsprint mill in Childersburg, Alabama, a joint venture of Kimberly-Clark and southern publishers. The region's newspapers had traditionally been printed on imported Canadian paper, partly because southern pulpwood was unsuitable for newsprint pulp production. But improvements in pulping technology enabled mills to process regional pulps, precipitating newsprint mill construction in many southern states in the postwar years. Shortly after the war, members of the Southern Newspaper Publishers Association approached Parker with a proposal to build a large mill at Coosa Pines, Alabama, to be managed by the Wisconsin papermakers. Parker had little interest in reentering American newsprint, a product line the company had abandoned in 1916, but he viewed the proposed plant as a valuable source of bleached sulfite pulp for the Memphis Cellucotton mill. In 1946 Kimberly-Clark joined more than one hundred newspaper publishers to form the Coosa River Newsprint Company, contributed $6.7 million to the $32 million dollar venture, and took a leading role in designing, building, and managing the mill. By the early 1950s the Coosa River mill was the premier pulp source for Kleenex disposable handkerchiefs manufactured at Memphis, which became the most important plant in Kimberly-Clark's postwar mill system.[7]

Plant improvement and construction programs also created newsprint-Cellucotton linkages north of the border, albeit on a smaller scale than in the South. The Spruce Falls mill in Kapuskasing, Ontario, which supplied *The New York Times* and other American papers, included a sulfite pulp mill whose daily capacity was 250 tons and whose output was mixed with groundwood pulp to produce newsprint. Beginning in the 1930s Kapuskasing shipped excess sulfite pulp to the Kimberly-Clark mill in Niagara Falls, New York, which produced Cellucotton, Kotex, and Kleenex. The Niagara Falls mill exported some of its output to Canada until 1945, when Kimberly-Clark built a Cellucotton plant with 30 tons daily capacity next to the Kapuskasing mill. Using an advanced process of chip distribution and independent acid recovery, the newsprint mill increased its output of bleached sulfite pulp, which was pipelined to Kimberly-Clark's new Cellucotton plant. The latter, operated by the wholly owned subsidiary Kimberly-Clark of Canada, Limited, shipped its entire output to a new manufacturing plant in Niagara Falls, Ontario, which converted it into Kotex and Kleenex.

Similar synergisms developed in the production of printing papers, where the postwar expansion program raised annual production capacity from 186,000 tons in 1946 to almost 245,000 tons four years later. In 1945 Parker announced a $5 million upgrade of the Niagara, Wisconsin, mill, the largest investment into Kimberly-Clark's printing paper business since 1920. The program added a single-story mill building, two fourdriniers, and a material handling system resembling that of the Memphis mill. Like the latter, Niagara procured most of its raw materials from a pulp mill located several hundred miles away, in this instance a major new plant in Terrance Bay, Ontario. The $15 million Terrance Bay mill, one of the largest built in postwar Canada by U.S. paper companies, came onstream in 1948 with a daily capacity of 250 tons, most of which went to the

Niagara mill for conversion into machine-coated grades. Niagara, Kimberly-Clark's largest printing paper mill, supplied publications such as *Business Week, Newsweek, Esquire,* and *New Yorker.*[8]

Several years after the expansion program that began in 1945 was completed, the company added important new mills on the West Coast and in the Northeast. The first new mill, a Cellucotton manufacturing and converting plant at Fullerton, California, was initially a topic of considerable controversy among executives. Citing a long list of failed paper mill projects in the region, senior engineers claimed that the buildup of freshwater-dependent manufacturing operations in water-scarce Southern California could result in long-term operational problems. Andrew G. Sharp, vice president of sales, and other marketing managers strongly endorsed the concept of "bringing the plant to market," arguing that the Fullerton mill would improve the competitiveness of consumer product lines in one of the nation's fastest-growing regional markets. The latter argument convinced Parker and a majority on the board of directors, which approved a $20 million appropriation for construction of the Fullerton plant. The mill, whose design incorporated advanced water purification and recycling technology, produced its first batch of Kotex in 1955 and became one of the largest plants in the Kimberly-Clark system. A similar Cellucotton mill was built in New Milford, Connecticut, in the late 1950s to supply metropolitan New York.[9]

The results of Parker's plant construction and reconfiguration program were mixed. Additional volume capacity enabled the company to cope with the staggering order backlogs of the late 1940s and early 1950s and to defend its market share in key product lines. Inflation-adjusted net sales grew by more than 230 percent from 1945 to 1955. The massive expansion of Cellucotton production reestablished Kleenex as the dominant product in disposable handkerchief markets, which had turned to competing products in the immediate postwar years because Kimberly-Clark lacked sufficient volume capacity to fill orders. Parker's claim that production linkages and plant efficiency gains would yield better financial results—an important rationale for the expansion program—stood on feeble grounds, however. Return on investment in fact declined during the early 1950s (table 4.2). Although corroborating evidence is lacking, one may speculate that Parker's attempt to network geographically dispersed plants (instead of building integrated pulp and conversion plants at single sites) contributed to a low return on investment because pulp shipments from Alabama to Georgia (280 miles) and from Northern Ontario to Nia-

TABLE 4.2
Kimberly-Clark return on investment, 1945–1952

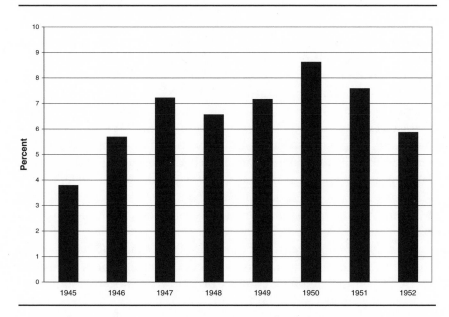

gara Falls (580 miles) resulted in higher transportation costs. John R. Kimberly, Parker's successor, nevertheless continued to foster production linkages between plants in disparate locales well into the 1960s, until the strategy came under attack by critics who attributed Kimberly-Clark's worsening cost structure to high transportation charges.[10]

Parker, who believed that disappointing earnings were the result of excessive volatility in Kimberly-Clark's core markets, advocated diversification into more stable product lines to prevent an earnings roller coaster. In 1951 he negotiated the acquisition of the Munising Paper Company, a manufacturer of sulfite bond papers that operated a two-machine mill in Michigan. The $4 million transaction marked a turning point in Kimberly-Clark's product diversification strategy, which had heretofore evolved new product lines from existing ones within in the company. Acquisitions-based product diversification, which became the norm over the next decade or so, was far from risk-free, however. Marketing of unfamiliar products frequently presented major challenges, particularly for companies like Kimberly-Clark whose marketing operations were highly centralized. Acquired product lines were often poor fits with a company's extant core business, blocking the types of production linkages and technological synergisms which Parker fostered in pulp and Cellucotton production. Then there was the possibility that acquisitions would prove to be lemons, as Kimberly-Clark learned in the case of Munising Paper. Touted as a leader in fine papers with advanced manufacturing operations and a strong record of product development, Munising's mill was poorly maintained and required a major repair program that curtailed operations for months. As Kimberly-Clark stockholders learned in 1953, "[D]uring the year certain conditions [manifested] themselves [that] called for expenditures . . . and [for] further expenditures in later years substantially in excess of those previously contemplated. This, plus some easing in demand for pulp and the Munising types of paper during the year, affected profits adversely."[11] Subsequent plant upgrades failed to improve the performance of Munising's pulp division, which was shut down permanently in 1961.[12]

Shortly before his retirement in 1955, Parker laid the groundwork for the acquisition of the International Cellucotton Products Company (ICPC), completed by his successor John R. Kimberly. Established as a wholly owned subsidiary to market Kotex and Kleenex, ICPC had evolved into a semi-independent corporation during the 1930s when the parent company sold some its stock holdings to Kimberly-Clark managers and employees. Although it developed a separate management organization (headquartered in Chicago) and controlled valuable trademarks and patents for Kotex and Kleenex independently, ICPC remained a marketing arm for Kimberly-Clark's consumer product lines. Seeking to solidify Kimberly-Clark's position in consumer markets, Parker and Kimberly engineered the acquisition of ICPC through a stock swap involving 3 million Kimberly-Clark shares. ICPC headquarters were moved to Neenah and integrated into the Kimberly-Clark marketing organization, which took direct control of Kotex and Kleenex advertising, promotion, and sales.[13]

II.

By the time of the acquisition, ICPC had accumulated a strong marketing record that stretched back to the early 1940s. Capitalizing on the success of *Marjorie May's 12th Birthday*, first issued in the United States in 1932, it launched major advertising campaigns to enhance brand name recognition for Kotex among teenagers, the fastest-growing consumer group of the 1940s and 1950s. These efforts were partly designed to fend off competitors in the sanitary napkin market, notably Johnson & Johnson, whose brochure entitled *Growing Up and Liking It* had gained popularity among teenagers. Meanwhile, tampon producers marketed their products aggressively as more "modern" alternatives to feminine pads. In 1942 Tampax Corporation published a series of ads headlined "I didn't know it was so simple to use Tampax—No Belts, No Pins, No Pads, No Odor"— all direct references to sanitary napkins, which required belts and pins as fasteners.[14]

In 1940 ICPC responded with an advice booklet entitled *As One Girl to Another* which inaugurated a new phase in menstruation discourses. The booklet replaced the fictional mother/daughter exchange presented in *Marjorie May's 12th Birthday* with a factual narrative. It also substituted flowery prose ("'Mother, dear, you are the best in the whole world,' said Marjorie May after her birthday guests had gone home") with lively, everyday-life language: "Girls have all sorts of crazy nicknames [for menstruation]," it read. "You may have heard them talk about 'falling off the roof'—or 'getting the pip'—or 'grandma is coming to visit.' Some call it 'the monthlies.' And if you're a shark at Latin you can guess why. For menstruation comes from the Latin word menses . . . meaning month."[15] Like most other pieces of advice literature, *As One Girl to Another* rarely mentioned physical or emotional discomfort, cheerfully reassuring readers that menstruation "causes most girls no trouble at all!" Admitting nebulously that menstruation is "a bit of a nuisance at times," the text hastened to add that this was "nothing *like* was it used to be, before Kotex was invented!"[16] After stressing that age variation and slight irregularities in the menstrual cycle were normal, it encouraged the use of a menstrual calendar (helpfully provided in the back of the booklet) so "you don't get caught unprepared." "If you're going off on an all-day outing in the country it's awfully easy to slip a Kotex pad and belt in your purse or pocket." Grabbing the opportunity to pitch another ICPC product, the text then counseled consumers to "fold [pad and belt] up in a piece of Kleenex . . . [and] pop a rubber band around them."[17] Advocating "normal" physical activity, including sports, *As One Girl to Another* cautioned against diving into cold water and swimming because it could result in temperature shocks, purportedly seen by many physicians as detrimental to menstrual health. (In truth, pad makers discouraged diving and swimming because highly absorbent sanitary napkins were unsuited for use under water.)

Young women who felt uncomfortable engaging in strenuous physical activity could expect understanding from their peers, including the opposite sex. "You know, boys know all about menstruation," the booklet claimed optimistically. "They don't think it's peculiar; it's a perfectly natural life process that they respect highly. They won't mention it . . . but they'll take the hint if you prefer the movies, or listening to the radio to playing some strenuous game."[18]

Although the bulk of *As One Girl to Another* marked a step toward a more candid menstruation discourse, the last several pages contained a problematic discussion of tampons that capitalized on popular myths and prejudices. In a transparent attempt to safeguard Kotex's market dominance, the authors claimed that "most authorities say young girls shouldn't use tampons without *first* consulting their doctor."[19] Without going so far as to raise the specter of accidental deflowering in as many words, the text pointed out that "there's . . . a membrane called a hymen which partly closes the entrance to the vagina—from which comes the menstrual flow. Therefore, Kotex sanitary napkins are more comfortable, and better suited to a young girl's needs, than tampons of any type"—hardly the logical explanation it purported to be.[20] After having thoroughly discouraged tampon use, the booklet recommended Fibs for the "particular case [where] it's all right to use tampons."[21] If anything, the lukewarm endorsement for "particular cases" was a telling comment on the relative insignificance of Fibs tampons in the ICPC product line. For more than a decade Kotex marketers continued to play on unspoken fears that tampons could rupture hymens, a myth authoritatively dispelled by gynecologist Robert L. Dickinson in *The Journal of the American Medical Association*.[22]

Like many other marketers who jumped on the patriotic bandwagon during World War II, ICPC launched a series of advertisements that linked sanitary protection to military themes. The ads were designed by San Francisco–based Foote, Cone & Belding, successor to the Lord & Thomas advertising agency which had handled Kotex advertising since the early 1920s. A Kotex ad released in 1944, for example, depicted a camouflaged sniper (one of the first men to appear in a sanitary napkin ad since 1920), whose "safety depends on *concealment*" (figure 4.1). "Useful at home, too. For its sharp strategy to hide your feelings at times . . . 'certain' times, especially." Unlike post–World War I marketers, FCB carefully avoided suggestions that menstruating women had anything in common with wounded soldiers—a widespread practice in wartime advertising, which preferred

FIGURE 4.1 "Are You in the Know?" advertisement, 1944

conquering warriors over battlefield casualties. The ad carried its mil-
itaristic metaphor to the extreme by claiming that Kotex enabled
young women to "'Dress to kill' in your fetchingest [*sic*] frock!"—not
unlike the sharpshooter who went hunting for the enemy attired in a
burlap suit. The accompanying artwork depicted young men and
(presumably menstruating) women dancing in a conga line and listening to the radio with Red Skelton's telltale cry "I dood it" blaring
from the speaker.

In 1946 ICPC supplemented its print advertising campaigns with
the promotional film *The Story of Menstruation*, a Walt Disney production that was viewed by more than 100 million high school students over the next several decades. The film was part of a rapidly
growing marketing trend when corporations commissioned "infor-
mational" productions to peddle their wares. Postwar pioneers of
these so-called ephemeral films included the Electric Auto-Lite Company, which released *The Right Spark Plug in the Right Place* in

1945, followed by Westinghouse's *The Dawn of Better Living* and Johnson & Johnson's *Bathing Time for Baby*. While most early productions were shown in movie theaters before feature presentations, *The Story of Menstruation* was one of the first corporately sponsored films distributed to high schools, whose vast captive audiences received free printed material to supplement the film, including instructional guides for teachers and student handouts. In a telling comment on postwar education, *The Story of Menstruation* and other, similar attempts to commercialize the classroom rarely attracted criticism from teachers who used films as teaching tools. Many, in fact, enthusiastically endorsed corporately sponsored motion pictures, which were usually more carefully crafted than dull public-service films thanks to higher production budgets. Moreover, the Kotex film producers preempted criticism by deliberately avoiding excessive product pitches, showing a box of Kotex only at the end of the film. The accompanying teaching material, including the student booklet *Very Personally Yours,* featured more frequent Kotex references and expanded on recent advertising themes by discouraging tampon use.

Work on *The Story of Menstruation* began in 1945, when Disney produced the first script drafts and conceptualized the visual material. Concerned that "adverse criticism from the medical profession could wreck the entire undertaking," the producers hired gynecologist Mason Hohl as a consultant to ensure scientific accuracy, enhancing the likelihood that school nurses and physicians who would preview the film before classroom screenings would give it a thumbs up.[23] As a result, all script drafts placed stronger emphasis on biological themes than other ICPC marketing material and adopted a far more reserved tone than the snazzy *As One Girl to Another.* "Mother Nature controls many of our routine bodily processes through automatic control centers called glands," the final draft adopted in June 1945 explained.[24] In adolescents the pituitary gland released a "maturing hormone" via the bloodstream to the ovaries to precipitate egg growth. Because unfertilized eggs did not require "the thickened lining [of the uterus that provides] nourishment for the budding human being," the lining was discharged from the body, producing "the flow which we call menstruation."[25] The remainder of the script admonished teenagers to keep a calendar, maintain normal levels of physical activity, and bathe regularly. All questions relating to menstrual hygiene were answered in the "very interesting booklet called *Very Personally Yours* [that] has been prepared to enlarge upon what you learn from this brief film," a script phrasing that linked the film inextricably to the promotional brochure.[26]

Unlike the script, visual material for *The Story of Menstruation* underwent major revisions before ICPC officially released the film. Eschewing costly full-scale production of the visual components, the Disney team outlined the film on seventy-six storyboards for presentation to high school test audiences. The test screenings, conducted in late 1945, resulted in major changes. Teachers objected to the depiction of a smiling embryo—not on scientific grounds, but because the image violated school policies that prohibited the showing of nude figures in classrooms. Students took exception to a scoreboard that compared the menstrual cycle to the change of seasons, inserted by the producers because it "had great possibilities for charm and beauty."[27] "Here we go again—back to the birds, the bees and the flowers," said one high school senior summing up student reaction. The idea of using animated Disney characters for *The Story of Menstruation* was quickly discarded because "no girl will identify herself with Disney cartoon characters." A draft of the opening credits included the film title and the words "presented by," followed by an image of a box of Kotex. Adult viewers were unconcerned about the sequence's commercialism but complained that it could unnerve high school audiences by starting the presentation with a product that caused "apprehension." The producers moved the Kotex box to the end, "where it appeared after the confidence of the audience had been won." The film's animation format—selected because it created "impersonal objective qualities"—won universal approval from test audiences and was heartily endorsed by ICPC because "the picture was kept dateless—was assured long life," enhancing amortization of production costs.[28]

While Disney worked on full-fledged production of the film, ICPC developed supplemental material, including a resource manual for educators that included a chart of menstrual physiology and a teaching guide. The latter encouraged teachers to address menstruation informally in fourth grade and follow up with more systematic discussions in seventh grade. Copies of *Very Personally Yours* would be distributed several days prior to screenings, and mothers would be invited to view the film together with their daughters in class. The manual also included a list of standard questions and answers. The recommended answer to "Can girls of 14 wear tampons?" was, without further explanation, "It would be wise to see a doctor before attempting to use tampons."[29] The use of Kotex was presumed in most standard exchanges, including "Can one prevent odor during the menstrual period . . .?" The suggested answer was, "Kotex sanitary napkins should be changed frequently."[30]

The Story of Menstruation received an enthusiastic reception when it premiered before an audience of high school teachers in 1946. A school director of health commended the film for its time-saving features, claiming, "In this day of increasing demands on teachers' time, it covers in ten short minutes far more subject matter than a teacher could handle in forty-five minutes, even with careful preparation."[31] Although nobody addressed the issue publicly, showing a film also reduced the amount of verbal explanation a teacher had to provide. Some students liked the film because it made them "feel relaxed. I enjoyed it instead of feeling hush hush," one girl remarked in comments that were included in ICPC marketing material for *The Story of Menstruation*.[32] The Library of Congress, claiming that the film had "potential historical significance," ordered two prints for its collection. The American Medical Association reviewed it favorably, as did *Parents' Magazine*.

Retrospective analyses were far less sanguine, criticizing the film's aseptic depiction of the female body and its normative assumptions of womanhood. Historian Joan Jacobs Brumberg, commenting on a revised version released in the 1950s, writes:

> In the Disney world, the menstrual flow is not blood red but snow white. The vaginal drawings look more like a cross section of a kitchen sink than the outside and inside of a woman's body. There are no hymen, no clitoris, no labia; all focus is on the little nest and its potentially lush lining. Although Disney and Kimberly-Clark advise exercise during the period, the exercising cartoon girls (who look like Disney's Cinderella) are drawn without feet; bicycles magically propel themselves down the street without any muscular or mental direction from the cyclist. The film ends happily ever after, with a shot of a lipsticked bride followed immediately by a shot of a lipsticked mother and baby.[33]

In addition to suggesting a problematic link between menstruation and motherhood, *The Story of Menstruation* squandered an opportunity to introduce some of the informal and at times funny vocabulary of *As One Girl to Another* into high school sex education. Instead of imitating casual teenage language, the producers offered scientific phraseology that set a tone of grave seriousness for classroom discussions. ICPC, convinced that "a detail that might cause a snicker" would ruin the film, in fact marketed it to schools by stressing its "objective," "scientific," and "unemotional" presentation that left no room for smiles.

Postwar "Are You in the Know?" advertisements, by contrast, were modeled after the lively wartime ads that juxtaposed Kotex pitches with advice on etiquette, dating, fashion, and grooming. The series, which continued well into the 1960s, imitated the question-and-answer format of advice columns in teenage magazines. The latter were periodically surveyed by ICPC marketers who selected frequently asked questions as a basis for "Are You in the Know?" ads. They also discussed ad drafts with editors of teenage magazines as well as with test audiences composed of young women. Text and artwork were designed to "*intrigue* girls and women into reading by appealing to their vanity," marketers claimed.[34] A typical ad released in 1949 abounded with teenage slang, coupled with references to recent developments in aircraft propulsion. Showing a waiter cleaning a patron's dress, the ad asked, "If he spilled a soda on your best dress, would you: [A] grieve and leave [B] grin and forget [C] call the manager." A young woman "in the know" would select B because "that's good sportsmanship. And it jet-propels your rating. Your confidence, too, hits the stratosphere—where you hurdle 'certain' handicaps with Kotex." The depiction of self-confident and at times wisecracking young women who enjoyed the admiration of smiling male companions in Kotex ads contrasted with marketing material developed by arch-rival Johnson & Johnson, which often conveyed more conservative messages. A Modess sanitary napkin advertisement released by Johnson & Johnson in 1949 criticized the tone of recent Kotex ads, asking suggestively whether "it's out-of-date to be tactful. . . . The wisecrack 'candid kid' may get laughs—even applause," the ad declared soberly. "But it's still good old tact that wins, and holds, friendship."

Encouraged by the widespread use of *The Story of Menstruation*, ICPC approached Disney in 1949 with a proposal for a promotional film for Kleenex disposable handkerchiefs entitled *How to Catch a Cold*. Taking a leaf from the underhanded commercial strategy that allowed ICPC to bill the Kotex film as educational material, the Kleenex marketing manager in charge of the project told team members, "[W]e do not want to load [*How to Catch a Cold*] with commercials. I would think that credits at the beginning and at the end of the picture, plus a few shots of cold sufferers taking tissues from the

Kleenex package in the picture itself, would suffice."[35] Disney, which had recently phased out promotional motion pictures, agreed to take on the project as a public service message. Produced under the scientific supervision of a consulting physician, the color film featured a boy hero named Common Sense who helped his sneezing friend The Common Man avoid colds. Unlike *The Story of Menstruation,* it was intended to make audiences laugh at The Common Man's clumsy mistakes, including golfing in wet weather and failing to cover his sneeze. Common Sense, always present with helpful advice, handed The Common Man a Kleenex at the end of the ten-minute presentation.[36]

The $150,000 production, released in 1951, was initially distributed to high schools and community organizations. Reviews indicated that ICPC's strategy of keeping commercial elements at a minimum paid off. "Even though the box of disposable tissues thrust by Common Sense under the running nose of The Common Man at the close of the picture is unmistakeably [*sic*] labeled 'Kleenex,' we think it should be acceptable in the classroom, as well as for industrial and community use," *Film News* noted.[37] The film's decisive breakthrough as a public service production came in autumn 1952, when the National Broadcasting Corporation selected *How to Catch a Cold* for a demonstration of color television and continued to broadcast it for several years. Over the next decade the film was seen by more than 200 million viewers, more than any other Disney production.[38]

Although *The Story of Menstruation* and *How to Catch a Cold* marked milestones in product promotion, they had little appreciable impact on ICPC's market shares. Kleenex accounted for 50.2 percent of all sanitary napkins sold in the United States in 1950, a figure that remained almost unchanged for the next three years, when viewership of *How to Catch a Cold* skyrocketed. Aware of its limited value for Kleenex marketing, ICPC kept advertising and distribution budgets for the film at a bare minimum through much of the 1950s. In 1955, after absorbing ICPC into its central marketing organization, Kimberly-Clark raised appropriations for the film by almost 40 percent, again without significant impact on Kleenex's market share. Management started to look for other ways to improve the balance sheet.[39]

III.

In 1955 Kimberly-Clark chairman Cola Parker was succeeded by John R. Kimberly, grandson of one of the company's founders. Born in 1902, he graduated in 1926 from the Massachusetts Institute of Technology with a degree in chemical engineering; he rose through the ranks to become manufacturing manager in the late 1930s. After a brief stint at the federal Office of Production Management, he was appointed vice president of sales in 1943 and executive vice president in 1952. A strong supporter of Parker's product diversification strategy, he was instrumental in acquiring the Munising Paper Company and ICPC. In addition to growing the company through further domestic acquisitions and plant improvements, Kimberly launched an ambitious international expansion program. Western Europe emerged as an area of particular interest in the late 1950s because paper consumption was projected to increase by 50 percent in 1965, compared to 39 percent in the United States.[40]

Kimberly began his twelve-year tenure as chairman by further diversifying the company. The $2 million acquisition of the Neenah Paper Company, completed through a stock swap in May 1957, marked Kimberly-Clark's return to cotton papers, a product line it had largely phased out more than seven decades before. Demand for cotton-based grades had declined precipitously in mainstream markets but remained strong in the niche market for fine business papers, where Kimberly-Clark had sought to stake a claim with the Munising acquisition. Designed to supplement the latter, the purchase of Neenah Paper enabled Kimberly-Clark to offer a complete line of business papers.[41]

The acquisition of Schweitzer Incorporated in February 1957 added cigarette and other thin specialty papers to Kimberly-Clark's product line. Schweitzer's origins dated to 1920, when Russian immigrant Peter J. Schweitzer acquired a paper mill in Jersey City, New Jersey, to produce cigarette paper and other thin grades. In 1922 his sons Louis and William Schweitzer incorporated and expanded the business, adding a major new mill in Elizabeth, New Jersey, which manufactured cigarette paper from flax pulp. The latter formed the basis for Schweitzer's meteoric rise in the 1930s and 1940s, when it became the leading paper supplier of the American Tobacco Company, Phillip Morris, and other major American cigarette companies. Determined to avail himself of the advanced French cigarette paper production technologies, William Schweitzer acquired Papeteries de Mauduit, a leading French company headquartered in Quiperlé, and formed a partnership with Papeteries Bollore, which operated three mills at Odet, Casadec, and Troyes. When Kimberly-Clark acquired Schweitzer for $18 million in 1957, it gained not only seven major cigarette and specialty paper mills in New Jersey, Pennsylvania, and Massachusetts (which produced more than 30 percent of the nation's thin paper output) but also a strong foothold in Western European markets through Schweitzer's French operations.[42]

The same year, Kimberly-Clark established a presence in British consumer product markets. Attempts to build up British operations dated to the 1920s, when Kimberly-Clark formed a subsidiary to market Kotex and Kleenex, but sales remained minuscule until after World War II. Initially shunning the establishment of full-fledged manufacturing operations in Britain, Kimberly-Clark negotiated a long-term agreement with Aylesford-based Albert E. Reed, Limited, which produced Cellucotton for exclusive distribution by a Kimberly-Clark subsidiary. John R. Kimberly, convinced that European markets for Kotex and Kleenex held considerable growth potential, engineered a joint venture between Kimberly-Clark and Reed to build a new Cellucotton production and conversion plant at Larkfield, which came onstream in 1957. Managed by the newly formed British subsidiary Kimberly-Clark, Limited, the plant helped sales grow strongly during subsequent years, and at the end of the 1960s sales had achieved more than 20 percent annual growth.[43]

British operations enabled Kimberly-Clark to expand into the West German market, where it teamed up with the Aschaffenburger Zellstoffwerke A.G. and the Dutch Unilever Corporation to form Zellwatte Limited as a joint venture ("Zellwatte" is a literal translation of "Cellucotton"). Zellwatte, whose conversion plant in Stockstadt churned out its first batches of Kotex and Kleenex in 1957, received the bulk of its Cellucotton supplies from the Larkfield mill. Sales presented major problems, however, because Zellwatte tried to compete with the German wholesalers that dominated consumer product markets. Attempts to sell directly to large retailers failed, resulting in a bulging inventory as Zellwatte missed projected sales by 70 percent in 1958. The joint venture remained a trouble spot throughout much of the 1960s as a result of poor operation and sales management.[44]

Kimberly's international expansion also produced mixed results in non-European markets, where Kimberly-Clark teamed up with local investors and paper companies in the late 1950s and 1960s. Kotex, Kleenex, and printing grades were exported to Mexico until 1955, when Kimberly-Clark formed a joint venture with Mexican investors to build a paper mill and conversion facilities in La Aurora, managed by the newly formed Kimberly-Clark de Mexico. Kimberly would have preferred to run Mexican operations through a wholly owned subsidiary, but "there is considerable pressure on foreign-owned companies to offer substantial interests to the Mexican public," he reported to the board of directors in February 1961.[45] Like Scott Paper, which faced similar pressure when it established a Mexican subsidiary in 1955, Kimberly-Clark willy-nilly agreed to reduce its ownership by 40 percent by offering stocks to Mexican investors. Printing paper sales waxed strongly from the start, but consumer products sales and profits lagged in the early 1960s because Kimberly-Clark de Mexico tried to circumvent wholesalers by marketing Kotex and Kleenex directly to large retailers. Unlike Zellwatte, it managed to turn the tide by signing a long-term distribution agreement with an exclusive wholesaler, markedly improving sales and earnings. At the end of the 1960s Kimberly-Clark de Mexico was one of that nation's largest consumer products companies and reported annual sales growth exceeding 30 percent, precipitating the construction of a large new mill in Orizaba in 1969 which supplied Central American markets.[46]

In 1958 finance manager William Clifford recommended substantial investments in South Africa. Arguing that "South Africa appears to have a favorable political climate for further foreign investment," Clifford suggested to the board of directors that Kimberly-Clark of South Africa, a small sales organization formed in 1936, be turned into a full-fledged manufacturing subsidiary.[47] A proposed consumer products plant near Johannesburg would procure Cellucotton supplies from South African Pulp and Paper Industry, a leading African company that operated a paper mill nearby. A Neenah executive who visited South Africa in 1958 concluded, "This proposal appears to be considerably more attractive than the alternative building of our own machine."[48] Kimberly-Clark of South Africa signed a ten-year contract with South African Pulp and Paper to secure Cellucotton supplies for its new Johannesburg conversion plant and became one of Africa's largest sanitary napkin producers.[49]

In contrast to overseas, where local conditions often forced Kimberly-Clark to rely on joint ventures and long-term supply contracts with other manufacturers and wholesalers, domestic operations were highly integrated. Kimberly, like Parker a proponent of vertical integration, advocated plant improvements and acquisitions to create new production linkages. A textile mill in Berkeley, North Carolina, that had been acquired during Parker's tenure received several upgrades that enabled Kimberly-Clark to manufacture the bulk of cotton gauze and nonwoven fabrics used as sanitary napkin wrappers without having to rely on outside sources. To gain additional pulp production capacity, Kimberly-Clark invested $8.4 million into Irving Pulp & Paper Limited, which operated a pulp mill in St. John, New Brunswick, with an annual capacity of 75,000 tons and 100,000 acres of timberland. "Our objective," Kimberly later recalled, "was to render ourselves *fully* self-sufficient in the area of quality pulp for as far into the future as our estimates and requirements could be projected."[50] Kimberly-Clark, which shared ownership of Irving Limited with Canadian investors, took over management of the pulp mill, whose output was processed by a new Cellucotton production and conversion mill nearby, completed in 1960.[51]

Kimberly's attempts at vertical integration ran into trouble in California during the 1960s. At the beginning of the decade the company completed a $9.6 million acquisition of the Ralph L. Smith Lumber Company, which owned extensive landholdings and operated four lumber mills in northern California, where Kimberly-Clark planned to build a pulp and paper mill in Anderson to supplement the Fullerton mill in Southern California. By 1965 the Fullerton mill received the bulk of its pulp supplies from the new Shasta mill in Anderson, which also produced printing papers. Sanitary products, printing papers, and other items manufactured at the Fullerton and Shasta mills were marketed by Blake, Moffitt & Towne (BMT) of San Francisco. BMT, a major paper distributor with thirty-four outlets in the western United States, was acquired in 1960 for $5.4 million in stocks. It was the largest western paper distributor with $65 million in annual sales which accounted for 15 percent of the region's paper merchant sales. The acquisition raised eyebrows throughout the industry because BMT scaled back its purchases from Kimberly-Clark competitors to concentrate on the marketing of Kimberly-Clark products. The antitrust division of the United States Justice Department, which viewed Kimberly-Clark's acquisition of BMT as part of a disturbing trend in paper wholesaling (Champion Paper, Mead Corporation, and Nekoosa Edwards all acquired major paper distributors in the early 1960s), launched an antitrust suit in 1962. Five years later a U.S. District Court ruled that the acquisition violated Section 7 of the Clayton Antitrust Act and ordered a divestiture. The divestiture, completed in 1968, removed a cornerstone of Kimberly-Clark's California operations, forcing the Fullerton and Anderson mills to develop sales partnerships with independent distributors in competition with other paper companies.[52]

In manufacturing, Kimberly's attempts to foster production linkages between mills failed to yield cost-efficiency gains. High manufacturing costs had been a persistent problem across product lines, particularly in printing papers, where Georgia-Pacific and other rivals had eroded Kimberly-Clark's market share with better products. In response Kimberly had launched a costly equipment update and quality assurance program which narrowed the gap between production costs and sales prices throughout the early 1960s. The picture was hardly more encouraging in consumer products, despite efforts to improve the cost structure through plant networking. A consumer division task force admitted in 1965 that "several competitors were putting their products into the market at a lower cost than Kimberly-Clark, charging comparable prices, and thus achieving higher return on sales."[53] Far from reducing manufacturing costs, intermill production linkages in fact worsened the cost structure because the geographic dispersion of networked plants burdened Kimberly-Clark with high transportation costs, the task force claimed: the Fullerton, California, mill was supplied by the Anderson, California, mill, separated by 560 miles, causing as much as 30 percent in extra shipping expenses per ton. Arguing that competitors like Procter & Gamble enjoyed the advantage of "integrated mills that produced pulp at the tissue manufacturing site," the task force recommended the construction of an integrated pulp and conversion plant in Beech Island, South Carolina, completed in 1968.[54]

IV.

A strong research and development organization had long been one of Kimberly-Clark's most important competitive assets. Its laboratories, which had developed Cellucotton, sanitary napkins, insulating material, and scores of other products, employed more research scientists and engineers than any other paper company lab by the end of World War II. In 1946 Kimberly-Clark abolished its technical department where scientists and engineers had worked together under technical director Henry Rothchild, replacing it with separate R&D and engineering departments. All R&D activities, previously housed in various mill buildings, were centralized at the old Neenah paper mill, converted into a 60,000-square-foot research center staffed by 160 scientists and support personnel. Headed by Rothchild until 1953 the center included an experimental paper machine and Cellucotton production equipment, as well as chemical and mechanical pulping facilities. The engineering division, which moved into a separate building in Neenah, employed one hundred engineers and their support staff who were responsible for paper machine installation, maintenance, and general repairs. The organizational separation of R&D and engineering, which came under criticism during subsequent years because researchers developed products without paying sufficient heed to practical engineering problems, was reversed in 1964.[55]

R&D played a key role in postwar product diversification. Capitalizing on wartime plastics research, scientists developed resin-impregnated paper trademarked Kimpreg which was marketed to industrial customers as a plywood surface and a core stock for laminates. To boost Munising's fine business paper sales, researchers experimented with new sulfite-based pulps for bond paper, ledgers, and mimeograph grades. Collaborating with cigarette paper specialists in the Schweitzer division, the Neenah research center developed tea bags and reconstituted binder tobacco for cigar manufacturers. To support the American Envelope Company, acquired in 1959, it developed new glues for mailing envelopes. Experiments with diverse new products required the hiring of additional specialists, almost doubling the staff of the Neenah research center, which employed more than 300 people by the early 1960s.[56]

The new research initiatives diverted resources from Kotex development, which became lackluster in the postwar years. During the late 1940s scientists improved the design of the "equalizer strip" used in high-absorbency pads by embossing the strip with curved lines to stop moisture from running to the ends of the pad. Following the commercialization of the improved equalizer strip in 1950, the Neenah lab abandoned Kotex development for almost five years, leaving the task of safeguarding the market share of Kimberly-Clark's most profitable product to Foote, Cone & Belding advertisers. Kotex, which generated 35 percent of the company's gross domestic profits, received a paltry 6 percent of the overall research budget, an internal review noted in 1958. "The professional research effort devoted to this major profit producing product for Kimberly-Clark appears much too small," it concluded.[57] Part of the blame rested with Rothchild, head of Kimberly-Clark's R&D operations since the late 1920s, who was convinced that Kotex required little product development to capitalize on the breakthroughs of the interwar period. However, aggressive marketing failed to maintain Kotex's market share, which dropped from 72 percent (1951) to 62 percent (1957), reducing Kimberly-Clark's profits by an estimated $32 million.[58]

The key factor in Kotex's declining market share was successful product development by Johnson & Johnson which caught Kimberly-Clark off guard. Johnson & Johnson, which produced Modess sanitary napkins, had challenged Kimberly-Clark's market dominance during the Depression in a bruising price war, followed later by advertising campaigns that stressed more conservative themes than the "Are You in the Know?" series. In the late 1940s its research division developed a soft masslin cover for the pad's absorbent material. (Masslin is an oil-impregnated, synthetic fabric.) Initial results were discouraging because the wrapper lacked the absorbency of conventional gauze, leaving side stains and a clammy feel that received low marks in consumer tests. Instead of abandoning the initiative, however, Johnson & Johnson researchers continued to work on the wrapper's absorbency, achieving significant improvements in the early 1950s. These efforts went hand-in-hand with advertising campaigns claiming, "New Design Modess is wrapped in a whisper-soft fabric that's smooth, gentle . . . cannot chafe . . . more absorbent than gauze!" From 1950 to 1957 net Kotex sales grew by 3 percent compared to a whopping 80 percent increase in Modess sales. Kimberly-Clark product managers, who had initially dismissed claims that Johnson & Johnson had developed a superior product, admitted internally in the 1957 report, "Modess held a quality advantage over Kotex for five or six years."[59]

Aware that Kotex development had suffered neglect in the early 1950s, Kimberly-Clark's new director of research and development Walter Swanson assembled a research team to catch up with Johnson & Johnson. In less than a year his team developed an innovative woven gauze that replaced the coarser Cellucotton cover. Labeled "Lenosoft," the new Kotex wrapper was introduced in early 1956, supported by an advertising campaign touting the "New Kotex—Softest Ever." Sawnson's confidence that Kimberly-Clark had recaptured quality leadership was shattered in spring 1956, however, when Johnson & Johnson test-marketed an improved version of its masslin wrapper featuring a highly absorbent perforated surface. "This new product immediately caused us much concern," a product manager stated in 1957. "It was tested by Politz [test marketers] in the 1956 summer product tests and found superior to leno Kotex, 52% to 40%, with 8% of the respondents having no preference."[60] "Thus, the Kotex napkin has measured up to Modess in quality only one year since 1950," another commented.[61] Johnson & Johnson, keenly aware of its competitive advantage, triumphantly announced in a new advertising campaign, "Discovery! Feminine Fabric . . . sheerest luxury . . . perfected protection." Partly in order to recover the staggering $2.4 million in advertising costs, Johnson & Johnson raised wholesale prices for Modess in August 1957, giving Kotex a temporary advantage. However, no one doubted that "greater competition is coming in the sanitary protection field," as the 1957 memo concluded. The "feminine hygiene war," precursor to the tissue and diaper wars of the 1960s and 1980s, was on.[62]

An internal study completed in 1958 detailed the reasons for the decline in market share and laid out Kimberly-Clark's long-range response. A comparison of Kimberly-Clark's and Johnson & Johnson's marketing budgets led reviewers to believe that "we cannot [attribute] our present market position to insufficient expenditures in advertising."[63] But Johnson & Johnson committed its entire, 202-member consumer goods sales force to the marketing of Modess pads, while Kimberly-Clark's 255 salesmen peddled a wide variety of consumer products in addition to Kotex pads, including sanitary belts, Kleenex tissues, table napkins, and paper towels. To avert a repeat of Kimberly-Clark's failure to prevent loss of market share through timely product development, closer coordination between the sales and marketing divisions was imperative. Sanitary napkin R&D required more appropriations and manpower to develop a non-woven pad cover resembling the Johnson & Johnson wrapper, as well as other Kotex improvements. More strategically, the study recommended systematic diversification into "entirely new sanitary protection products."[64]

The Kotex research team quickly followed up on these recommendations. In addition to a nonwoven wrapper and brighter wadding, it developed a rayon-based material dubbed Kimlon that was designed to enhance pad absorbency. Placed between two layers of Cellucotton, nonabsorbent Kimlon slowed moisture penetration, resulting in a more even distribution of moisture in the two layers. Thanks to better coordination between Kotex R&D and marketing, researchers received detailed information about competitors' product changes, enabling them to respond quickly with further Kotex improvements. When Johnson & Johnson added a polyethylene baffle to the Modess pad in the early 1960s in order to improve absorbency, the Neenah research team developed a similar additive that went into commercial production only six months after the research initiative had been launched. Combined with aggressive advertising and discounts, continued product development slowed but failed to halt the erosion of Kotex's dominant market position. The annual decline in market share averaged 2.2 percent from 1951 to 1959, and 1.75 percent from 1960 to 1965.[65]

At first glance Kimberly-Clark's overall standing in sanitary napkin markets was more encouraging because the company introduced a second brand, trademarked Fems, as a niche market product. The brainchild of Kotex product manager David Smith, Fems pads were slightly longer than Kotex to fit plus-size women, whose share in the U.S. population had doubled since the 1930s. The introduction of Fems in 1958 was part of a broader trend toward specialty designs in sanitary napkins. Johnson & Johnson developed form-fitted Modess Vee pads in the late 1950s, followed in 1960 by Scott Paper, which entered the sanitary napkin market with the Confidets brand featuring a triangular-shaped design that was tapered to body contours. Kimberly-Clark introduced Fems in a $1.6 million marketing program that was "the most powerful ever to launch a K-C consumer product," Smith claimed, including $714,000 for advertising and $570,000 on consumer coupon campaigns.[66] The brand captured almost 3 percent market share within a year, raising the possibility that Fems could not only offset continuing Kotex losses but even increase Kimberly-Clark's overall market share in sanitary napkins. In 1961, however, Scott Paper introduced the innovative Confidets design, which quickly gained popularity among specialty pad consumers. Scott also launched what Smith deemed an "extremely aggressive move"[67] to establish itself in niche markets through large discounts and lavish advertising. Confidets, in fact, reached 6.7 percent market share by 1965, largely at the expense of Fems, whose share leveled off at less than 5 percent. Faced with strong competitive pressure from other new entrants, Kimberly-Clark withdrew the product in the early 1970s.[68]

V.

Following the recommendations of the 1957 review, Kimberly-Clark started a new tampon development initiative in 1959. Previous attempts to break Tampax Corporation's quasi monopoly in tampon markets had failed, most notably in the ill-fated Fibs program of the 1930s which fizzled out during the postwar years. An effort was launched in 1943 to develop a cotton-based, high-quality tampon

with the brand name Kotams; the new product went into pilot production at the Lakeview mill but was abandoned eleven years later
because of engineering problems and high raw material costs. Moreover, ICPC focused its marketing effort on Kotex and made "no serious commitment . . . to the tampon business," a product manager
complained.[69] A marked increase in competitors' tampon sales from 3
to 8 percent annually during the late 1950s, combined with the recommendations of the Kotex study, precipitated new research initiatives that resulted in the development of stick tampons in 1959.[70]

Mindful that earlier attempts to produce premium tampons had
suffered from excessive costs, project managers decided to develop an
inexpensive product to compete at the low end of the market. A Kimberly-Clark research team headed by scientist Howard Whitehead
shelved early attempts to develop a design- and cost-intensive tube
applicator, preferring a stick applicator that was deemed "less messy
and easier to dispose of" than the Tampax applicator.[71] Instead of
expensive plastic sticks considered early on in the project, Whitehead's research team selected lollipop paper sticks. Eschewing Cellucotton, which had proved unsuitable for tampons during the Fibs
debacle, the team developed an inexpensive cotton-rayon absorbent
that could be inserted with the stick applicator and removed with a
string.[72]

Following established practice in menstrual hygiene product
research, the Whitehead team developed regular as well as highly
absorbent versions of the stick tampon. In February 1962 they compared the Kimberly-Clark tampon to competing brands in a clinical
test to determine absorbency. In addition to Tampax, the test included a new tampon with the brand name Colleens. In a replay of the
flawed Fibs tampon tests of the 1930s, researchers played down product deficiencies that bedeviled the Kimberly-Clark tampon, claiming
"regular and super absorbent [Kimberly-Clark tampons] and Tampax
absorbed approximately the same grams." "That does not appear to
be at all obvious from the data," a tampon review team commented
more than a decade later.[73] Worse, the authors of the 1962 test report
underestimated the Colleens tampon: "Because the outward appearance of Colleens are [sic] so very similar to Tampax and because of a
possible higher price, a consumer wouldn't be inclined to change to
an unknown, new brand name."[74] The International Latex Corporation, a girdle manufacturer that subsequently acquired the Colleens
brand, evidently agreed that the product needed a better brand name.
In 1967 it relaunched Colleens as Playtex, an established trademark

for International Latex's girdle products. Playtex tampons became the fastest-growing menstrual hygiene brand of the late 1960s and 1970s.

Kimberly-Clark's tampon testing programs remained substandard during subsequent years. "The major flaws in the testing conducted in this 6-year period [1960–1965] seem to be: (1) Bias in the tests or analyses, leading to underrating of competitors and excessive praise of K-C products, and (2) incorrect use and interpretation of statistical methods," a review concluded.[75]

Engineers and mill staff meanwhile built tampon production lines at the Berkeley, North Carolina, mill. From the outset the program suffered from insufficient coordination between research scientists and engineers. The latter were not consulted in the early stages of the tampon project, a common problem since 1946, when the breakup of the old technical department had separated research and engineering. The result was an awkward "machine design that strings together a bunch of jigs and fixtures developed by Research for clinical and use testing," a product reviewer noted.[76] Blending cotton with rayon in a batter to produce absorbent material involved problems because the batter devised by the Whitehead research team lacked precision controls, resulting in weight variations of ±15 percent in high-volume production. "Our blending operation is . . . best described as an art form," the product reviewer commented. "Unfortunately, critical product attributes such as absorbency, string pull and stick pull are dependent on the blend."[77] The finished cotton-rayon batts were calendered, conditioned, and formed into a fibrous web, which was rolled into long cylinders. Air jets tucked the tab into the cylinder, which was then wrapped into a protective cover and cut to tampon length. Taking a leaf from Tampax production technology without infringing on vital patents, the Whitehead team had devised a hydraulic turret that precompressed the tampon and molded it into its final shape. The turret design, however, received low marks from production engineers, who complained that the precompressor stopped each time it picked up or ejected a cylinder. To compensate for the precompressor's low productivity, engineers installed seventeen tampon lines at the Berkeley mill to achieve sufficient volume capacity. Each line was staffed by an operator who performed quality controls, stacked tampons on trays, and fixed the failure-prone equipment.[78]

Brand manager David Smith, adding tampons to his extant responsibilities for Kotex and Fems pads, developed a marketing strategy for the stick tampon. Simulating a $1 million advertising campaign, a market test launched in June 1960 introduced the prod-

TABLE 4.3

Tampon market shares by company, 1965–1974

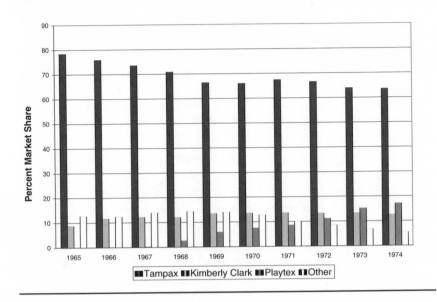

uct in eight metropolitan regions. Consumer surveys resulted in the adoption of the brand name Kotams. Based on the test results, Smith predicted that Kotams would quickly capture about 10 percent of tampon markets, but he noted that "peak market shares were reached in 4–6 months and then leveled" in test marketing—a fairly accurate forecast of the actual performance of Kotams stick tampons in national markets (table 4.3).[79] Consumers reportedly liked Kotams because of their low price and convenience, but they frequently switched to lower-priced rival brands once Kimberly-Clark phased out initial promotional deals. Attempts to boost market share by substituting the Kotams brand name with "Kotex Tampon" led nowhere. In summer 1965 Kimberly-Clark responded to stagnant sales by suspending all Kotex tampon promotion, advertising, and research because was the product was "a failure as a profit producer and sales getter," a product manager believed.[80] Refusing to admit defeat, however, Kimberly-Clark restarted the Kotex stick tampon initiative in February 1966 with an "aggressive cost cutting program" to reduce production costs by 30 percent. A $1.7 million program budget for fiscal year 1966–1967 included heavy consumer discounts; it increased market share by 0.5 point, to 12.2 percent, and was considered a failure.[81]

The tampon initiative also suffered from product management deficiencies. Researchers and engineers, like Smith busy with diverse projects, failed to adhere to a long-range product development agenda. A review blamed "some apparent compulsion by technical managers that each professional must have several projects in addition to his primary project, i.e., there is too much shotgunning and too much daily reordering of priorities." Personnel turnover exacerbated these problems, the report noted. "It takes three to five years to bring a technical man to the point of making a contribution in the tampon area and the constant parade of new faces has worked against tampon development."[82]

Kimberly-Clark's inability to stake a claim in tampon markets impaired its leadership in feminine hygiene products. Tampon sales tripled over the course of the 1960s while sanitary napkin sales remained flat early in the decade and in fact declined at an average annual rate of almost 2 percent from 1966 to 1969 (table 4.4). The company dominated what was widely seen as a stagnant market.

TABLE 4.4

Sanitary napkin and tampon sales, 1960–1970

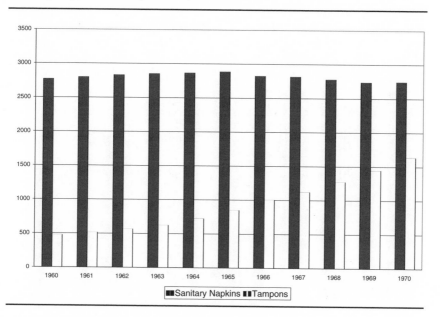

■ Sanitary Napkins ■ Tampons

VI.

Parallel developments in disposable handkerchiefs became a major source of concern for Kimberly-Clark because Kleenex—one of the company's most reliable profit makers—yielded market share to new competitors (table 4.5). During the 1950s Kleenex was still the predominant product, controlling about 50 percent of the market, with store brands accounting for much of the remainder. Scott Paper tried to stake a claim in facial tissue markets through heavy advertising of its Scotties brand, but the product captured less than 10 percent of the market. In 1959, however, Procter & Gamble, the Cincinnati-based consumer products company, launched a strategic offensive in paper-based consumer products, including facial tissues, paper towels, toilet paper, and paper napkins. Procter & Gamble was quickly followed by other new entrants, transforming the competitive dynamics of markets that had traditionally been controlled by two companies, Kimberly-Clark in facial tissue and Scott Paper in paper towels and toilet paper.

Procter & Gamble was widely "judged one of the best-managed American corporations," according to *Time* magazine.[83] Thriving on

TABLE 4.5
Kleenex market share, 1949–1965

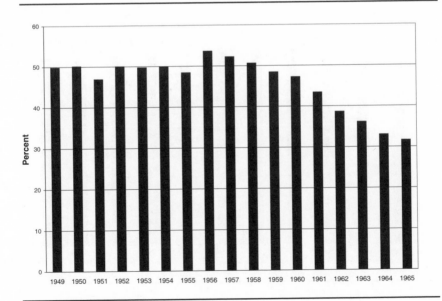

its core business in soaps, laundry detergents, and toothpaste, it entered papermaking in 1958 with the acquisition of Charmin Paper Mills, Incorporated, of Green Bay, Wisconsin, described by a Procter & Gamble executive as "a pilot plant and a little pilot marketing area with which to learn the [paper] business."[84] A market survey conducted shortly after the Charmin acquisition determined that consumers wanted greater softness and absorbency in paper tissues. Company researchers quickly launched an R&D initiative to improve the quality of Charmin, developing an innovative pulp fluffing process that separated fibers in a hot air stream. Procter & Gamble introduced two new products that were based on dry fluffed pulp: White Cloud toilet paper and Puffs facial tissue.[85]

These moves raised eyebrows at Scott Paper and Kimberly-Clark. Harrison F. Dunning, president of Scott Paper, stated belligerently, "If they [Procter & Gamble] want to pour in money, and try to blast their way into sanitary tissues, that's their business—but I'll tell you this: We aren't sitting around here in fear and trembling of anybody."[86] Kimberly-Clark's reaction was more subdued. Lewis Phenner, vice president in charge of consumer products, reported to the board in April 1959: "Procter & Gamble is testing a new facial tissue, Puffs. It is understood that this product will be pushed with a very heavy promotional program."[87]

In 1960 Procter & Gamble introduced Puffs nationwide with a multimillion dollar advertising campaign that touted the new product's superior softness, coupled with a promotional program that offered consumers steep discounts. Although detailed statistics on Puffs' market share are unavailable, the campaign appears to have had a serious effect on Kleenex, whose market share tumbled from 47.3 percent in 1960 to 36.2 percent in 1963—a development most analysts attributed to Procter & Gamble's entry into the facial tissue field. Furthermore, in the early 1960s Crown-Zellerbach joined the fray with its own line of facial tissue, and Scott ratcheted up attempts to improve Scotties sales through heavy advertising and promotion, as did distributors of private labels.

Kimberly-Clark's first major move in what the business press called the "tissue war" was a new packaging format named Space Saver, featuring compressed tissues in smaller boxes than those used for regular Kleenex. Test marketing results were encouraging, Phenner told the board in December 1960. "Despite Procter & Gamble's very heavy promotional expenditures, Kleenex tissues . . . held their own in the one area where the Space-Saver box was in distribution."[88]

Subsequent marketing research determined that Space Saver boxes containing at least 300 tissues were popular with consumers, and the format went into national distribution in November 1962.[89]

Kimberly-Clark also tried to fend off Procter & Gamble and other competitors with heavy discounts. Phenner explained to the board in April 1961, "[T]he facial tissue market is feeling the impact of the Procter & Gamble Puffs promotional program and Scott has stepped up its promotion in response. In May we are commencing a heavy free-goods promotion, one case of Kleenex tissues free with 20 cases of any product."[90] Kleenex sales increased temporarily, but earnings declined in 1961 compared to the previous year as a result of heavy promotional activity, which became a permanent feature of the facial tissue market. "Competition in consumer products lines today makes heavy promotion a necessity," Phenner believed.[91] Price competition increased during subsequent years. Procter & Gamble and Scott cut wholesale prices for facial tissue 5 percent in mid-1963, forcing Kimberly-Clark to follow suit in November. To limit the effect on earnings Phenner initiated a cost-saving program in Kleenex production, including new manufacturing standards that mandated higher per-worker output. The program yielded annual savings of $2.5 million throughout the consumer products division, offsetting some of the staggering costs of promotional activity and price cuts. However, what one executive called the "cost-price squeeze" remained a constant source of concern.[92]

Paralleling attempts to shore up its position in sanitary napkins with the addition of a new brand, Kimberly-Clark introduced Kleenex Boutique facial tissue in 1967. Development of this new brand was motivated by surveys indicating that "consumers viewed virtually all brands of facial tissues as soft and/or absorbent, leaving package size (sheet count) and price the major differences. This lack of palpable difference between products and brands was unsatisfactory in a mature market situation." Product uniformity across brands did not meet "the requirements of a changing life styles [sic] and a changing market (more young people, greater affluence, greater attention to décor relative to other products used in the home, etc.)."[93] Kleenex managers expected that Boutique tissues "would be additive to present business and would hopefully increase the volume of total market instead of merely cannibalizing or taking business away from other Kimberly-Clark facial tissue products."[94] Featuring a large variety of deep colors, the new brand was first introduced in Seattle and Indianapolis in early 1967 as "new and excitingly different tissue."[95]

Foote, Cone & Belding, which handled advertising, suggested the name Boutique to appeal to the "younger, better educated, affluent and urban housewife who wants a little more—and a little more style—in the product she buys."[96] Marketing was key to the brand's success because "the central idea behind Boutique [was] a mood, spirit or feeling about the product rather than any kind of performance identification."[97]

Encouraged by the results of successful test marketing, the board approved an ambitious advertising program to introduce Boutique nationally in 1968. Television advertising figured prominently, requiring considerable sums to position the brand. In 1968 alone, Kimberly-Clark spent more than $2 million on Boutique advertising, amounting to 22 percent of advertising expenses in the entire tissue paper industry. The result was a 2 percent market share at the end of 1968. By comparison regular Kleenex, with a market share of 30 percent, received a $3.5 million advertising budget in 1968. A year later Boutique captured a 6 percent market share, raising Kimberly-Clark's aggregate share from 32.5 percent in 1968 to 34 percent in 1969. About one-third of Boutique users had previously used regular Kleenex, but the remainder switched from competing brands. The 1.5 percent gain in the company's aggregate market share came at a steep price, however. Boutique did not take substantial market share from Kleenex, but it cannibalized the latter's advertising budget. By 1971 the company had spent $6.5 million in Boutique advertising, reducing the amounts available for regular Kleenex advertising from $3.5 million annually in 1968 to $1.9 million in 1971. A product manager noted in 1971, "Boutique alone will account for about 19% of total industry advertising dollars to support only about 6% of industry sales"—hardly an encouraging statistic.[98]

While Kimberly-Clark sought to maintain market leadership in facial tissues with new box designs and colors, Procter & Gamble exploited opportunities in product development, single-handedly creating the market for disposable diapers which it dominated with the Pampers brand for almost two decades. The program had a rough start. In 1957 a research team headed by director of exploratory development Vic Mills launched a diaper development initiative that capitalized on market surveys conducted by Charmin Paper Mills, the papermaker acquired by Procter & Gamble. After several failed design attempts, the Mills team completed a diaper featuring an absorbent pad encased in a plastic cover. Like Kimberly-Clark in tampons, Procter & Gamble encountered unexpected engineering problems when it tried to build a full-scale production line, an engineer recalled: "It seemed a simple task to take three sheets of material—plastic sheet, absorbent wadding, and water repellent—fold them in a zigzag pattern and glue them together. But the glue applicators dripped glue. The wadding generated dust. Together they formed sticky balls and smears which fouled the equipment. The machinery could run only a few minutes before having to shut down and be cleaned."[99] Unlike the designers of Kimberly-Clark's tampon production line, however, Procter & Gamble engineers had greater control over machinery design and thus were able to work out the kinks.

Marketing diapers initially presented major challenges. Surveys determined that mothers found disposable diapers more convenient than washable cotton diapers, but some "felt that the amount of time they spent caring for their babies reflected the amount of love the babies were receiving. Using disposables made these women feel guilty because they spent less time caring for their babies' physical needs."[100] To address these concerns Procter & Gamble chose a brand name that suggested that mothers pampered their babies by using disposable diapers. Advertising downplayed Pampers' convenience for mothers, highlighting instead the comfort babies derived from dry bottoms. These marketing strategies, combined with low prices, established Pampers as one of the fastest-growing consumer nondurables of the decade. Despite strenuous attempts by major pulp and paper companies to stake claims in the $200 million diaper market, Procter & Gamble remained the undisputed leader, producing about 90 percent of all diapers sold at the end of the 1960s.[101]

VII.

Financial results reflected Kimberly-Clark's loss of competitiveness in the 1960s. At first glance overall figures were impressive, particularly compared to other pulp and paper companies. Inflation-adjusted net sales increased by 118 percent from 1956 to 1969, compared to Crown-Zellerbach's 98 percent and International Paper's (IP's) 43.8 percent. Closer examination revealed disturbing trends, however. Kimberly-Clark's profits averaged 6.6 percent from 1956 to 1969, one-half percentage point below the IP and Crown-Zellerbach averages (table 4.6). This was a far cry from the 1930s, when Kimberly-Clark had bested every large paper company except Scott.

TABLE 4.6

Net earnings of Kimberly-Clark, IP, and Crown-Zellerbach, 1956–1971

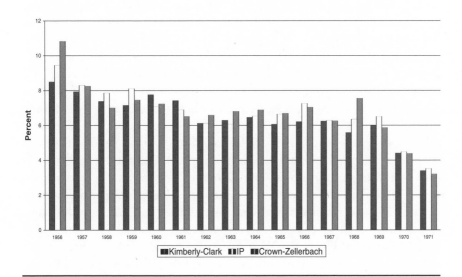

IP, still the world's largest pulp and paper company, staged a comeback that dated to the late 1930s, when it started to focus on consumer nondurables. In addition to cutting its newsprint capacity in half by selling a large Canadian mill that dragged down profits, it terminated an ill-conceived foray into hydroelectric power through divestiture in 1941. Simultaneously, IP expanded its linerboard capacity to supply manufacturers of corrugated containers and bleached milk cartons through a large-scale kraft mill construction program. In 1940 it integrated forward into linerboard conversion through the acquisition of Agar Manufacturing Company, a corrugated carton producer, followed six years later by the acquisition of Single Service Containers, Incorporated, which converted bleached linerboard into milk cartons. The latter transaction laid the groundwork for a liquid packaging division that produced the bulk of IP profits during the postwar decades. Investing heavily into plastic-coated carton research and development during the 1950s, IP became the nation's leading supplier of milk and juice cartons. Net profits during the 1950s averaged more than 9 percent, two points ahead of the Kimberly-Clark average.[102]

The gap narrowed in the 1960s, when IP's average profits dropped to 6.5 percent compared to Kimberly-Clark's 6.2 percent. The drop was partly attributable to an overall trend in the U.S. pulp and paper industry, whose profitability declined as a result of overcapacity and heightened price competition. IP's earnings ratio fell disproportionately because of its ill-conceived diversification into lumber products through the acquisition of Long-Bell Lumber Company, whose poor performance during the 1960s dragged down profits. Furthermore, instead of shoring up its core business through a capital investment program into its aging kraft paper mills in the late 1960s, IP tried to diversify into the burgeoning diaper market by building a $50 million mill on the West Coast. This product line, however, required advanced marketing capabilities, traditionally one of IP's greatest weaknesses. Like Kimberly-Clark in tampons, IP abandoned the venture at a multimillion-dollar loss. When kraft paper sales fell sharply in 1970 during that year's recession, IP suffered disproportionate financial losses, precipitating what one analyst described as the "dispossessing of [IP's] chief executive officer," Edward Hinman, who was replaced by a former AT&T executive.[103] Unlike Kimberly-Clark, IP remained bedeviled by management turmoil and disappointing financial results in the 1970s.[104]

Crown-Zellerbach's greatest postwar challenge was the entry of Kimberly-Clark, IP, and other extra-regional competitors into the West Coast paper market, where the San Francisco–based newsprint and white paper producer had long been the predominant player. As a result of mill construction programs and acquisitions launched by competitors, Crown-Zellerbach's share in the West Coast paper market declined from more than 35 percent in the 1930s, to 24.4 percent in the late 1950s. Crown-Zellerbach responded by encroaching on IP's and Kimberly-Clark's home turf, acquiring in 1955 Gaylord Container Corporation with mills in Louisiana and Ohio and launching a joint venture with Time, Inc., the magazine publisher, to build a coated paper mill in Louisiana. It also added new kraft paper capacity in California and British Columbia, primarily to supply punch cards to International Business Machines (IBM), one of its largest customers. Crown-Zellerbach's Canadian subsidiary produced newsprint for the *Los Angeles Times* until 1965, when the newspaper company started its own mill, creating havoc at Crown-Zellerbach Canada, Limited, for the remainder of the decade. Simultaneously, International Paper competed fiercely with Crown-Zellerbach for the IBM punch card business, precipitating price erosion in this once-prof-

TABLE 4.7

Net earnings of Kimberly-Clark and Johnson & Johnson, 1956–1971

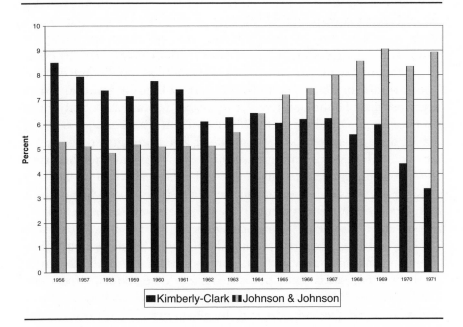

itable market during the late 1960s. Pollution problems, combined with more stringent environmental regulation, meanwhile forced Crown-Zellerbach to close three pulp mills, contributing to a steep fall in profits.[105]

While Kimberly-Clark shared the problem on declining profitability with other large paper companies, comparisons with consumer products companies illustrated strategic trends that disturbed pulp and paper executives. Throughout the 1950s Kimberly-Clark's profit ratio was consistently higher than that of Johnson & Johnson, but the latter started to make significant headway in the early 1960s (table 4.7). By 1964 both companies reported close to identical profitability. However, while Kimberly-Clark's rate began to stagnate, Johnson & Johnson's continued to grow, and by 1969 Johnson & Johnson was 50 percent more profitable than Kimberly-Clark. The growing gap was partly the result of Johnson & Johnson's continued success in sanitary napkin development, as well as its successful move into pharmaceuticals through the acquisition of McNeil Pharmaceutical Company, makers of the profitable Tylenol painkiller. More importantly, Johnson & Johnson's financial performance was not

weighted down by printing grades and other general paper com-
modities, whose lackluster performance became a growing source of
concern for Kimberly-Clark executives because the paper industry's
profitability started to lag behind that of other manufacturing industries.[106]

Scott Paper's postwar financial history confirms that paper commodity lines compared unfavorably to consumer goods (table 4.8).
Unlike Kimberly-Clark, Scott remained far more profitable than other
paper companies, maintaining the lead it had established during the
interwar years. Until the late 1960s Scott shied away from printing
grades and remained focused on paper-based consumer products,
adding Confidets sanitary napkins to its extant business in paper towels and toilet paper. Furthermore, the company improved its marketing with television advertising and the establishment of the Scott Store
Advisory Service, which offered store managers free advice and counsel on various aspects of store management. By the mid-1960s Scott
not only was the nation's most profitable large paper company but
also compared favorably to Johnson & Johnson and other consumer
product companies. Scott's performance deteriorated in the late
1960s, however, when it launched an unsuccessful attempt to gain a
foothold in the soaring disposable diaper market. Trademarked
BabyScott, its diaper featured a flushable pad in a reusable panty that
compared unfavorably to the one-piece Pampers among consumers. A
$2.4 million BabyScott advertising campaign launched in 1970 (com-
pared to Procter & Gamble's $4.9 million advertising budget for
Pampers) failed to improve its marketability, forcing Scott to abandon
its foray into diapers in 1971 at a major loss. More important, Scott's
declining profitability was the result of the ill-conceived, $134 million
acquisition of S. D. Warren, a producer of printing grades. Echoing
Kimberly-Clark's experience, Scott's printing paper business started
to dilute the profits of its consumer products division. In 1971 chairman Dunning admitted that the company had entered a period of
"stress and strain" as a result of the unsatisfactory performance of the
acquisition.[107]

These developments reflected larger trends in the comparative
financial performance of the pulp and paper industry. In the 1950s its
aggregate corporate earnings rate had been 0.5 to 1 percent higher
than that of all manufacturing industries. But the trend lines crossed
in 1962, when the paper company earnings rate dropped below the
general manufacturing average, where it remained for the rest of the
decade.

TABLE 4.8

Net earnings of Kimberly-Clark and Scott Paper, 1957–1970

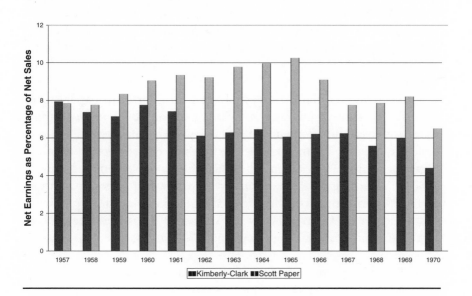

Investors, concerned about decreasing dividends, started to shun pulp and paper shares during the 1960s. By mid-decade, only one of the fifty stocks most widely held by mutual funds was issued by a paper company (IP), compared to three chemical, five electrical and electronic, and eleven oil company stocks. Paper company shares performed poorly in the stock market, rising a paltry 8 percent in the first half of the decade, compared to a 61 percent increase in the industrials average. James W. Davant, managing partner of Paine, Webber, asked in 1966: "Is the public giving inadequate recognition to the strengths and prospects of the paper industry? Or does its lackluster interest merely reflect performance by the paper industry itself?" The latter, he argued, was

> closer to the point. . . . In the past ten years, corporate profits have increased about 67 per cent while paper company profits have advanced only 40 per cent. This is not only below the pace of total corporate earnings, but well below the leading profit gainers during this period. Profits per share of some leading paper companies are where they were ten years ago; some are actually below those levels.[108]

Kimberly-Clark's dividends per share, for example, fell from $2.84 in 1955 to $2 in 1966. Davant attributed the downward trend partly to "the industry's failure to come up with the kind of marketing and research break-throughs [*sic*] that might have solved many . . . capacity and pricing problems."[109] This prognosis applied to the Wisconsin papermaker, whose unsuccessful attempts to break into tampon markets was a prime example for the industry's R&D shortcomings.

Other analysts blamed investors' lack of interest in paper stocks on price volatility. Lawrence Ross of Burnham & Company argued that "the instability of demand and earnings is sufficient . . . to prevent the industry from offering the investor the consistent earnings patterns seen in such defensive industries as public utilities, oils or food." According to Ross, the chief culprit was a latent encouragement of overproduction which destabilized the relationship between costs and prices. In an industry notorious for its capital intensity, its large overheads, and its high depreciation charges,

> mill managers are pushed to run their machines full, because full operation provides the greatest number of tons over which to spread . . . fixed costs. The simultaneous presence of steeply falling cost curves, a fractioned market structure and much commodity tonnage results in a basically unstable price structure and contributes to the instability of earnings. It is a perverse fact of this industry's economics that when unit costs are poor, at low operating rates, that can be the very time that prices are weak, as pressure to run at higher rates increases. And when the mills are full and overhead absorption best, that's the very time it's a seller's market with good prices.[110]

These problems were magnified by attempts of major companies to encroach on one another's home turf, both geographically and in terms of product lines, often motivated by hopes that expansion into new markets could offset declining profitability in core businesses. Kimberly-Clark, IP, and St. Regis built new mills on the West Coast, putting competitive pressure on Crown-Zellerbach, which responded in kind. Scott started to compete with Kimberly-Clark in facial tissue and sanitary napkins, while the Wisconsin firm diversified into paper towels.

Busy trying to wrest market shares from one another, paper companies failed to develop innovative paper products like disposable diapers, leaving the job to outsider Procter & Gamble, which entrenched itself as the market leader in the fastest-growing paper market of the 1960s. When paper companies launched belated efforts to catch up, Procter & Gamble beat all comers. IP with its inadequate marketing capabilities was not likely to succeed, but Procter & Gamble also managed to fend off Scott, who was (along with Kimberly-Clark) the savviest marketer in the American paper industry and whose extensive marketing campaigns failed to position BabyScotts for success.

Later developments in disposable diaper markets demonstrated that Procter & Gamble was hardly invulnerable. Kimberly-Clark assumed market leadership with the Huggies brand, relegating Pampers to second place in the 1980s. The key to that success was not simply expensive advertising but a combination of effective marketing and product development. The latter was largely neglected by Scott and other paper companies of the 1960s—a telling verdict on the state of the American pulp and paper industry.

VIII.

Kimberly-Clark's senior management identified the "cost-price squeeze" as a serious and persistent problem in the late 1950s, when president Kimberly asked executive vice president William Kellett to propose strategic solutions. Kellett, a chemical engineer who had joined the company in the 1920s, had served as superintendent of the Niagara Falls, New York, consumer products plant in the early 1930s and later managed the Badger-Globe and Lakeview mills in Neenah. He became general superintendent of manufacturing during World War II and joined the board of directors in 1945. During the 1950s he served as vice president of manufacturing and as executive president. Known as a tough and experienced production man with a strong record of cost control, Kellett proposed a large-scale reorganization plan that decentralized Kimberly-Clark's management structure in 1959. Under the old structure the company had been organized into centralized functional divisions (Engineering, R&D, Manufacturing, Administration, Personnel, and Finance and Law) supervised by Kellett as executive vice president. Kellett, who noted that "the principal objective of [the reform plan] is to pinpoint profit responsibility," divided senior executive functions into three separate areas of responsibility (table 4.9).[111]

TABLE 4.9

Kimberly-Clark organization chart, 1959

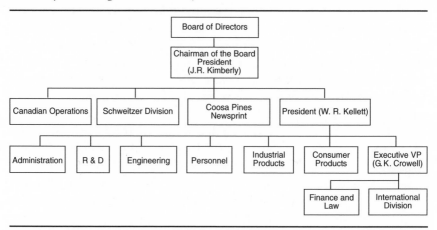

Kimberly headed long-range planning as chairman of the board and remained directly responsible for Canadian operations, for cigarette and other thin papers in the Schweizter division, and for the Coosa Pines newsprint operation in Alabama. Kellett, who took over Kimberly's office as president in 1959, managed the remaining functional divisions, as well as the new industrial and consumer products divisions. G. Kenneth Crowell, succeeding Kellett as executive vice president, headed finance, legal affairs, and international operations. The new products divisions, headed by senior vice presidents, became responsible for mills that had heretofore been managed through centralized functional divisions. Following recent trends in postwar capital budgeting systems, Kellett also implemented earnings, sales, and investment targets for each division. Executives assessed the division's performance and needs based on quarterly (later monthly) cash-flow reports that detailed progress toward the financial targets.[112]

Using statistics generated through Kellett's budgeting system, comptroller Charles W. Schueppert reported to the board in June 1961 on the "factors which adversely affected anticipated earnings per share. The principal items were as follows: [1] increased labor costs [2] reductions in printing paper prices [3] imposition of 15% tax on dividends paid by Canadian Companies [4] interest in proposed new debenture issue [5] deconsolidation of Kimberly-Clark de Mexico."[113] Determined to meet the 1962 targets by improving operating efficiency, Kellett immediately proposed a cost reduction program for his product divisions. In August 1961 he reported, "[W]hile these programs got under way very slowly, it appears that gains are being made and that ultimate savings in the neighborhood of five million dollars a year are possible. Revised personnel policies have been established which it is believed will reduce total employment by several hundred within a year."[114]

Kellett's "revised personnel policies" marked a turning in Kimberly-Clark's employment practices, which had heretofore avoided permanent layoffs through reductions in overtime and shorter work-weeks. A key aspect of company paternalism—guaranteed employment even in slack times—fell victim to formal capital budgeting as management struggled to improve the company's competitiveness. The failure of Kimberly-Clark's company unions to challenge Kellett's program facilitated the rise of independent unions affiliated with the American Federation of Labor (AFL), which replaced company unions as collective bargaining representatives at several Kimberly-Clark mills in the early 1960s.

Kellett's cost control program continued unabated. In January 1962 he appointed a committee to study Kimberly-Clark's major service divisions (financial, administrative, and personnel). Its purpose was to "determine what services they were providing, whether such services were necessary and were being fully utilized, whether there was any overlap, and what changes, if any, might be made to improve efficiencies and reduce costs."[115] The ax fell a few weeks after the committee had issued its report: in addition to laying off 5 percent of hourly workers, Kimberly-Clark reduced salaried personnel by 3.5 percent. But cost savings were largely offset by declining orders for printing papers which forced Kimberly-Clark to reduce its prices by $10 per ton. The consumer products division meanwhile reported the largest annual decline in Kleenex market share to date, from 43.5 percent (1961) to 38.7 percent (1962), precipitating a 5.6 percent drop in sales. Kimberly-Clark's overall earnings ratio fell from 7.4 percent (1961) to 6.1 percent (1962). Alarmed directors issued a statement in December 1962: "that the Corporation must take all steps necessary to remain competitive and that continued emphasis on quality and customer service are [sic] vital. To counteract current price weaknesses, continued effort must be exerted on the cost control programs now in effect throughout the organization."[116] Kellett obliged in early 1963 with a top-to-bottom review of fringe benefits that resulted in a recommendation to reduce employee life insurance benefits.

Kellett's proposal strained industrial relations as five AFL unions mounted a defense of established fringe benefit programs. Contract negotiations reached a deadlock in June 1963, when union members at five Kimberly-Clark mills voted to strike. The unions agreed to a short-term extension of negotiations. Kellett "hoped a solution satisfactory to all parties might be found during the forthcoming negotiations, but in the event that it was not, there was the possibility of a strike."[117] Management and union representatives worked out a last-minute compromise, averting what would have been the first strike at Kimberly-Clark mills in more than fifty years, but pressure to improve the company's cost structure continued to build. Contract negotiations finally broke down in 1964, when the Shasta, California, and Moraine, Ohio, mills were shut down by strikes. Combined with poor profits in consumer products, the strikes contributed to Kimberly-Clark's poor financial performance in 1964, when profits barely exceeded 6 percent.[118]

Strikes became a persistent problem during subsequent years. Stung by management's cost-saving programs and company unions' failure to object to changes in work schedules and benefits policies, Kimberly-Clark workers joined AFL unions in growing numbers. The movement quickly spread from the company's newer mills in California and Canada to the Wisconsin mills, which had long been bastions of company unionism. In October 1966 a one-week labor conflict over Sunday work idled the Lakeview and Badger-Globe mills, with "adverse effect on earnings for the [last] quarter" of 1966, management reported.[119] This conflict was followed in summer 1968 by a series of labor disputes over wages and benefits which shut down the Anderson, California, pulp and paper mill; two Canadian consumer products plants; the Irving pulp mill in St. John, New Brunswick; two U.S. consumer products plants; two U.S. business paper mills; and the Schweitzer specialty paper mill in Lee, Massachusetts. The strikes forced the consumer products division to defer several long-planned promotional programs for Kotex pads and tampons, Fems sanitary napkins, and Kleenex in fall 1968. Profits for the year dropped to 5.5 percent, the lowest rate since the late 1940s. The decrease was particularly galling to management because its cost-savings programs had closed the profitability gap with large competitors in the paper industry during the previous year, but IP—largely unaffected by strikes—once again pulled ahead of Kimberly-Clark in 1968.[120]

Reorganization and ill-advised investment strategies exacerbated these problems. In the early 1960s Kimberly-Clark bought out its investment partners in the Coosa River Newsprint Company, turning the joint venture into a fully integrated newsprint division. Management had originally invested into the Coosa River venture to secure pulp supplies for the Memphis, Tennessee, Cellucotton plant, shunning a full-scale return to American newsprint. Citing possible antitrust problems, however, the southern newspaper publishing companies that owned the bulk of Coosa River Newsprint Company shares asked Kimberly-Clark to take over the entire investment. Despite weak newsprint prices the Kimberly-Clark board and shareholders approved the plan. Arguing that newsprint "has plenty of long-term growth ahead," John R. Kimberly convinced the board to invest $45 million into the Coosa River mill to expand annual output by a staggering 150,000 tons, turning it into the nation's largest newsprint mill.[121] Combined with additional newsprint capacity installed by competitors, the investment raised aggregate industry output by 680,000 tons in 1967 alone, precipitating an immediate softening in prices. The industry tried to raise prices, but "history—if not economics—suggests that newsprint producers will have a good deal of difficulty making the price rise stick in the face of sagging demand," *Forbes* magazine surmised.[122] Asked whether "producers have enough market leverage to put the increase into effect," Kimberly replied, "I sure hope so. All our costs, particularly labor costs, are up."[123] Surprisingly, the newsprint industry did manage to implement a $4 price increase per ton, but even at that level "newsprint prices have not kept up with labor and other costs," Kimberly-Clark reported in 1969.[124]

Similarly questionable investments into additional white paper capacity reinforced the "cost-price squeeze." Softening demand for printing and business grades notwithstanding, vice president for industrial products Andrew Sharp recommended a five-year, $43.7 million investment program to raise annual capacity by 140,000 tons in the early 1960s. Kellett, a major supporter of Sharp's proposal, argued that "such a plan is essential to the orderly development of our manufacturing facilities."[125] Kimberly-Clark implemented a slightly scaled-down version of the program by installing two new fourdriniers, reconfiguring extant machines, and upgrading the aging printing paper mill in Niagara Falls, New York. Growing competitive pressures forced Kimberly-Clark to cut printing paper prices during subsequent years, however, frequently making it impossible for the industrial products division to meet its earnings targets during the 1960s. A sharp drop in prices depressed the printing paper business in 1968, followed by a slow recovery a year later, "but not enough to offset increased raw material and labor costs," management told stockholders.[126]

The buildup of vast newsprint and printing paper capacities changed Kimberly-Clark's image on Wall Street. In the early 1960s investment analysts frequently commended the company for its attempts to maintain and expand its position in consumer non-durables, whose growth potential exceeded that of conventional pulp and paper products. However, Kimberly-Clark's $100 million investment into its paper business during the 1960s, coupled with its inability to develop viable new consumer products, led some observers to believe that the company was turning into a conventional papermaker. Investment analyst Joseph Olmsted argued in 1971, "Kimberly I think, as well as Scott, is somewhat in a transition period, going from a marketing trademark product basis to sort of a commodity product basis."[127] Given the increasingly problematic performance of conventional paper commodity lines, this was hardly an encouraging assessment. In 1970 consumer products accounted for 56 percent of Kimberly-Clark's operating profits but received a mere 21 percent of net capital expenditures.[128]

The mounting strategic and structural problems of the late 1960s coincided with the resignation of John R. Kimberly, who reached the company's mandatory retirement age of sixty-five in 1968 and was succeeded as chief executive by Guy Minard. Born in 1907 in Ottawa, Ontario, Minard joined the company in 1928 and became technical director of the Spruce Falls newsprint mill. Promoted to vice president in 1951, he succeeded Kellett as president in the 1960s and was elected chairman at age sixty-one in 1968.[129]

Given the company's mandatory retirement policy, Minard was little more than a caretaker CEO. But he insisted on serving as president after his election as chief executive, instead of appointing a younger executive to assume responsibility for operational management. The latter required close attention and determined leadership because Kimberly-Clark faced some of the most serious challenges in its history. Sanitary napkin sales were flat. Kleenex's market share had shriveled to little more than 30 percent. Attempts to develop tampons had reached dead ends. Return on the printing paper investment program of the 1960s was effectively zero. Shortly after Minard's election, the company was engulfed in labor conflicts that left industrial relations in tatters. Even when the company recovered from strike-related losses, profits failed to break the 6 percent mark in 1969. A chastened Minard finally agreed to delegate operational management to Darwin E. Smith, former vice president of administration, who was elected president in late 1969 at age forty-four.[130]

The energetic Smith could do little to avert the crisis that exploded a few months into his tenure, when the recession of 1970 took a tremendous toll on Kimberly-Clark. Triggered by overproduction, inflation, and rising interest rates, the recession wreaked havoc on corporate profits in most industries. Already weakened by long-term difficulties, Kimberly-Clark's profits fell by 26 percent, "a deep disappointment," management admitted in its annual report.[131] "Changes in consumer spending habits became noticeable as the year progressed," the report stated. "Many shoppers, apparently reacting to the lag in the economy, held off buying our products until coupons or other promotions made them available at reduced prices. As a result, our promotional costs were far above normal and adversely affected profitability."[132] A series of disastrous labor conflicts, precipitated by disagreements over wage increases, exacerbated these problems. In fall 1970 a strike idled the giant consumer products mill in Memphis, Tennessee, for forty-nine days. Printing paper operations fared even worse. "The publishing industry, already off in circulation and lineage at the beginning of the year, was further depressed throughout the year," the annual report stated. "This, coming at a time when capacity to produce coated and uncoated papers was at a new high, resulted in extremely competitive conditions."[133] Wage strikes shut down three printing paper mills, including the Neenah and Niagara, Wisconsin, mills, for a total of 245 days. Management explained that labor conflicts remained "a source of great concern, not only because of their adverse impact on current earnings but also because of the longer range implications which would have occurred by attempting to avoid the strikes through the granting of demands which could have jeopardized the vitality of the Corporation and the job security of the striking employees." Promising to do everything in its power to avoid future strikes, management pleaded with "our unionized employees, their locals and their internationals to exert the same effort."[134]

Minard's prediction that 1971 would bring a turnaround was disputed by industry analysts, who pointed to long-term structural problems in the industrial products division. Investment analyst Milward Martin claimed, "Kimberly's major earnings problems today are in the white printing–communications area, and I think this will have a slow cyclical recovery like some similar companies."[135] The 1971 financial results were in fact worse than those of the previous year, despite peace on the labor front. Net earnings dropped one-seventh, to 3.4 percent. In light of a moderate upturn in consumer products

sales, the decline was largely attributable to the horrendous performance of the industrial products division, observers agreed. An analysis of historical data concluded that Kimberly-Clark "over the past
five years . . . has made no return on assets in these business areas."[136]
Turnaround was nowhere in sight. Analysis of future market trends
determined that "there was little likelihood of making a return over
the next five years which would meet our criteria."[137] John R. Kimberly's $40 million capital investment program into printing papers,
which had diverted precious resources from Kimberly-Clark's consumer products business during the 1960s, had produced a financial
albatross.

IX.

In one respect Kimberly-Clark's performance in the early 1970s
echoed the Depression years: the 1971 earnings ratio was the company's worst since 1934. In the latter year, however, it had still performed far above industry average while major competitors accumulated staggering losses. By 1971 there were only marginal differences
in the financial results reported Kimberly-Clark, IP, Crown-Zellerbach, and other large paper companies. Kimberly-Clark had joined
the industry mainstream.

During the postwar decades, the company pursued far more conventional corporate strategies than it had in the interwar years,
including acquisitions-based product diversification and multinational expansion. Abandoning the focused approach to product development that had sustained Kotex's and Kleenex's market dominance in
the 1920s and 1930s, the company vastly expanded the scope of its
R&D activities to support product diversification, spreading itself
wide and thin. This created strategic openings for nimbler competitors, notably Johnson & Johnson, which wrested leadership in sanitary napkin development from Kimberly-Clark, followed by Procter
& Gamble in facial tissues.

Kimberly-Clark's responses to these challenges varied by product
line. In sanitary pads the company launched sustained product development initiatives that slowed the decline in market share during the
1960s. At the end of the decade Kotex still maintained a considerable
lead over competing products. By contrast, Kimberly-Clark's response
to Procter & Gamble's entry into the facial tissue market focused on
new packaging formats and discounts. Reflecting management's belief

that facial tissue had essentially turned into a commodity product whose market performance depended more on price and packaging than on quality, this competitive strategy produced less satisfactory results: in the 1960s Kleenex's market share declined more rapidly than that of Kotex. The costly and ultimately futile attempt to safeguard market share with Boutique tissues—strictly leveraged as "image products"—shed further doubt on the wisdom of marketing-focused competitive strategies.

Kimberly-Clark's failure to gain a foothold in tampon markets revealed weaknesses in R&D strategy that were shared by many pulp and paper companies. In contrast to the interwar period, when Kimberly-Clark had leveraged Kotex as a high-quality product at premium prices, postwar tampon initiatives sought to carve out a niche at the low end of the market. Based on flawed market research, this strategy resulted in a substandard product. International Latex, meanwhile, banked on premium-priced Playtex, the first tampon that had successfully challenged Tampax's market dominance. In the 1970s Kimberly-Clark derived crucial lessons from its defeat in tampons for its foray into disposable diapers: like Kotex and Playtex, Huggies were design-intensive products that competed at the high end of the market, successfully challenging Procter & Gamble's quasi monopoly.

Kimberly-Clark's strategic offensive in diapers was part of a larger effort to reposition itself as a consumer products company at a time when pulp and paper, its traditional mainstay, descended into a long-term structural crisis. Kimberly-Clark's large-scale mill construction and reconfiguration program of the 1960s contributed to the downward spiral of excess capacity, price competition, and overproduction that weakened the industry years before the onset of the economic crisis of the 1970s. Pulp and paper companies faced an economic quagmire in the new decade. Ambitious expansion programs could only serve to deepen the lingering overproduction crisis. Lack of investor interest in paper company stocks compelled most firms to finance capacity expansion through borrowing, driving up their debt-to-equity ratios. Forced to service large debts, many companies soon lacked sufficient resources for ambitious product development and diversification initiatives. Kimberly-Clark's management, painfully aware that pulp and paper had dragged down its consumer products business for much of the 1960s, avoided some of the problems that bedeviled the industry in the following decade by opting for the most radical solution. Catapulting itself out of the mainstream, Kimberly-Clark liquidated its coated paper business in the 1970s.

"The Diapers That Help Stop Leakage":

THE TRANSFORMATION OF KIMBERLY-CLARK, 1971–1990

N THE 1987 comedy *Raising Arizona,* convenience store robber H. I. (Nicolas Cage) is married to police photographer Edwina (Holly Hunter). Desperate for a child, the couple kidnaps an infant and hits the open road; suddenly H. I. realizes that the boy needs diapers. Gun tucked in his belt, he walks into a late-night convenience store, grabs a pack emblazoned "New! Elastic Waist and Added Absorbency," and instructs the store clerk, "Wake up, son. I'll be taking these Huggies and . . . uh . . . whatever cash you got." During the ensuing police chase, H. I. holds tightly to his package of Huggies (medium-sized, 12–24 pounds), until he is forced to relinquish it in a hail of bullets.

Producer and writer Ethan Cohen pointed out that the filmmakers received no product placement fee. Cohen selected Huggies because it "sounded funnier than any other brand name," he told a reporter.[1] "Go ahead and laugh, says Kimberly-Clark—as long as Huggies keep disappearing from the store shelves," *The Wall Street Journal* commented. "Today, three out of 10 disposable sold in America are Huggies. Kimberly-Clark's success in the highly profitable, ultra-competitive diaper business has amazed people in the consumer-products industry."[2] Investors, impressed with Kimberly-Clark's dividend performance, flocked to the stock through much of the 1980s, just like the young parents who were grabbing package after package

160

of Huggies from the shelves. Kimberly-Clark's inflation-adjusted stock price quintupled over the course of the decade.

Business analysts and commentators have attributed Kimberly-Clark's transformation from a Wall Street stepchild into an investor darling to Darwin Smith, the maverick chairman and chief executive officer who led the company from 1971 to 1991. Born in 1926, Smith attended Harvard Law School, briefly became a member of the Chicago law firm Sidley & Austin which handled Kimberly-Clark's legal affairs, and then joined the company's legal department in 1958. Quickly rising through the ranks, he was appointed president of the company in 1969, effectively serving as CEO Guy Minard's chief operating officer. What happened next literally became the stuff of corporate legend. *Business Week* reporter Kevin Kelly noted, "When he [Smith] became CEO in 1971, he inherited a stodgy papermaker with shrinking markets. By the mid-1980s he had transformed Kimberly into a well-known consumer products company with such market-leading brands as Huggies diapers, Kleenex tissues, and Kotex sanitary napkins."[3] Author Jim Collins, who cited Smith as an example of exemplary corporate leadership in his 2001 bestseller *Good to Great: Why Some Companies Make the Leap . . . and Others Don't,* concurred: "Smith created a stunning transformation, turning Kimberly-Clark into the leading paper-based consumer products company in the world. Under his stewardship, Kimberly-Clark generated cumulative stock returns 4.1 times higher than the general market . . . It was an impressive performance, one of the best examples in the twentieth century of taking a good company and making it great."[4] Many other observers have traced Smith's success to what Collins has called "the most dramatic decision in the company's history: Sell the mills. Shortly after he became CEO, Smith and his team had concluded that the traditional core business—coated paper—was doomed to mediocrity . . . [L]ike the general who burned the boats upon landing, leaving only one option (succeed or die), Smith announced the decision to sell the mills, in what one board member called the gutsiest move he'd ever seen a CEO make. Sell even the mill in Kimberly, Wisconsin, and throw all the proceeds into the consumer business, investing in brands like Huggies and Kleenex."[5]

These obsequious accounts of Smith's tenure hardly amount to an accurate portrait of Kimberly-Clark's transformation in the 1970s and 1980s. Nor do they do justice to Smith, an unpretentious man and a stickler for facts. As he would have pointed out to Collins and others, the liquidation of four coated paper mills attributed to him was in fact based on a strategic review initiated by his predecessor Minard, who was also the driving force behind the decision to sell the mills shortly before his retirement in 1971. Likewise, Smith would have objected to Kelly's description of Kotex as a "market-leading brand." By the mid-1980s Kimberly-Clark's share of the sanitary napkin market had shriveled to 15 percent. Simultaneously, the humble but tough-minded CEO would have taken credit for accomplishments that have largely escaped the attention of his admirers. In 1979, for example, he initiated an exquisitely timed sale of California timberlands that raised four times more cash than the liquidation of the entire coated paper business. Moreover, far from turning Kimberly-Clark from a papermaker into a consumer products company—a transformation that had started in the 1920s—Smith's most important contribution was a partial reorientation of the consumer business itself, toward research and design-intensive products that competed in premium markets.

Rather than a simple matter of selling the company's mills, the transformation of Kimberly-Clark was a multifaceted process, rich with failures and achievements. Executing his predecessor's plan to reduce the company's presence in stagnant commodity paper markets, Smith engineered the sale of four revenue-draining coated paper mills. This move lifted a significant burden, enabling the company to improve its long-term profitability and concentrate its managerial, financial, and marketing resources on the remaining product lines, particularly consumer nondurables.

The divestiture was not as drastic and thorough as Collins and other recent observers have proposed, however. Kimberly-Clark retained a sizable newsprint business and remained a leading producer of cigarette paper. Moreover, Kimberly-Clark's attempts to compete in hygiene products were far from flawless, especially in feminine care products. Despite investments into new products and processes, the company was unable to maintain its sizable lead in a market segment that it had dominated for almost five decades. Although it recaptured some ground in the early 1980s, when menstrual toxic shock syndrome associated with tampons boosted demand for pads, its market share shriveled to less than 20 percent in 1986, compared to more than 40 percent in 1970.

Kimberly-Clark's decisive breakthrough came in premium disposable diapers. Its earliest attempts to break Procter & Gamble's quasi monopoly dated to the late 1960s, when it introduced the Kimbies brand. Riddled with technological and marketing difficulties, the disappointing results with Kimbies convinced a majority of company managers to terminate the foray into disposable diapers. Realizing the potential of disposable diapers, however, Smith urged Kimberly-Clark to stay in the market. As a result, the company launched a new product design and marketing program in the mid-1970s that positioned it for competition in the premium diaper market. Within a decade Smith's gamble paid off. Huggies became the nation's leading diaper brand in the 1980s, wresting market leadership from Procter & Gamble's Pampers and Luvs.

Kimberly-Clark's success in diapers was a departure from its own corporate strategies of past decades and from business trends of the 1970s and 1980s. For the first time in its history, Kimberly-Clark gained leadership in a consumer market pioneered by a major prime mover that enjoyed high brand loyalty. This was a notoriously difficult feat, as evidenced by Pepsi-Cola's decades-long attempts to unseat Coca-Cola as the leading soft-drink maker, as well as similar efforts by Johnson & Johnson in sanitary pads and Colgate-Palmolive in toothpaste. Kimberly-Clark's success in premium diapers was all the more remarkable because it was achieved on the home turf of Procter & Gamble, arguably one of the most resourceful and marketing-savvy players in the consumer products business. Equally important, Kimberly-Clark diversified into diapers by developing extant resources in research, development, production, and marketing, instead of taking the more conventional route of product diversification through mergers and acquisitions. The latter strategy was popular among companies whose core business stagnated or declined, which Kimberly-Clark experienced in the 1950s and 1960s. Buying into market leadership was also fraught with risks because it often produced organizational synergy problems and did little to reinvigorate the diversifier's existing assets. Smith, whose reputation as a maverick CEO was partly due to his dislike of mergers and acquisitions, envisioned the Huggies program as an attempt to redeploy the company's core assets and capabilities. Smith's leadership and his disdain for mergers and acquisitions enabled Kimberly-Clark to avoid the financial pitfalls of divestiture that occurred across the business world in the late 1970s and 1980s as companies shed acquisitions that had failed to meet profit targets. A long-forgotten but notable example was General Electric, which endured the "Neutron Jack" days during Jack Welch's early years as CEO, when he downsized tens of thousands of employees and sold off countless acquisitions that did not lead in their respective markets.

Kimberly-Clark's comeback—which was neither a complete makeover nor an unmitigated success—was based on a strategy of partial asset redeployment, product development, and new departures in marketing where successes outweighed failures. The company's emphasis on developing extant assets and capabilities put Kimberly-Clark ahead of other corporations that were forced to implement similar strategies years later, during the hostile takeover and leveraged buyout craze of the 1980s. For the first time since the interwar period, Kimberly-Clark found itself on the cutting edge of corporate strategy.

The sources used as the basis for the present chapter require comment. All internally generated financial data since 1975 remain confidential, as do minutes of board meetings. Furthermore, given the increasingly competitive nature of the consumer products and paper businesses, access to internal information on product strategies, production technology, and other sensitive data generated since 1975 remains restricted. Financial and other statistics presented in this chapter, as well as discussions of corporate and brand strategies and related matters, are based largely on publicly available sources. These limitations admittedly render the present chapter more tenuous than previous ones, but they still permit what amounts to an outline of Kimberly-Clark's transformation in one of the most turbulent phases in American economic and business history.

I.

The company's partial withdrawal from the commodity paper business evolved over a five-year period. It started in November 1970, when Minard—disappointed with recent earnings—appointed a task force to conduct an in-depth analysis of coated paper operations. A group of nine executives, headed by executive vice president Harry Sherrin, pored over "sales budgets by mills and by product lines, profit trends, profitability by grades, and factors currently affecting the paper industry."[6] The task force quickly determined that both short-term and long-term prospects were discouraging. Kimberly-Clark's coated paper mills suffered from excessive inventory buildup that required repeated write-offs, even as the committee was compiling its report. The mills operated at barely 80 percent capacity, precipitating the firing of 390 workers, more than 10 percent of the coated paper workforce in the first six months of 1971 alone. Most of the paper machines were "comparatively old, narrow and slow—a serious disadvantage when competing against newer, wider and faster machines."[7] The high cost of labor, energy, and environmental control had "combined to produce a total cost structure which has not been and is not projected to be appropriately offset by changes in product mix, gains in productivity or price increases."[8]

The market outlook was bleak, bolstering the need for action. Industrywide expansion of papermaking capacity during the 1960s, combined with the disappearance of several major publications at the end of the decade and an overall decline in magazine advertising during the 1970 recession, resulted in sharply lower prices. The Sherrin committee's conclusion—that a significant turnaround was nowhere in sight—was shared by Minard, who told *Forbes* that the U.S. magazine business was "heading the way of the dodo and the great auk."[9]

In August 1971 the Sherrin committee presented its report and recommendations to the board. Its key suggestion was to sell the coated paper mills at Anderson, California; Niagara Falls, New York; and Niagara, Wisconsin. What was left of the magazine paper business was to be consolidated at the last remaining coated paper mill in Kimberly, Wisconsin. Other major items considered for liquidation were the company's extensive timberlands and a forest product business in Northern California that had been acquired in 1961 to provide a pulp source for the Anderson mill. Although the housing boom of the early 1970s created strong demand for building timber that rendered the Anderson forest and timberland properties profitable, a prospective buyer of the mill would in all likelihood ask Kimberly-Clark to sell them to ensure a pulpwood supply for the mill, the task force argued.[10]

Donald Hibbert, executive vice president for corporate finance and a member of the Sherrin task force, presented financial data that were premised on the hypothesis that the board would adopt all of the committee's recommendations. Hibbert noted that in the year of disposal, "nonrecurring losses would be substantial but that in the following year, earnings improvements in the range of $12 million could be expected [without a sale of the Anderson forest and timberland operations] and $10.5 million [with a sale of the Anderson forest and timberland operations]."[11] At Minard's urging, the board unanimously approved the Sherrin committee's recommendations, setting into motion the asset liquidation.[12]

Minard, however, did not stick around to enact the measures that he had vigorously supported and had pushed the board of directors to authorize. The unenviable task of implementing divestiture fell to Smith, who succeeded Minard as CEO in October 1971. The properties on the block employed 2,920 workers and operated 13 paper machines with a daily capacity of 1,230 tons of paper. Except the ten-year-old Anderson mill, the plants were comparatively old and small by industry standards and suffered from high transportation costs because they imported most of their pulpwood from remote timberlands. These liabilities, combined with the structural problems cited by the Sherrin task force, made it difficult for Kimberly-Clark to obtain attractive bids.

The Niagara Falls, New York, mill, built by Kimberly-Clark in 1920 and once considered the technological marvel of the U.S. pulp and paper industry, went to the Cellu-Products Corporation for $16 million, or 10 percent below book value due to its dilapidated condition. The Niagara, Wisconsin, mill was another hard sell, partly because workers had launched a spirited defense of wages and benefits during a seven-month strike in 1971. A year later Pentair Industries Inc., a Minneapolis-based conglomerate, submitted a $10 million bid, provided that the Niagara mill workers agreed to a three-year wage freeze and that the state of Wisconsin would postpone a previously scheduled pollution abatement program. The sale went through in 1972 when the outside parties agreed to Pentair's conditions, which became a particularly bitter pill for the workers because inflation turned the wage freeze into a *de facto* 20 percent cut. The Anderson mill went to the Simpson Lee Paper Company, a forest products company in the Pacific Northwest, for only $7.5 million, partly because Smith insisted that Kimberly-Clark keep the timberlands.[13]

Divestiture produced satisfactory results for Kimberly-Clark. As Hibbert had predicted, short-term effects were painful. Mill disposal required a $42 million nonrecurring write-off, which—combined with poor ordinary income—produced a 1.1 percent net loss for 1971. There was reason for optimism about long-term prospects, however. Management reported in February 1972, "First, a drain on reported earnings is eliminated . . . Our short-term objective for the plan was to improve net earnings in the range of $6 million during the first twelve months following its consummation. Second, a drain on cash is eliminated and a source of cash is created . . . [We] estimate it will exceed $50 million, much of which will be realized over the next two years. Third, a drain on managerial talent and energy is eliminated. We can concentrate on areas promising greater rewards for our stockholders."[14] Actual results for 1972 exceeded the conservative estimate of a $6 million improvement in net earnings, contributing to a 66 percent increase in net profits compared to 1971, excluding the latter year's nonrecurring charge.

These results would have been even better if Kimberly-Clark had liquidated its entire coated paper business, which dragged down the operating profits of the paper and specialty products division. The latter accounted for 24.5 percent of net sales but only 19 percent of net operating profits. By comparison, consumer products accounted for 59.6 percent of net sales and 65.8 percent of net operating profits, while newsprint contributed 15.6 percent and 14.7 percent respectively.[15]

The main culprit was the eighty-year-old Kimberly mill. Cost and quality improvements launched in 1971 produced no discernible changes over the next three years. What management called "irresponsible rumors spread by competitors that the company is considering the shutdown of this facility" precipitated an exodus of customers for magazine paper in 1974.[16] In February 1975 Smith pointed out to board members that "the very poor performance of the Paper Division's coated specialties business as reflected in recent business reports [is] primarily due to the Kimberly mill, which continues to be a major problem."[17]

In a last-ditch effort to save it, Smith reassigned the mill from the paper and specialty products division to an autonomous operating unit headed by Hibbert. (The move helped double the operating profitability of the papers and specialty division in the next twelve months.) Under Hibbert's direct management, the mill still accounted for an operating loss of $7 million in 1975. The loss convinced Smith of the necessity to liquidate the Kimberly mill, despite its historic and cultural significance as a symbol of the company's past successes.

In March 1976 the Midtec Paper Corporation offered to buy the property, provided that unions signed a three-year contract that stipulated a wage freeze for 1977, with subsequent raises contingent upon $1.5 million or more in net earnings. When a majority of the 1,050 Kimberly workers rejected the proposal, Kimberly-Clark threatened to close the mill for good and started shutting it down in July 1976. Faced with a do-or-die proposition, the workers voted in August to overturn their earlier rejection of the contract, enabling Kimberly-Clark and Midtec to proceed with the $14.5 million sale. The transaction marked Kimberly-Clark's final exit from magazine papers, which had been one of its core businesses since the turn of the century.[18]

Hindsight suggests that Kimberly-Clark's abandonment of coated papers had considerable merits. In order to compete with industry leaders Weyerhaeuser, Champion International, and St. Regis Paper in the weak magazine paper market of the 1970s, Kimberly-Clark would have had to launch major plant reconfigurations to update the dilapidated Niagara, Kimberly, and Niagara Falls mills, with little prospect of reaping a substantial return on investment anytime soon. At Niagara Falls, Pentair Industries had to spend $8.2 million—half as much as it had paid for the entire plant—to raise the mill's output by a mere 7 percent. In addition, the recession of the early 1980s hurt large producers of coated paper, including St. Regis, whose net income dropped from 6.2 percent in 1981 to 1.7 percent in 1982. Demand for magazine paper rebounded during the subsequent general economic recovery, precipitating an 8 percent price increase in 1984 and a scramble for new capacity. However, the sums involved in building new mills and updating old ones with state-of-the-art equipment reflected the rapidly growing capital intensity and increased competitiveness of the coated paper business. Weyerhaeuser built a $380 million mill in Mississippi, Bowater Incorporated (a U.S. spin-off of a British papermaker) spent $340 to expand its South Carolina plant, International Paper (IP) converted a newsprint machine in Arkansas to coated paper at a cost of $200 million, and Scott Paper invested $220 million into a new paper machine at a New England mill. Companies that were willing to invest such amounts often reaped substantial returns on investment in the mid-1980s, but high demand cyclicity and falling prices—the familiar scrooges of the commodity paper business—again took their toll at the end of the decade. Repap Industries, a Montreal-based paper company that had acquired the old Kimberly-Clark mill in Kimberly, Wisconsin, and had become one of largest North American suppliers of coated paper in the 1980s, barely broke even in 1989 and 1990. When demand for magazine paper fell throughout the early 1990s, Repap lost an aggregate $510 million over four consecutive years, twice as much in inflation-adjusted dollars as IP had lost in the Great Depression. The liquidation of its coated paper business enabled Kimberly-Clark to avoid substantial investments in the 1980s and major losses at the beginning of the following decade.[19]

As Sherrin explained in 1973, "[W]e didn't pull out [of commodity papers], we pulled back from these fields."[20] This move was reflected in the company's organizational structure with its three main product divisions: consumer and service; newsprint, pulp, and forest products; and papers and specialties. The last category comprised the Schweitzer thin paper operations with eight plants in the northeastern United States and several in France, two business paper plants in the Midwest, and four envelope plants in Ohio. Combined net sales in the mid-1970s comprised 11 percent of Kimberly-Clark's overall sales, and the division's operating profit exceeded that of the consumer and service division. This was largely the result of the satisfactory performance of the Schweitzer unit, which was one of the nation's largest suppliers of cigarette paper and which remained profitable in later years as the principal supplier for Philip Morris and R. J. Reynolds. A development program launched in the early 1980s by Schweitzer researchers in France resulted in an innovative manufacturing process that facilitated the use of tobacco stems in cigarette production. The process also permitted the manipulation of the nicotine content in cigarette tobacco, leading to charges by health advocates that Kimberly-Clark was legally liable for the effects of cigarette addiction. The company spun off its cigarette paper business in 1995, when it still accounted for 5.5 percent of net sales.[21]

The company's pullback from commodity papers in the 1970s did not include its newsprint business, the centerpiece of the newsprint, pulp, and forest products division. Retaining newsprint was a gamble, particularly because most American newspapers lost readers and advertisers to television during the early 1970s, leading to reduced demand especially in northeastern markets. *The New York Times,* for example, which procured most of its supplies from the Kapuskasing mill in Ontario that it owned jointly with Kimberly-Clark, reduced its daily circulation by more than 100,000 copies from 1970 to 1976. Simultaneously, however, capacity reduction by major U.S. and Canadian producers buttressed tonnage prices, which almost doubled over the course of the decade. A major strike against large Canadian producers in 1973 provided a boost for Canadian mills unaffected by the labor conflict, including Kapuskasing as well as U.S. mills. Newsprint profitability started to decline in the second half of the decade, though. In 1975 the Kapuskasing mill was shut down by a six-week strike. Stricter enforcement of federal and state regulations compelled Kimberly-Clark to implement a $42 million environmental improvement program at the Coosa Pines mill, followed by similar investments in the 1980s. At the same time, the company scaled back other plant improvements at Coosa Pines, concentrating its newsprint capital investments on the Kapuskasing mill. The latter added modern thermomechanical pulping facilities that doubled the amount of pulp derived from logs, and in 1985 it launched a $26 million general plant development program. When the recession of 1990 resulted in significant losses, however, Kimberly-Clark and The New York Times Company grew increasingly desperate to dispose of the mill, offering it for free to the 1,420 workers it employed. The deal went through in 1991, when Kapuskasing became an employee-owned mill which struggled for survival for the remainder of the decade. Insufficient investments into the Coosa Pines mill, combined with market problems, meanwhile resulted in quality problems and a deteriorating cost structure. Smith acknowledged as much in 1989, when he told mill workers that Coosa Pines newsprint was "considered among the worst in the industry."[22] A $200 million mill and quality improvement program conducted in cooperation with unions during the late 1980s and early 1990s provided only a temporary reprieve. In 1997 the company sold the Coosa Pines mill to Montreal-based Alliance Forest Products Incorporated for $600 million.[23]

In retrospect, Kimberly-Clark's continued presence in newsprint created more problems than it solved. In the 1970s the South was the only newsprint market that posted strong gains, in contrast to northeastern markets served by the Kapuskasing mill. To supply southern markets, Weyerhaeuser, Georgia-Pacific, and Crown-Zellerbach embarked upon large-scale facility-improvement and facility-expansion programs at the end of the decade. These projects contributed to excess capacity and falling prices in the early 1980s. They also presented smaller newsprint companies with the uncomfortable choice of either losing profits and market share or investing into their southern plants to catch up with the productivity gains that industry leaders derived from more modern mills and technology. Kimberly-Clark opted for the former, costing it dearly in the early 1980s, when severe price declines ravaged the newsprint industry. The operating profits of Kimberly-Clark's newsprint business fell 40 percent in 1982, followed by an even larger decline the next year. Some of these problems could have been avoided if Smith had included both newsprint mills in Minard's asset liquidations of the early 1970s.[24]

While the company's half-hearted commitment to newsprint produced disappointing results, Smith's decision to keep the Anderson, California, timberlands proved highly beneficial. Instead of selling the 323,000-acre property as part of the Anderson mill liquidation, as the Sherrin committee had contemplated, Kimberly-Clark built a sawmill on the property. Once it had completed a difficult startup in 1972, the sawmill employed more than 670 people and produced building lumber. With housing starts reaching record levels of more than 2 million units annually in the early 1970s, and with lumber prices rising as much as 70 percent in some markets, the Anderson lumber operation contributed healthy profits to the newsprint, pulp, and forest products division.

Home construction and prices fell off in the 1973 recession, declined dramatically for two years, and started to rebound in late 1976. Housing starts again reached 2 million units in 1977 and remained on an upward trajectory the next year, leading to a sharp appreciation of timberland assets. Smith, eyeing a way to raise cash for the Huggies diaper program, contemplated selling the forestlands in early 1979. Arguing that the Northern California property was "neither a wood source for any of our pulp mills nor intended to support the long-range fiber needs of our other principal businesses," he sold the property to Oregon-based Roseberg Lumber Company in September 1979.[25] The transaction was remarkable for two reasons. First, the forestlands fetched $262 million, a 1,000 percent inflation-adjusted increase over what Kimberly-Clark had paid for the property in 1961. Second, Smith concluded negotiations with Roseberg in the nick of time, shortly before the onset of the economic recession of 1979 precipitated a 20 percent decrease in new home construction and a sharp drop in timberland prices in the following months. The liquidation of John R. Kimberly's venture into Northern California provided a welcome infusion of cash for the consumer products business.[26]

II.

Feminine care products were a key area in which Kimberly-Clark sought to expand its consumer nondurables business in the 1970s and 1980s. Initiated by Minard, the strategy complemented the liquidation of the coated paper business, whose proceeds were earmarked for major investments into diapers, sanitary napkins, tampons, and a variety of other consumer products. The plan seemed to have considerable merits when Minard first formulated it in 1971. Demand for feminine care products bounced back quickly after the 1970 recession, producing healthy profits as early as spring 1971. Setbacks in previous decades notwithstanding, Kimberly-Clark was still the nation's largest feminine care products company of the early 1970s with more than 40 percent market share overall, trailed by Johnson & Johnson, a distant second with 25 percent. However, Kimberly-Clark's

TABLE 5.1

Feminine care products market shares, 1970–1986

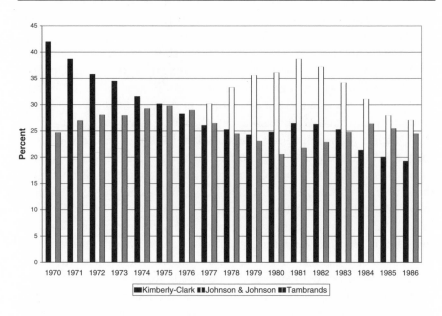

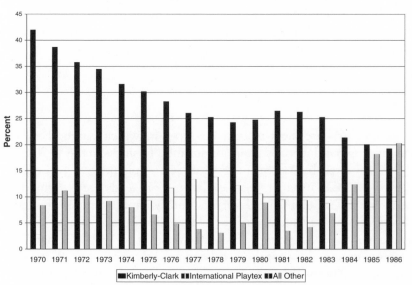

position deteriorated during the ensuing years. In 1976 it was briefly eclipsed by tampon giant Tambrands. A year later Johnson & Johnson became the nation's largest producer of feminine care products, a position it retained in subsequent years (table 5.1.)

Kimberly-Clark's problems in feminine care products were the result of seismic technology and market shifts. Product technology changed fundamentally in 1969, when Johnson & Johnson introduced a tabless pad that gained increased popularity with consumers. Fighting to stay competitive, Kimberly-Clark's feminine care division scrambled to develop comparable designs but was unable to close the market share gap with Johnson & Johnson. The resulting decline in financial performance was partly offset by the success of the Kotex panty liner, which accounted for the bulk of the company's profits in feminine care products during the 1980s.

Although losing market share was painful in each consumer segment, Kimberly-Clark's greatest disappointment came in sanitary napkins, where the Kotex brand underwent a swift decline from more than 50 percent market share in 1970 to 15 percent in 1986 (table 5.2). Overall pad output had stagnated during the 1960s because consumers exhibited a growing preference for tampons, which by 1970 accounted for more than one-third of all menstrual care products sold in the United States.

Consumer surveys indicated that younger women viewed sanitary napkins as old-fashioned and cumbersome because they required sanitary belts or pins to hold tabbed pads in place. Kimberly-Clark, despite being aware of these changes in consumer preference, was reluctant to rock the boat with new products, partly because sanitary belts represented a sizable and profitable part of its feminine care business. This failure to act created an opportunity for Johnson & Johnson, which launched a product development initiative in the late 1960s to develop the Stayfree tabless sanitary napkin. Stayfree was successfully test-marketed in 1969 and introduced nationwide two years later. The Stayfree Mini-Pad consisted of a narrow piece of absorbent material with an adhesive strip that enabled women to attach the pad to their underwear. Although the new design did not entirely eliminate chafing—a source of frequent consumer complaints since the 1920s—the adhesive strip reduced it by keeping the pad securely in place, resulting in a product advantage that proved unbeatable. With the Stayfree pad, Johnson & Johnson had created a new market segment in the feminine care products business. By 1976 the market share of tabless sanitary napkins exceeded that of tabbed ones, which later almost disappeared (table 5.3).

TABLE 5.2
Feminine care external products market shares, 1970–1986

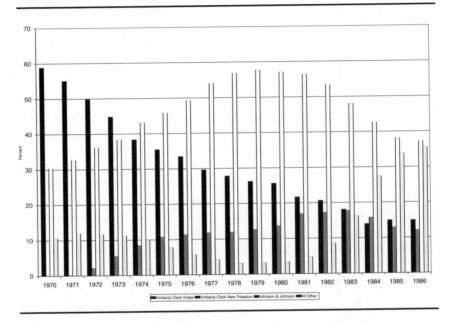

Kimberly-Clark and other pad makers were slow to realize that Johnson & Johnson had not simply added a new feature to an existing product but had actually created an entirely new product that would replace its predecessor. Kimberly-Clark's initial response to the introduction of tabless pads echoed its handling of previous challenges to Kotex's market dominance. As in the late 1950s, when it introduced a softer pad cover to fend off Johnson & Johnson's attempt to gain market share with its improved Modess design, Kimberly-Clark launched its own tabless pad only six months after Johnson & Johnson had introduced Stayfree nationwide. However, inept product positioning overshadowed this research and development achievement. Instead of immediately redesigning Kotex as a tabless pad, Kimberly-Clark first introduced the new design nationwide under the separate New Freedom label in 1972. This two-brand strategy amounted to a replay of the largely unsuccessful attempt to halt the decline in Kotex's market share during the 1960s with the introduction of the Fems specialty pad brand. Although New Freedom steadily gained market share in the 1970s, it was unable to offset the losses accrued by the Kotex brand, whose design as a tabbed pad remained unchanged until the mid-1970s.[27]

TABLE 5.3

Feminine care products market share, 1970–1986

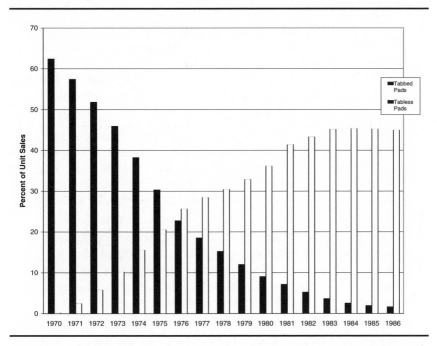

The competitive disadvantage resulting from Kotex's obsolete design was confounded by the rise of television advertising for feminine care products in the 1970s. At the beginning of the decade the National Association of Broadcasters (NAB) relaxed its long-standing restrictions on tampon and sanitary pad advertising, enabling Johnson & Johnson, International Playtex Corporation, and other companies willing to spend money on expensive commercials to increase their market shares. Kimberly-Clark initially resisted the trend, refusing in 1972 to join other feminine care products companies in their effort to lobby for the NAB policy change. Arthur Schulz, chairman of Foote, Cone & Belden, the ad agency responsible for Kotex marketing, explained that Kimberly-Clark took "a stand in opposition to the lifting of the television ban despite the clear advantage it would give them. To this date, they have prevailed, and I hope they will continue to. This was a decision based on good taste and respect for consumer attitudes, rather than on sales and profits alone."[28]

The decision, a reversal of the company's decades-long attempts to enhance the advertisability of sanitary napkins, made more business sense than Schulz gave Kimberly-Clark credit for. Expensive television advertising was likely to reduce the profitability of long-established labels like Kotex and Tampax tampons. Similar considerations probably motivated Tampax Incorporated to resist television advertising, enabling its bolder competitor, International Playtex Corporation, to launch the nation's first tampon television commercials in the early 1970s and to erode Tampax's market share. Kimberly-Clark likewise postponed Kotex television advertising until 1974, whereas Johnson & Johnson took advantage of the NAB policy change immediately after it was announced. Delayed entry into television advertising safeguarded Kotex's operating profits, which exceeded 30 percent before the launch of the first Kotex commercials in 1974 and then dropped by half.[29]

Kimberly-Clark meanwhile sought to defend Kotex's position with incremental product changes and new print ads. In the early 1970s, researchers developed a new Kotex cover (trademarked as Air Weave) and a new, superabsorbent filler for the pad. An ad campaign headlined "Kotex invents the Dry Napkin" claimed that "the Air Weave surface stays drier. And you stay drier. And fresher feeling than you can imagine. And really, isn't that the way you like to feel?"[30] Unfortunately for Kimberly-Clark, this new advertising and product improvement hardly amounted to a strategic boost for Kotex. Although the new cover and filler were quite innovative, the redesign failed to turn Kotex into a tabless pad. Moreover, the ad depicted a woman in loose-fitting pants standing far away from the camera, in contrast to recent Johnson & Johnson ads that showed close-up shots of women in tight clothes to illustrate that new pads were barely visible. The claim that "there's never been anything like it," combined with the explanation that "the fluff draws wetness away from you, and deep into the napkin center" was debatable.[31] In truth, there was nothing innovative about a high-absorbency pad core that soaked up menstrual discharge—this was simply how pads had worked for decades.

Product obsolescence and inadequate marketing were the chief factors behind a 20 percent decline in inflation-adjusted Kotex net sales from 1971 to 1974. In February 1974 Sherrin—acutely aware of "the very rapid increase in market share attained by the tabless napkin in the last three years"—acknowledged the inadequacy of Kimberly-Clark's response, chiding the company for the "slowness in entering this segment of the market, and the resulting loss in market share."[32] An industry observer later remarked more bluntly that Kimberly-Clark "has had a firm grip on the dying end of the business."[33]

Sherrin recommended a crash product development and marketing initiative in feminine care products to reverse these trends. Kotex was successfully redesigned as a tabless pad in 1975, but advertising remained a consistent problem. To sustain Kotex's 35.5 percent market share in sanitary napkins in 1975, Kimberly-Clark expended less than 15 percent of the total advertising dollars spent by the nation's pad makers in that year. Johnson & Johnson, by contrast, controlled 46 percent of the pad market in 1975 but expended 48 percent of all advertising dollars spent on sanitary napkins. These statistics illustrated long-term trends. Kotex's share in total advertising expenditures consistently lagged behind its market share during the 1970s and 1980s (table 5.4), in contrast to Johnson & Johnson in pads (table 5.5) and International Playtex in tampons. The Kotex brand, already bruised by the delayed switch to a tabless design, continued its fall largely as a result of inadequate advertising.[34]

Kotex's decline was partly attributable to Kimberly-Clark's two-brand strategy that required major advertising to establish name recognition for the New Freedom label. Like the Boutique brand, whose introduction in the late 1960s emasculated Kleenex's advertising budget, New Freedom received a disproportionate share of Kimberly-Clark's pad advertising dollars. In the first three years of its launch, New Freedom accounted for 62 percent of the company's pad advertising budget but only 12 percent of net pad sales (table 5.6). Like Playtex in tampons, New Freedom's share in the pad industry's advertising expenditures remained ahead of its market share until 1984, underwriting the brand's continuous growth.[35]

New Freedom also marked a departure in terms of ad content. Building on the tabless design, advertisements developed by Foote, Cone & Belding (FCB) in the early 1970s stressed that the pad featured "no belts, no pins," which positioned the brand for competition with tampons. In a way, Kimberly-Clark had finally found an answer to Tampax's 1942 claim that tampon use involved "No Belts, No Pins, No Pads, No Odor." An ad series released in 1974, headlined "New Freedom 'Small Pads'—No pins. No belts. No doubts!" explained that the brand was a "highly absorbent *little napkin,* so slim and lightweight, you hardly know you're wearing anything."[36] Borrowing from Fibs tampon marketing of the 1930s, the ad recommended New Freedom for days when the consumer experienced lighter flow, claiming that the pad was "just what you need for your tapering on and tapering off days." It then went on to pitch "New Freedom Full-Size Pads, too, for your regular and high flow days."[37]

TABLE 5.4

Kotex market share and advertising, 1970–1986

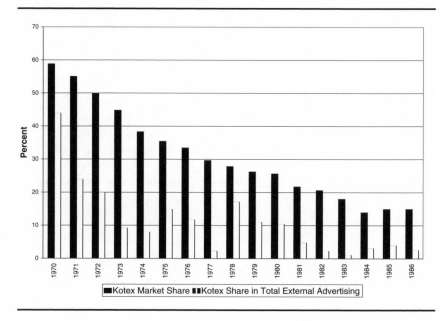

TABLE 5.5

Johnson & Johnson pad market share and advertising, 1970–1986

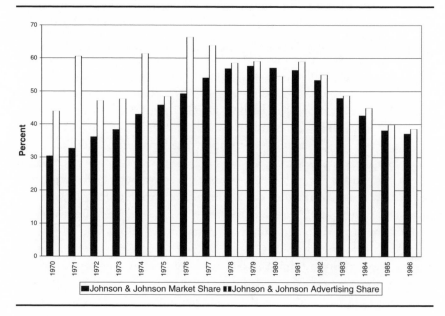

TABLE 5.6
New Freedom pad market share and advertising, 1972–1986

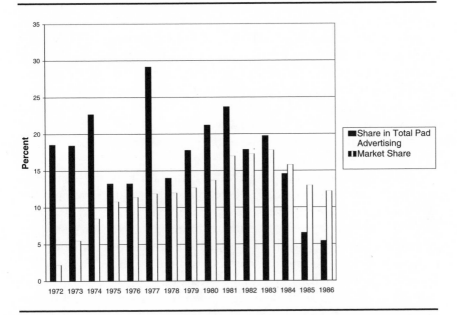

Meanwhile, FCB worked on television advertisements for New Freedom, including a thirty-second commercial developed in 1974. It began with a woman in her mid-twenties who proclaimed, "Sure I'm sure. It's all I ever need," followed by a freckled teenager, who opined, "I call it terrific. Yup, really terrific." An announcer then declared, "New Freedom Mini Pads. Better for the way you live today." (This segment was later revised to define the product's performance advantages more clearly, stating: "New Freedom Mini Pads. The most absorbent, most comfortable, most protective mini pads you can buy.") The commercial then continued with a shot of a mother in her early twenties watching her baby on a swing in the park, who chimed in, "*Some days,* there's just nothing better." This contradicted the first woman's claim that the New Freedom mini pad was "*all* I ever need," ruining the commercial's message.[38]

Although documentary evidence is unavailable, one may speculate that the poorly designed pad commercials may have contributed to Kimberly-Clark's decision to reassign New Freedom television advertising from FCB to Kelly Nason, an innovative ad agency which later gained responsibility for print advertising as well. In 1975 Kimberly-Clark terminated its fifty-two-year association with FCB, citing "irreconcilable differences."[39] This drastic move set New Freedom marketing adrift for the next several years. Kelly Nason, known as something of a rabble-rouser in the marketing industry, also fared poorly and quickly lost the New Freedom account to the Chicago-based Leo Burnett agency. The latter developed a variety of New Freedom marketing programs, including several aimed at Hispanic consumers and other ethnic minorities, which helped double the brand's market share in the late 1970s and early 1980s. Leo Burnett's association with Kimberly-Clark ended in 1983, however, when New Freedom was reassigned to the renowned New York advertising agency Ogilvy & Mather, already in charge of most other Kimberly-Clark consumer products (see below).

While experimenting with new marketing formats and strategies, Kimberly-Clark supported New Freedom with product development. After launching the product as a tabless maxi pad, it added a mini pad version to compete head-on with Johnson & Johnson's Stayfree brand. A redesign of the maxi pad in 1978 added rounded ends and dimple embossing to improve comfort and reduce the pad's visibility. Intended to boost Kimberly-Clark's market share in maxi pads to more than 40 percent, the redesign failed to enhance product differentiation. By 1981, Kimberly-Clark's maxi pad market share had declined to 31 percent.[40]

This setback notwithstanding, inflation-adjusted New Freedom net sales jumped almost 80 percent from 1980 to 1983. The cause was menstrual toxic shock syndrome (TSS) associated with superabsorbent tampons. TSS killed more than 100 women in the early 1980s and made thousands of tampon users ill. TSS is triggered by *Staphylococcus aureus,* a bacterium that causes the human body to start an immunological self-assault resulting in fever, vomiting, diarrhea, dangerously low blood pressure, and in some instances the cutting off of the blood flow to the brain and death. Menstrual TSS, first reported in 1978, occurred in 1,066 cases in 1980. The Centers for Disease Control and Prevention (CDC) alerted the public in May 1980 that menstrual TSS was strongly correlated with tampon use, followed in September by an announcement that 70 percent of menstrual TSS victims surveyed in a CDC study had used Procter & Gamble's Rely tampon. Procter & Gamble immediately challenged the findings, claiming that the CDC test was "too limited and fragmentary for any conclusions to be drawn."[41] The company then suspended Rely production and distribution, offered customers refunds "for unused supplies," and continued to insist that the Rely tampon was safe. A business magazine later called these moves "one of the worst examples of crisis management" in the late twentieth century.[42]

In contrast, Kimberly-Clark, which had largely abandoned attempts to market its Kotex stick tampon but continued to sell it, was the first tampon producer to implement a campaign to inform consumers and physicians about menstrual TSS and ways to prevent it. The Rely withdrawal meanwhile cost Procter & Gamble a $75 million write-off that did not even include legal fees and settlements with some of the 300 claimants who sued the company for damages. Since CDC studies also implicated other tampon brands, the menstrual TSS scandal precipitated a massive drop in overall tampon sales, creating a major opportunity for pad makers to reclaim lost ground.[43]

Industry analysts doubted that Kimberly-Clark's pad business would reap strategic benefits from menstrual TSS. Forbes magazine noted as early November 1980, "Given Kimberly-Clark's record in the napkin market . . . it seems unlikely that the Wisconsin-based company can maximize any potential stemming from toxic shock."[44] Its share in the feminine care products market actually increased slightly in 1981 and 1982 but then resumed its long-term decline. Part of the problem was that Procter & Gamble launched a well-financed product development and marketing effort for its Always brand of sanitary pads. The product was test marketed in 1983 in the Minneapolis–St. Paul area with such deep discounts that one observer quipped, "If anyone wanted to buy a sanitary napkin, he should have gone to Minneapolis. They were practically giving them away."[45] The campaign foreshadowed Procter & Gamble's $18 million advertising campaign to introduce the product nationally in 1984, followed by even larger ad and promotional budgets over the next several years. This massive assault, which captured a 16.8 percent share for Always in the pad market just two years after its national introduction, came largely at the expense of established market leaders. Kimberly-Clark's New Freedom brand, which had slowly chipped away at Johnson & Johnson's market leadership in the 1970s until it reached 17 percent in 1981, slipped to 12.2 percent in 1986. From 1983 to 1986, Johnson & Johnson's and Kimberly-Clark's overall shares in the pad market fell by 23 percent each as Procter & Gamble emerged as the leading beneficiary of the menstrual TSS crisis.[46]

The introduction of tabless pads revolutionized the feminine care market as no other product had since the invention of the tampon. Johnson & Johnson invented a genuinely new product—much as Kimberly-Clark had with tabbed sanitary napkins in the 1920s and as

Procter & Gamble had with disposable diapers in the 1960s. As the feminine care products market entered a new era, Kimberly-Clark wasted valuable time defending an obsolete product, but it also brought its own tabless pad to market shortly after Johnson & Johnson launched Stayfree. Historically speaking, challenging a prime mover shortly after it had created a new market was no small feat. Kotex had enjoyed a quasi monopoly for almost a decade, as had Pampers. Kimberly-Clark's real problems in the tabless pad market were the result of poor marketing. An internal company study concluded in 1987, "We were second into the product segment, our brands were not sufficiently differentiated as to product performance benefits, we were consistently outspent by Johnson & Johnson in advertising support to establish and grow the new product forms and our advertising campaigns were intermittent and of inconsistent persuasive quality."[47] As a result, Kimberly-Clark was unable to stake a major claim in the new pad market, leaving the task of mounting the first decisive challenge to Johnson & Johnson's dominance to Procter & Gamble.

Kimberly-Clark turned the table in 1975 with the launch of the Kotex Lightdays Panty Liner, which established another new market segment in the increasingly differentiated feminine care business. Developed in the early 1970s by a Kotex product team at the Neenah research center, the design featured a bonded, carded web as a cover, a fiber substructure, a nonwoven baffle as an absorbent, and an adhesive strip to attach the liner to the panty. As the brand name indicated, it provided protection against light menstrual flow, could be used in combination with tampons, and prevented staining of underwear by intermenstrual discharge (experienced by one-third of all women under the age of 34). Smaller and more lightweight than mini pads, the Kotex Panty Liner was designed to compete with the Stayfree brand. It did so quite successfully, as Johnson & Johnson effectively recognized when it introduced its own panty liner under the new Carefree label in 1976, scrambling to catch up with Kimberly-Clark with a heavily financed advertising and promotion campaign. The campaign succeeded in capturing more than half of the rapidly growing panty liner market in the late 1970s, partly because the Kimberly-Clark product derived no benefits from its marketing under the Kotex brand. Kimberly-Clark responded in 1980 by adding the New Freedom panty liner, which—combined with incremental product improvements—helped boost its overall market share to 55 percent in the early 1980s, at Johnson & Johnson's expense. Procter & Gamble's entry into the market in 1984, when it introduced its own product as part of its Always rollout, cost both Johnson & Johnson and Kimberly-Clark substantial market share. Despite its inability to remain a market leader in a product category it had established, Kimberly-Clark continued to reap substantial benefits as a result of the rapid overall growth of the panty liner market (by 1987 the product accounted for 20 percent of all feminine care products sold in the United States). Production increased fourfold from 1976 to 1986, at a surprisingly modest cost of approximately $5 million in capital investments to purchase machinery for the Lakeview mill in Neenah and the Conway, Arkansas, mill. By the mid-1980s, panty liners accounted for a quarter of the company's feminine care business by volume and generated up to half of its total operating profits in feminine hygiene products.[48]

The introduction of new products and the decline of old ones required mill reconfigurations and the introduction of new technologies. In the early 1970s, manufacturing involved only two base technologies for tabbed pads and stick tampons, with the latter accounting for only 10 percent of total output. Production involved six mills: Memphis, the largest consumer products mill, manufactured Kotex pads in various sizes, as did the slightly smaller mills in Fullerton, California, and Lakeview, Wisconsin. Tampons were produced at the old Berkeley, North Carolina, mill and at a new facility in Conway.

The proliferation of feminine care products developed in subsequent years required the addition of six new base technologies for tabless maxi pads, tabless mini pads, panty liners, and several minor products, at a cost of more than $40 million from 1970 to 1980. Almost half of these capital expenditures went to the Conway mill, completed in 1969 specifically to manufacture tampons. When the latter product failed to gain significant market share in the 1970s, Kimberly-Clark retooled the mill extensively to produce New Freedom panty liners. The remaining expenditures were largely used on new equipment for the Memphis and New Milford mills, which switched from tabbed pads to tabless ones, and on the Lakeview mill to start up panty liner production. Although detailed information on capital expenditures and proprietary production technology remains confidential, it can be said that the plant reconfigurations of the 1970s were largely successful in increasing the operating profitability of the mills. Overall, however, these gains were not sufficient to offset skyrocketing marketing costs in the highly differentiated and competitive feminine care markets. As a result, the operating profitability of Kimberly-Clark's feminine care products business fell, creating a modest drag on operating profits in the consumer products division. Fortunately for Kimberly-Clark, the growing profitability of its diaper business eventually more than compensated for the downward trend in feminine care products.[49]

III.

The competitive dynamics of the disposable diaper market differed markedly from those of feminine care products, owing largely to product characteristics. Far bulkier than sanitary napkins or tampons, diapers were a retailer's nightmare because they consumed vast amounts of shelf space. In the 1970s most supermarkets and drugstores opted to carry only two diaper labels, sometimes supplemented by a store brand. Given Procter & Gamble's formidable lead as the prime mover that had invented the product, the company enjoyed high brand loyalty and controlled at least 80 percent of the market until the mid-1970s. The main task facing any new entrant was to crowd out other secondary producers. Entry into the disposable diaper market was a high-stakes gamble. Unless a diaper maker succeeded in establishing its brand as the second largest, it was doomed because there was literally no room for a third or fourth largest brand. This market dynamic explains abrupt decisions by Scott, Johnson & Johnson, International Paper, and others to abandon diapers after failing to establish their brands as one of the top two. Simultaneously, the potential rewards were enormous because disposable diapers were among the most profitable consumer nondurables of the 1970s. Rapid acceptance of the product, combined with continued population growth, turned disposable diapers into a $1 billion market by the mid-1970s. Any diaper maker that carved out a modest market share against Pampers and simply hung on to it without making further gains against Procter & Gamble could expect sales to triple as a result of sheer market growth.[50]

Kimberly-Clark's entry into the diaper market started in 1966, five years after Procter & Gamble first test marketed Pampers. At the time, Pampers had reached 50 percent of the national market share. In 1966 Scott Paper test marketed BabyScotts in Denver, Colorado, to compete at the lower end of the market with a product featuring a flushable pad in a reusable panty priced 40 percent below Pampers.

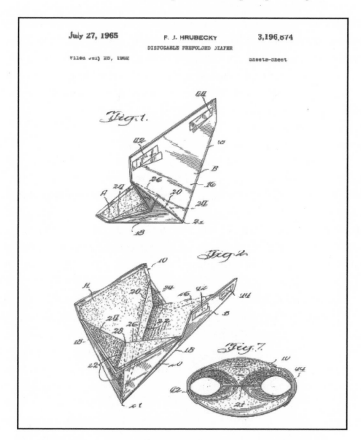

FIGURE 5.1
Hrubecky diaper design, 1965

BabyScotts had considerable environmental merits because the flushable pad did not contribute to solid waste, but consumers rejected it, citing its inconvenience compared to one-piece diapers, dooming the innovative design. To this day, most diapers are based on a three-layer construction featuring a fluid-pervious sheet covering the baby's bottom, an absorbent pad, and a plastic-based backing sheet to prevent moisture leakage from the pad. The design's environmental impact is monumental because tissue pads are firmly glued to plastic-based covers and backing sheets, making it nearly impossible to extract recyclable pad tissue. Moreover, ignoring strong objections from environmentalists, most diaper makers have replaced cellulose pads with polypropylene-based superabsorbent fillers that are not recyclable.[51]

The design of what later became the Kimbies diaper added a variety of new features developed by Kimberly-Clark scientist Frederick Hrubecky, who experimented with diaper technology in the early 1960s. His key contributions included a new folding pattern that provided a better fit with body contours than the standard fold, or so Hrubecky claimed (figure 5.1). Early consumer tests conducted in 1966, in which the Hrubecky fold was tested against the standard Pampers fold, actually determined that consumers preferred the latter, partly because the Hrubecky fold resulted in more leakage. Product managers, counseled by Foote, Cone & Belding, responsible for Kimbies marketing, were keen on introducing a uniquely shaped diaper and hence favored the Hrubecky fold, which was adopted as the base design. Even before Kimbies went into extended test marketing, Kimberly-Clark installed $1 million worth of Hrubecky-fold production equipment, including the first experimental folding machine, which went into production at the Memphis mill in 1968.[52]

More important from both a technology and a consumer standpoint, Hrubecky incorporated into the diaper adhesive tapes that replaced pins as fasteners. Developing an appropriate adhesive tape proved rather difficult, and Hrubecky reported that ordinary pressure-sensitive tapes "do not have a sufficiently aggressive adhesive to remain adhered to the surface of [the polyethylene-based diaper backing sheet] . . . When tack is increased to overcome . . . premature detachment problems, another problem arises in trying to provide a suitable protective release sheet for temporarily covering the adhesive."[53] Experimenting with a variety of pressure-sensitive tapes, Hrubecky settled on one with sufficient tack strength to stick to the backing's polyethylene surface when the baby moved around, without making it too difficult for the parent to remove the protective tape cover. Consumer tests conducted in 1968 in Denver and Salt Lake City determined that the replacement of pins with tapes were Kimbies' most attractive feature, forcing a redesign of Pampers in 1969, the same year Procter & Gamble had achieved national distribution of its diaper.[54]

Off to a promising start, the Kimbies program came unglued in the early 1970s. By 1969 the pilot production line at the Memphis mill was unable to keep up with orders pouring in from test markets, convincing Kimberly-Clark to install full-scale production lines at the new Beech Island consumer products mills in South Carolina and at the Memphis mill. Disaster struck in 1970, however, when a wage strike shut down the Memphis mill for two months, just as the Kim-

bies production line entered its startup phase. This threw off Kimberly-Clark's diaper test marketing program in the Southwest, effectively rendering its results useless. Moreover, poor financial results in
1970 and 1971 resulted in cutbacks in Kimbies research and engineering at the exact time when the product required more money to
work out design kinks and keep up with the competition. Leakage
resulting from the Hrubecky fold remained a persistent problem, and
the product's cover softness and pad absorbency compared unfavorably to those of Pampers and BabyScotts. New entrants were launching a variety of diaper development programs, including International Paper, American Can, Union Carbide, and Dow Chemical. Johnson
& Johnson, the most important new entrant, brought out a diaper
with a fastenable tape, wiping out Kimbies' only major product
advantage among secondary brands. Kimberly-Clark, however,
appropriated only 5 percent of its total budget for consumer products
research and engineering for the diaper program. Faced with the poor
financial results of 1971, management insisted that only three-quar-
ters of this paltry sum actually be spent, making it difficult for the
handful of scientists assigned to diapers to develop substantial product improvements.[55]

Conditions later improved temporarily, but the program continued to face major difficulties. As early as June 1971, shortly before
the decision to liquidate most of the company's coated paper business,
the board approved $17 million in appropriations for the Kimbies
program at Minard's urging. The bulk was spent on volume capacity
at the Memphis and Beech Island mills, which started six new diaper
machines in 1971 and 1972, with each machine producing 200 diapers per minute. This brought annual production capacity to one billion units in 1973, enabling Kimberly-Clark to expand distribution to
more than 60 percent of the national market. By 1974 Kimbies started to produce a modest operating profit, but the product remained
marred by continued marketing and design problems. After Procter
& Gamble and Johnson & Johnson had switched to fastenable tapes,
Foote, Cone & Belding recommended emphasizing the diaper's
unique triangular shape in Kimbies marketing, even though there was
no indication that consumers cared much about the product shape.
Researchers, unaware of this change as a result of insufficient coordination with marketers, meanwhile started to tinker with the glue
attaching the cover lining to the pad core, despite the fact that consumer testing indicated little consumer dissatisfaction with this element of the Kimbies design. In 1974 they replaced a plastisol adhesive

with latex adhesive. Driven by cost considerations—plastisol prices had recently increased—the switch proved disastrous because latex glue was weaker and less durable. Consumer complaints about diapers that arrived unglued or that disintegrated during use skyrocketed immediately following the switch to latex glue. As a result, Kimbies net unit sales dropped by 25 percent from 1974 to 1975. Attempts to correct the mistake came too late to maintain Kimbies as the nation's second largest diaper brand, a position it relinquished to Johnson & Johnson in 1975. In October of that year, Kimberly-Clark yanked the Kimbies account from FCB without immediately appointing a successor agency, effectively recognizing that the diaper program had reached a strategic dead end.[56]

A project review conducted in 1975 attributed the failure of the Kimbies program to five main factors. First, the decision to use the Hrubecky fold as a basic design resulted in leakage problems without providing a distinct marketing advantage. Second, the unfortunate timing of the Memphis mill strike in 1970 derailed test marketing, with serious consequences for subsequent brand positioning. Third, the company invested too little into research and engineering, contributing to the failure to position Kimberly-Clark for successful competition against Johnson & Johnson for the critical second place standing among diaper producers. Fourth, a considerable share of the inadequate research budget of the early 1970s was wasted on the development of latex glue that sent the product into a tailspin. Fifth, market research failed to discern critical trends in consumer preference, resulting in poorly conceived marketing strategies.[57]

At this critical moment most company executives were ready to terminate Kimberly-Clark's foray into disposable diapers. Smith, although disappointed with the results of a project he had inherited from his predecessor, made the decisive decision to give diapers another shot. After reading the Kimbies review closely, he ordered the consumer products division to develop an entirely new product and concurrent marketing plan that incorporated the lessons of the Kimbies debacle. The new diaper initiative was to be based on market research that took a hard look at actual consumer preferences, a shift from the previous strategy of telling consumers what they *should* want. In another departure from the Kimbies program, Smith willingly authorized significant amounts of money for research and engineering to develop a design-intensive product, channeling most of the proceeds of the $14.5 million Kimberly mill sale in 1975 into the new diaper program. Smith even reduced appropriations for feminine care products advertising to fund a new marketing offensive in disposable diapers.[58]

The new initiative, which resulted in the introduction of Huggies diapers in 1977, evolved amidst major changes in the disposable diaper industry. Parents had flocked to Pampers and the secondary brands throughout the early 1970s, but complaints about disposable diapers were widespread. Consumer surveys determined that tape fasteners often came detached, absorbency was unsatisfactory, and liners and backing sheets came unglued. Most important, rectangular diapers like Pampers and Kimbies frequently leaked, despite attempts to solve the problem through new folding patterns. The most comprehensive solution was to design a non–uniformly shaped diaper that conformed to body contours, but most diaper makers shied away from the high research and development costs involved, as well as heavy investments into plant retooling. The only major exception was Procter & Gamble, which in 1976 introduced the Luvs diaper featuring elastic leg gathers and an hourglass shape. To recapture development costs, Procter & Gamble introduced Luvs at a price that was 30 to 50 percent higher than that of Pampers, effectively creating a new market segment for premium diapers. Somewhat reluctant to take business away from its profitable Pampers brand, Procter & Gamble was uncharacteristically slow in taking Luvs into national distribution. This created a strategic, but temporary, advantage for competitors that were willing to spend significant amounts on research, development, and marketing in the new product segment. Time and geography were critical factors. As Procter & Gamble had demonstrated with Pampers in the 1960s, and as subsequent developments in premium diapers confirmed, being first in a regional market created a high degree of brand loyalty that competitors found difficult to overcome. Viewed from this perspective, the premium diaper wars of the late 1970s and early 1980s were attempts to secure as much unclaimed territory as possible, only later followed by head-on collisions between the combatants.[59]

Consumer surveys conducted in 1975 determined that mothers were primarily interested in three major design and performance characteristics. First, they preferred any product that kept babies' bottoms dry, confirming the results of the first Pampers surveys of the 1960s which indicated that mothers strongly correlated dryness with baby comfort. Second, they liked diapers that promised a substantial reduction or elimination of leakage, the most frequently cited problem with Pampers and other standard diapers, and they were willing

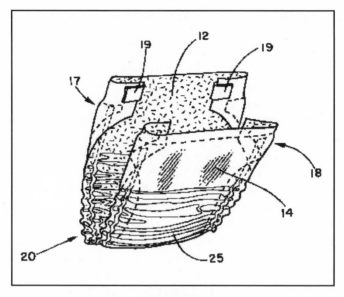

FIGURE 5.2
Huggies diaper design

to pay significantly more for diapers that eliminated the problem. Third, mothers liked the adhesive tapes introduced in the early 1970s but complained that extant technology did not permit refastening.[60]

Huggies incorporated the survey results in a sophisticated product design (figure 5.2). Taking advantage of a research and engineering budget that was four times larger than the Kimbies appropriations, a research team headed by scientists Lin Sun Woon and Dan Endres developed Huggies in 1975 and early 1976. Reviewing the state of the art of diaper design, they pointed out three major deficiencies bedeviling standard rectangular products. First, in the latter "there is excess bulk between the legs which may cause discomfort; second, the folds . . . are generally linear and the relatively non-conformable structure of disposable diapers prevents a closely conforming fit at the buttocks or thighs, often leaving undesirable gaps in those two areas which permit leaks to occur; and third, when applied to the child the non-conforming sides of the rectangular diaper tends to pull the waist down at the sides and thereby cause the diaper to gap at the front of the waist where leaks can then occur."[61] Attempts to reduce bulkiness between the legs with an hourglass shape had resulted in problems because it left gaps and reduced absorbency in the narrow section. Simply adding elastic bands to the entire length of the edges to close the gaps provided no solution because it caused excrement and urine to gather at the edges, precipitating skin irritation, and created gaps at the waist. A better solution, Woon and Endres argued, was to incorporate elasticized sections only into the narrow section of the diaper instead of the entire edge, and to thicken the pad slightly at the crotch to create additional absorbency. In their words, "Limiting the elasticized edges to the narrow crotch area foreshortens and provides transverse rugosities in the diaper batt only in the crotch area while minimizing the development of gaps at the waist."[62] Like the design of Luvs, the design also featured the refastenable tapes consumers had clamored for since the mid-1970s.

Developing manufacturing technology for this complicated design posed major challenges. Engineers, working closely with scientists in the product development team, devised a wide array of proprietary machine designs for the core mills in Memphis, Tennessee; Beech Island, South Carolina; and New Milford, Connecticut. A tissue machine combined layers of absorbent padding into sheets of varying thickness to form the wings and the crotch section, which was 15 percent thicker than the edges. Once the sheet had been cut into individual hourglass shapes, the latter received an elastic band at the crotch section and were combined with the cover and backing sheet to form the diaper.

The brand name for the new product had to incorporate the diaper's performance characteristics, while also appealing to emotional sentiment. Although detailed information on brand name development remains confidential, it can be said that "Huggies" meant to indicate that the new diaper fit snugly, effectively hugging the child. "Kleenex Huggies" sought to associate the diaper brand with the disposable tissue, still Kimberly-Clark's most well known trademark, and create an association with softness and high absorbency.

Huggies marketing began in December 1977. In contrast to Kimbies, which had made its debut in Denver, Colorado, where the competing Pampers brand was firmly entrenched, Huggies was first introduced in Wisconsin and Northern Michigan. Instead of taking on Procter & Gamble's Luvs brand directly in its core regions of Missouri and Ohio, Kimberly-Clark first competed with the Johnson & Johnson brand and Pampers, convinced that standard diapers were more vulnerable to direct competition with Huggies than Luvs. While the strategy was risky because it left key questions about Huggies' competitive performance vis-à-vis Luvs unanswered, it succeeded in beating back Johnson & Johnson, which had recently taken its brand national. In Milwaukee, Johnson & Johnson lost 29 percent of its market share in the six months after Huggies was introduced; in Denver, 36 percent; and in Seattle, Sacramento, and San Francisco, more than 50 percent. The West Coast, along with the Midwest, quickly became the core regions of Huggies distribution, where the brand gained considerably more market share than Kimberly-Clark had expected. Advertising and promotion cost almost $10 million annually, much of it financed through a war chest Smith had established after the sale of the company's Northern California timberlands.[63]

Marketing was handled by the advertising agency Ogilvy & Mather, which was responsible for research and analysis, as well as print and television advertising. Founded in New York in 1948 by British immigrant David Ogilvy, the agency was recognized as an advertising powerhouse that combined hard-nosed research with highly creative marketing initiatives. In the 1950s and 1960s Ogilvy & Mather had developed such renowned campaigns as the Hathaway shirt ads featuring a man with a black eye patch, as well as the luxury car slogan, "At 60 miles an hour, the loudest noise in the new Rolls-Royce comes from the electric clock." Kimberly-Clark was especially impressed with Ogilvy & Mather's record in consumer marketing, including its campaigns for General Food's cereal products as well as Maxwell House coffee. Dissatisfied with Kelly Nason, the maverick agency that had succeeded Foote, Cone & Belding as the lead marketer for feminine care and diaper products in the mid-1970s, Kimberly-Clark moved its entire consumer products account to Ogilvy & Mather later in the decade. The New York agency quickly proved its worth with (still confidential) market research on diaper buying patterns, pricing of premium diapers, and the comparative performance of Huggies, Luvs, Pampers, and other brands. It also developed the Huggies slogan, "Introducing a diaper that helps stop leaking," variations of which remained a staple of Huggies marketing for the remainder of the century.[64]

Reflecting the results of market research, the slogan suggested that Huggies assisted mothers in their battle against leakage, instead of assigning all credit to the product itself. Advertisements elaborating on the theme of parental expertise declared, "To anyone who's ever held a baby, or changed a baby, or changed a baby's bed clothes, [a diaper that helps stop leakage has] got to be terrific news."[65] Making the important link to the disposable handkerchief brand, ads proclaimed that Huggies "are extra absorbent, too. (They're from Kleenex, aren't they?)." Direct-mail campaigns developed by Ogilvy

& Mather reinforced the theme, informing mothers about "a brand new type of diaper called 'Huggies,' made by the folks at Kleenex (now there's a name you know you can trust!)."[66] Some women wrote unsolicited responses indicating that Kimberly-Clark had hit the right note. One wrote in February 1978, "I have a $1^1/_2$ year old and he is a heavy wetter and Huggies really take care of him. The Huggies cost a little more but I found because they absorbe [sic] more I use less."[67] The comment on pricing was somewhat understated because Huggies—like Luvs—were priced 30 percent more than standard diapers to recapture their considerable development and manufacturing cost, but the letter indicated a common perception among consumers. The only major complaint was that Kimberly-Clark had introduced Huggies in only four sizes, neglecting a toddler version that was quickly added in the late 1970s.[68]

Less than three years after it had been officially launched, the Huggies program achieved an important intermediate objective. In May 1980 Johnson & Johnson fired almost half the workforce at its diaper plant in Skillman, New Jersey, causing rumors "that the $4.2 billion health-care giant was calling it quits."[69] Johnson & Johnson's attempts to sidestep premium markets earned low marks from industry analysts. Smith Barney vice president John Wilkerson opined, "J&J came out with a Cadillac when everyone else had a Chevy, [then] P&G and Kimberly-Clark came out with a Mercedes."[70] Although Johnson & Johnson initially denied the rumor that it was preparing to pull out of the diaper market, it officially terminated the venture in February 1981. This move, which firmly positioned Kimberly-Clark in the critical number-two spot in the diaper market, was remarkable for its timing amidst the economic recession of the early 1980s. At a time of rampant inflation, declining real wages, and economic uncertainty, consumers flocked from Johnson & Johnson's moderately priced diapers to the Huggies and Luvs premium brands. This turned observers who had second-guessed Kimberly-Clark's decision to compete at the upscale end of the diaper market into ardent admirers of Darwin Smith. For the first time since the interwar period, Kimberly-Clark had a new product that deserved the label "recession resistant."[71]

Johnson & Johnson's withdrawal from the market coincided with the completion of Procter & Gamble's efforts to distribute Luvs nationally. This marked an important milestone because previous episodes in the premium diaper wars had confirmed that being first in a given market was key to a brand's success. In Denver and Phoenix, for example, where Huggies had beaten Luvs to the punch, the Kimberly-Clark brand held a 25 percent market share by 1980, compared to Luvs' 16 percent. The fact that Luvs had achieved national distribution first, coupled with Johnson & Johnson's withdrawal, precipitated changes in Huggies marketing. The choice was between comparative ad content and aggressive pricing. Following in-depth studies and discussions of the matter, Kimberly-Clark and Ogilvy & Mather decided to offer Huggies at a slightly lower price than Luvs, partly because it was difficult to differentiate the two premium brands on the basis of performance features. Instead of inventing brand differences for comparative advertising, Kimberly-Clark introduced Huggies in markets dominated by Luvs at a 6 percent overall discount, supported by coupon promotion and a $17 million advertising campaign in 1981 and 1982. Although the strategy temporarily reduced Huggies' profitability, it succeeded in making inroads into Luvs' share in the latter's core markets. Procter & Gamble's response indicated that the Cincinnati consumer products giant had lost some of its legendary surefootedness in diaper marketing. Instead of following suit with aggressive pricing in premium diaper markets or Luvs product improvements, it added refastenable tapes to its Pampers brand, but it then failed to advertise this significant new feature in print and television ads. From spring 1982 to spring 1983, Huggies achieved a 29 percent rise in brand share growth, Luvs gained 3 percent, and Pampers lost 10 percent. In 1983, when Huggies reached national distribution, Kimberly-Clark controlled 21 percent of the diaper market, compared to Luvs' 21 percent and Pampers' 40 percent (the remaining 18 percent largely represented store brands).[72]

Kimberly-Clark's management, carefully analyzing recent market trends, became convinced that premium diapers had the potential of capturing a majority share of the disposable diaper market. Richard Bowers, the company's manager for infant care products, predicted as much in October 1983, immediately cautioning, "We're not so naïve to think that P&G won't defend its products."[73] Indeed, Procter & Gamble quickly improved Pampers with what it called "stay-dry gathers" to defend the brand against Huggies. However, it introduced the new feature in a somewhat poorly conceived marketing campaign that failed to differentiate sufficiently between Luvs and Pampers, costing both brands market share. In 1984 Procter & Gamble took advantage of a growing trend in marketing that intertwined product promotion with popular children's movies, sending Muppets dolls to Pampers users who mailed in proofs of purchase during the release of the film *The Muppets Take Manhattan*. Kimberly-Clark quickly responded with a massive advertising and promotion campaign devised by Ogilvy & Mather that elaborated the "diaper that helps stop leaking" theme. This all-out effort featured hospital promotions, television advertising, direct mailings, and coupon distribution campaigns, each aiming at specific consumer groups ranging from expectant mothers to cloth diaper users. As a result of the $17 million program, Huggies' market share briefly exceeded Pampers' in spring 1985. Later that year Kimberly-Clark opened a new front by introducing Huggies in Canada, whose diaper market had previously been completely dominated by Procter & Gamble. In the next six months, Luvs' market share fell from 18.7 to 11.7 percent, Pampers' fell from 54.6 to 30 percent, and Huggies' increased to 30.6 percent.[74]

The next episode in the diaper wars centered on new performance features, most notably superabsorbent fillers. Diaper scientists at both Kimberly-Clark and Procter & Gamble had experimented with polymer-based superabsorbents since the late 1970s. The key problem was a phenomenon called gel-blocking, described as the swelling of two or more superabsorbent particles into a single dam "which prevents or inhibits water or other fluid from passing through the superabsorber 'dam' into the remainder of the absorbent structure."[75] In 1982 Procter & Gamble assembled a research team to propose solutions. Procter & Gamble later claimed that the team, whose senior members reported directly to the company's CEO, discovered a "revolutionary" technique of preventing gel blockage by densifying a superabsorber-fluff mixture, vastly enhancing absorbency. This finding had significant implications for disposable diaper design and marketing. To improve the absorbency of traditional all-wood-pulp-based fillers, diaper makers had simply increased pulp volume, complemented by product marketing that essentially told consumers that "thicker is better." The introduction of denser superabsorber-fluff mixtures enabled manufacturers to increase pad absorbency while decreasing pad thickness. Procter & Gamble recognized that the technique, combined with marketing that stressed the physical attractiveness of thinner diapers, could derail Huggies' swift rise to prominence.[76]

The result was the swift introduction in 1986 of Luvs Deluxe and Ultra Pampers Plus, whose fillers were based on the new technology. Kimberly-Clark immediately followed suit with Huggies Supertrim that featured denser superabsorber-fluff mixtures, as well as an elastic waistband that ensured a better fit of the diaper. The new Huggies were introduced under the slogan, "Elastic Waist and Added Absorbency," developed by Ogilvy & Mather and featured in *Raising Arizona* ("I'll be taking these Huggies and . . . uh . . . whatever cash you got."). Procter & Gamble's attempt to derail the introduction of Huggies Supertrim through a patent infringement suit against Kimberly-Clark ended in a judgment in favor of the defendant. In 1988 Huggies replaced Pampers as the nation's leading diaper brand.[77]

Kimberly-Clark solidified its position with the introduction of Huggies Pull-Ups Training Pants, designed for toddler toilet training. Although the combination of diaper technology and cloth underwear that formed the basis for the Pull-Ups design was far from revolutionary, diaper makers hesitated to develop a marketable product because it threatened to reduce conventional diaper use by up to two months. Kimberly-Clark, however, deriving a crucial lesson from its ill-advised reluctance to introduce Kotex tabless pads swiftly in the early 1970s because the new design threatened to erode demand for tabbed napkins, embarked on a secretive, years-long, $12 million development program in the mid-1980s. Product design involved a series of technical challenges, particularly pant elasticity, required to enable toddlers to remove the training pants unassisted. In 1987 the manager of the Pull-Ups program, Wayne Sanders, an engineer by training, proposed using an innovative synthetic fabric that did the trick. Pull-Ups were rolled out in May 1989 after only a few months of hasty test marketing on the West Coast, partly to prevent competitors from developing a comparable design. The strategy worked admirably, according to industry analyst Bruce Kirk, who surmised, "Procter & Gamble has been totally blindsided by Pull-Ups."[78] Business journalist Fara Warner—unable to resist the rich metaphorical potential of the matter—agreed, claiming "Cincinnati [got] caught with its pants down."[79] Huggies Pull-Ups in fact reigned unchallenged for the next three years, capturing 9 percent of the diaper market and generating more than $200 million in annual sales for Kimberly-Clark. (Sanders, the architect of Kimberly-Clark's Pull-Ups feat, succeeded Smith as CEO in 1991.) Procter & Gamble meanwhile maintained its stunned silence, leaving the task of challenging Huggies Pull-Ups to Drypers Corporation, a joint venture of VMG Enterprises and Veragon Corporation which became the first diaper maker to introduce a comparable product in 1992.[80]

Industry analysts, trying to explain the remarkable success of the Huggies diaper program, pointed out that Kimberly-Clark had learned crucial lessons from Procter & Gamble. Drexel Burnham

Lambert's Hercules Segalas (not necessarily an unbiased observer because he was a former Procter & Gamble executive) claimed, "Kimberly-Clark stole a page right out of Procter's manual of how to succeed: get an excellent product and execute well."[81] *Business Week* and *The Wall Street Journal* concurred, noting that Kimberly-Clark had recruited several former Procter & Gamble marketing managers in the early stages of the Huggies program development. In a slight variation of the same argument, some observers suggested that Procter & Gamble found itself in the midst of a difficult transition period when Kimberly-Clark struck in the early 1980s. In a marked shift from its traditional strategy of developing most of its innovative products in-house, the argument goes, Procter & Gamble sought to strengthen its muscle by acquiring companies like soft-drink maker Crush International, citrus processor Ben Hill Griffin, and Richardson-Vicks, a major producer of cold remedies and skin lotion. Sidetracked by the formidable task of making these acquisitions profitable, Procter & Gamble neglected traditional product lines, creating strategic opportunities for competitors to erode its market shares. This line of reasoning is not without merits, as evidenced by Colgate-Palmolive's successful attempts to loosen Procter & Gamble's grip on toothpaste markets. Kimberly-Clark and private brands meanwhile widened the breach in disposable diaper markets, to a point in the early 1990s when Pathmark, Toys "R" Us, Safeway, and other major retailers stopped selling Luvs altogether, precipitating rumors—unfounded, as it turned out—that Procter & Gamble would fold the label into the Pampers brand. The argument can be carried only so far, however, because Procter & Gamble used its still-formidable marketing and product development capabilities to elbow its way into sanitary napkins and panty liners with the Always rollout, which coincided with its defeats in diapers and toothpaste.[82]

There is little doubt that Kimberly-Clark's consumer products division, instructed by CEO Darwin Smith to knock "the you-know-what out of Cincinnati,"[83] learned much from Procter & Gamble's successes and failures in disposable diapers. The early test market success of the Luvs brand in 1976, for example, hastened Kimberly-Clark's decision to introduce Huggies in regional markets as quickly as possible. Analyses that remain focused on Procter & Gamble ignore important lessons that Kimberly-Clark learned by looking at its own failures, however. These failures included not only the Kimbies debacle—extensively reviewed by the consumer products division and by senior corporate executives—but also the strategic mistake of maintaining Kotex's obsolescent tabbed pad design for four years in the early 1970s. Internal reviews of these and other episodes offered a variety of product-specific explanations for failure, but most attributed Kimberly-Clark's lack of success in standard diapers, sanitary napkins, and tampons to the company's reluctance to vie for market leadership with research- and design-intensive premium products. This helped lay the groundwork for Kimberly-Clark's success in disposable diapers, which became the company's biggest profit maker.

IV.

At first glance Kimberly-Clark's financial performance in the 1970s and 1980s hardly seems particularly noteworthy. Net income as percentage of net sales exclusive of nonrecurring charges more than doubled from 1971 to 1973, reflecting the liquidation of unprofitable coated paper mills (table 5.7), and this figure dropped slightly during the subsequent recession. Profits then climbed above the 7 percent mark in 1976, where they remained until 1981. Once the company had overcome the newsprint crisis of the early 1980s, net income oscillated above the 6 percent mark and started to rise toward the end of the decade. Historically speaking, these trends amounted to something of a replay of the company's sterling financial performance in the 1950s, followed by the slightly lower earnings of the 1960s, except the drop-off toward the end of the latter decade.

Kimberly-Clark's earnings statistics, however, look quite impressive when compared to those of other paper companies. Kimberly-Clark, Scott, and International Paper all reported abysmal earnings of less than 4 percent in 1971, but Scott trailed Kimberly-Clark the next year, followed by IP in 1976. Scott's financial performance became erratic in the late 1970s and 1980, while IP experienced a prolonged drop in the mid-1980s. By the end of the end of the 1980s, earnings divergence had largely disappeared, with all three companies reporting income of more than 7 percent. In short, for almost two decades Kimberly-Clark exhibited a far more stable earnings trend than Scott and IP. Its long-term financial performance was more comparable to that of Johnson & Johnson, whose average earnings from 1971 to 1990 exceeded Kimberly-Clark's by 2 percent but were similarly stable throughout the period.

The earnings statistics only hint at the high drama of American business history in this era, the most tumultuous since the Great

TABLE 5.7

Net income as percentage of net profits (excluding all extraordinary charges and gains), 1971–1990

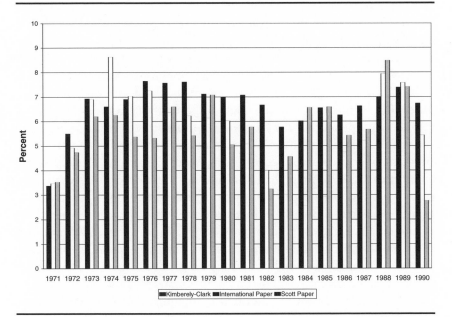

Depression. The bill came due in the 1970s— especially for companies that were in stable-tech industries and mature markets and that had embarked on international expansion, mergers, acquisitions, and product diversification to compensate for declining return on investment in their domestic core businesses. Weakened by insufficient investments into core product lines, many became soft targets for resourceful domestic and foreign competitors, resulting in lower earnings and dividends. Corporate strategies started to diverge at this critical juncture. Some companies began shedding recent acquisitions and mobilized resources for capital investment programs, with the strategic goal of boosting earnings, dividends, and share prices. These moves contributed to the first great wave of divestitures in the early 1970s. In many other cases, however, management was more interested in maintaining old divisional fiefdoms and creating new ones than in raising what later came to be called "shareholder value." Exacerbated by macroeconomic trends—high inflation, high unemployment, slow growth, and the crisis of the Bretton Woods system— managerial inertia contributed to a severe crisis in core sectors of the

U.S. economy. It also precipitated the Wall Street revolt of the late 1970s and early 1980s, when investors and their institutional allies tried to force management to improve profitability, dividends, and stock performance.[84]

Leveraged buyouts (LBOs), pioneered by the merchant bank Kohlberg Kravis Roberts & Company (KKR), created vast corporate debts that compelled companies to shed poorly performing assets and improve the profitability of remaining operations to generate cash flow. Corporate raiders chose the more drastic technique of hostile takeovers of undervalued and poorly performing companies. Based on the assumption that the parts of a company were worth more than the whole, hostile takeovers often resulted in the large-scale dismemberment of corporations, contributing to the second wave of divestitures in the 1980s. Whether LBOs and hostile takeovers succeeded in improving the long-term viability of their target companies remains a matter of debate. But there is little doubt that they contributed to management's growing willingness to "create" shareholder value through divestiture and investments into core businesses, as well as a renewed emphasis on higher earnings and dividends—even without the immediate threat of a hostile takeover or an LBO.[85]

International Paper exemplified companies that delayed restructuring until the 1980s. When its earnings suffered in the 1960s, IP had diversified into disposable diapers, a venture it abandoned in the early 1970s. The company also built up a massive overseas presence in Latin America, Asia, and the Caribbean, where it produced mostly kraft paper for liquid packaging containers and corrugated cartons. In the short run, multinational expansion yielded significant benefits, reflected in IP's impressive earnings gains in the early 1970s. Simultaneously, however, the strategy helped undermine the domestic kraft paper and Canadian newsprint operations, which were hollowed out by insufficient capital investments. Unlike Kimberly-Clark, which abruptly abandoned its prior expansion of coated paper capacity to strengthen its consumer business, IP maintained kraft paper plants and Canadian newsprint mills through much of the 1970s. However, it neglected much-needed capital investments, instead spending $278 million to acquire General Crude Oil Corporation at mid-decade. Billed as an attempt to help the company exploit petroleum resources on IP lands, the transaction did little more than create another management fiefdom while failing to halt the precipitous decline in earnings and dividends. IP's core business meanwhile continued to deteriorate, forcing management to close a flagship plant at Springhill,

TABLE 5.8

IP annual stock closing price adjusted for stock splits, 1971–1990

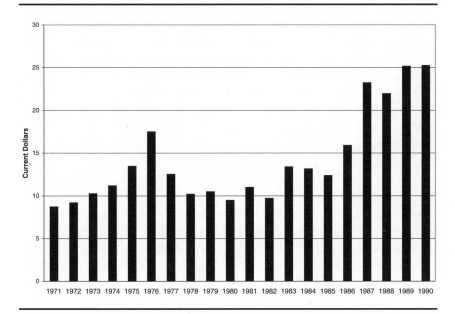

Alabama, and sell a major kraft mill in Panama City, Florida, in the late 1970s. Wall Street, worried about IP's cost and profitability problems, started to shun the share, whose average annual closing price adjusted for stock splits fell by almost one-half from 1976 to 1980 (table 5.8). *Business Week* noted in 1978 that IP was "regarded on the Street as a plodding giant," citing management problems and disappointing financial results, as well as the company's "antiquated paper mill base in the South."[86]

Attempts to turn the tide in the 1980s led to further turmoil. After selling most of IP's interest in General Crude Oil, CEO Edwin Gee liquidated the company's vast newsprint and timberlands empire in Canada for more than $900 million in 1981—a decade after Kimberly-Clark had started to sell off its coated paper mills. The proceeds contributed to a six-year, multibillion-dollar mill reconfiguration program in the southern United States, but the initiative came too late to halt an accelerating decline in net earnings as a result of poor operating profitability at existing mills. Earnings fell continuously from 6 percent in 1980 to less than 3 percent at the height of the Reagan boom. Veteran industry analyst Lawrence Ross warned in 1984, "With operating rates already at a very high level and operating earnings remaining unimpressive, IP has a long way to go to meet analysts' expectations."[87] From 1982 to 1986, when the Dow Jones Industrial Average rose 60 percent, the average annual IP share closing advanced by little more than 30 percent, turning the asset-rich company into a potential takeover target. At mid-decade, management tried to fend off uninvited tenders by putting the most valuable holding, seven million acres of timberland, into a limited partnership and by seeking authority to issue new stock. Shareholders balked at these and other management attempts to establish a poison pill against a hostile takeover, creating turmoil at stockholders' meetings. Management successfully derailed investor revolts, in part by firmly committing itself to boosting the stock price. It followed up almost immediately by allocating a larger share of earnings to dividends. This, combined with the $1.1 billion acquisition of Hammermill Paper in 1986, finally rekindled investor interest in IP stocks, whose price rose by one-third in 1987 alone.[88]

Scott Paper's history reflected other problematic aspects of corporate strategy and structure in the 1970s and 1980s. Long one of the paper industry's marketing and earnings powerhouses that had thrived on consumer nondurables, Scott had acquired the textbook papermaker S. D. Warren in 1967. Not only did the $134 million transaction fail to produce a significant return because the commodity paper market started to stagnate; it also diverted resources from Scott Paper's battle with Procter & Gamble for market leadership in paper towels and toilet paper.

By the 1970s Scott Paper's erstwhile quasi monopoly in these markets had shriveled to 40 percent in paper towels and 30 percent in bathroom tissue. The BabyScotts debacle meanwhile ended with nothing to show for it other than a $6.5 million write-off. Scott's mills, once considered the best equipped in the industry, suffered from neglect because they failed to produce an acceptable return on investment. Adding to company woes, management pushed for diversification into foam products and plastic lawn chairs, even acquiring a furniture company. To strengthen the marketing of its paper product lines, Scott in 1979 filled the position of president and chief operating officer with Morgan Hunter, a former Procter & Gamble executive responsible for Procter & Gamble's success in towels and toilet paper—and responsible for Scott's decline. Initially hailed as "a strong-minded executive and a good marketing man,"[89] Hunter presided over a 30 percent drop in net earnings. He resigned abruptly in 1981, saying, "They [Scott] made a mistake. I made a mistake."[90]

Simultaneously, a decline in share prices attracted Brascan Limited, a Canadian investment company controlled by the Bronfman family, which acquired a 20 percent stake in Scott in 1981. Scrambling to avert an uninvited takeover, Scott CEO Philip Lippincott quickly disposed of the foam division and the furniture business, as well as 240,000 acres of valuable timberlands. Lippincott also committed Scott to rebuilding its dividends and share price by strengthening its paper business with a five-year, $1.6 billion plant improvement program. In contrast to earlier decades, Scott positioned itself for fierce price competition at the low end of the market, abandoning all attempts to enter more design-intensive paper products, such as diapers and feminine care items. Lippincott's strategy served the company well in the mid- to late 1980s, when new volume capacity came on-line and produced healthier earnings and dividends.[91]

The list of undervalued paper and consumer products companies that came under severe pressure from raiders could be extended. In pulp and paper, Sir James Goldsmith "arrive[d] with his ax"[92] at Crown-Zellerbach, St. Regis, and other asset-rich companies notorious for their poor earnings records and stock performances. Goldsmith proceeded to dismember the companies. In 1986, when Paul Bilzerian preyed on Hammermill, it was "rescued" by IP, which in short order closed down several loss-producing Hammermill plants while trying to capitalize on the acquisition's paper marketing expertise. In consumer products, Richardson-Vicks Incorporated faced an uninvited bid from Unilever in 1985, with Procter & Gamble intervening as a "white knight" with a successful $1.25 billion cash offer. In 1989 an investor group led by Kohlberg Kravis Roberts & Company took control of R. J. R. Nabisco in an epic struggle with management and other bidders. While it would be gratuitous to attribute corporate restructuring in the 1980s *per se* to hostile takeovers and LBOs, it is difficult to deny that these transactions—and in many instances the mere threat of a raid—helped trigger divestiture of poorly performing assets and forced companies to develop their core businesses. The question of whether these machinations were successful remains to be answered elsewhere.[93]

Kimberly-Clark's transformation long predated the LBO and raider era. The initiative for restructuring in the 1970s came from top management, not takeover artists, LBO wizards, or shareholders disgruntled about poor earnings and stock performance. The timing of the liquidation of the coated paper business was largely attributable to the earnings crisis of the late 1960s and early 1970s, which

TABLE 5.9

Kimberly-Clark annual stock closing price adjusted for stock splits, 1971–1990

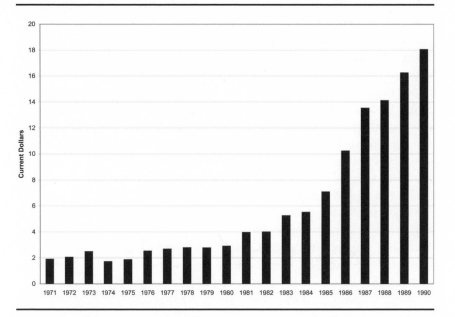

company executives viewed as particularly severe in light of the company's good financial performance in prior years. In retrospect, the recession of the early 1970s was a warning shot that many executives chose to ignore. However, Kimberly-Clark's management, sensitive to its long-term implications, conducted a strategic review that predicted future market trends in coated papers with considerable accuracy, leading it to the decision to sell underperforming assets. Though not quite as drastic as many observers have suggested, the move spared Kimberly-Clark some of the turmoil that IP, Scott, and many other paper companies suffered over the next decade or so.

Equally important, Smith sought to improve Kimberly-Clark's stock performance long before "shareholder value" became a core principle of corporate governance in the 1980s. Determined to "[insulate] dividends against inflation and, consistent with longer range capital needs, [provide] a measure of real growth," he more than doubled quarterly dividends from 1972 to 1978.[94] While investors hardly flocked to the stock through much of the 1970s, Smith's policy contributed to an uneventful stock performance (table 5.9), in contrast to the IP share and similar industrials, whose market value deteriorated over the course of the decade.[95]

The strengthening of consumer nondurables quickly produced the desired results, enabling management to report healthier profits. Major challenges remained, however, especially in feminine care products, where profits came at the expense of product development and advertising. The exception was panty liners, the only major breakthrough in product development and the area that became responsible for the bulk of the feminine care profits at modest outlays. Given the loss of market share in sanitary pads, combined with higher advertising costs for feminine care products, Kimberly-Clark urgently needed a new source of profits.

For a while it seemed that expansion into foreign consumer products markets could fit the bill. Hoping to turn overseas operations into a significant earnings factor, Kimberly-Clark invested $200 million in Europe, Asia, and Latin America. Major additions included a joint venture with an Australian paper company to expand a consumer products mill near Sidney, a similar project in the Philippines, and new converting equipment for Kimberly-Clark Limited of England. By the mid-1970s almost 20 percent of the company's assets were located outside North America, with the bulk in Western Europe and Mexico. Unfortunately for Kimberly-Clark, however, profits from its important British operations not only stagnated over the course of the decade but also suffered from sterling devaluation and the long-term slide of the British pound in international currency markets. Kimberly-Clark de Mexico performed well through much of the 1970s, but it became a financial albatross early in the following decade as a result of peso devaluation which reduced the currency's value by 82 percent in 1981 alone. Combined with the slide of newsprint prices in the same period, the Mexican crisis became the largest drag on overall profits from 1981 to 1983.[96]

Given the inability of multinational expansion to create sources of robust, long-term growth, the success of the Huggies diaper program became critical for the company's overall financial performance. As could be expected, high initial development and advertising costs, required in order to position the product, made it difficult for Kimberly-Clark to derive even marginal profits from the diaper program in the late 1970s. By 1981, however, increased unit sales of Huggies began to yield significant operating profits. Three years later, amidst the fierce battle with Procter & Gamble for market leadership, Smith reported, "The highly favorable performance in diapers . . . more than offset a disappointing year for our feminine care products which declined in unit volume due largely to intense competition."[97] For the remainder of the 1980s, Huggies accounted for the bulk of the company's net earnings.

Wall Street's love affair with Kimberly-Clark stocks—inevitably dubbed "huggable shares"[98]—was largely attributable to the breakthrough in diapers. As early as 1980 Kimberly-Clark was, as *Forbes* magazine speculated, "beginning to draw a following on Wall Street," partly because the product's early success fueled expectations that "there is a chance that Huggies will get as much as 20% of the big disposable-diaper market."[99] Average annual stock closing prices in fact advanced 25 percent from 1980 to 1983, despite investor concerns over Kimberly-Clark's poorly performing newsprint business and despite losses associated with the peso devaluation. When the profit drain subsided in 1983, investors flocked to the stock, whose average annual closing price, adjusted for a two-for-one stock split, doubled over the next three years. The successful introduction of Huggies Supertrim further bolstered the share, which outperformed the leading indexes through much of the decade. Investment analysts were soon gushing with praise. Kimberly-Clark "just knocked the cover off the ball with all [its] products," one opined. "The company conducts a very impressive capital spending program, without wrecking the balance sheet and borrowing very much. This certainly puts [Kimberly-Clark] in a class by itself. . . . Earnings per share growth of the last five years has [*sic*] been in excess of 15 percent, even though net income grew at a considerably smaller rate, and pretax [income] grew only around ten percent." "Kimberly avoided all the pitfalls of the paper industry," noted another. "The CEO's done a tremendous job managing the consumer operation. . . . Kimberly-Clark always delivers. It's one of the few companies that I follow that usually surprises the Street on the upside."[100]

The soaring share price provided a measure of protection against raiders, but Smith took no chances. When takeovers reached a fever pitch, he announced a $300 million share buyback program in January 1987 that brought 6.5 percent of outstanding stocks back into company coffers, immediately boosting share prices by 10 percent. In June 1988, when Revlon CEO Ronald O. Perelman was rumored to contemplate a hostile bid, analysts "scoff[ed] at the idea of Kimberly being taken over."[101] Smith, less certain that a takeover was not in the cards, suggested to his board that Kimberly-Clark should respond by buying paperboard maker Stone Container Corporation for $3 billion to make the company less attractive to Perelman. Rumors that Smith intended to poison the reputed takeover backfired, however, driving down Kimberly-Clark's share price 5 percent in a week because investors worried about the effects of a Stone acquisition on Kimberly-Clark's debt-to-equity ratio. Fortunately for Smith, analysts who had doubted that Perelman seriously considered making a run at Kimberly-Clark were right. Perelman wasn't heard from again, Smith shelved his proposal to buy Stone, and the company's stock recovered. More important, the hostile takeover fever that had gripped businesses and financial markets through much of the decade subsided shortly afterwards because KKR's outlandish $30 billion bid for R. J. R. Nabisco raised doubts about the wisdom of corporate raiding. Kimberly-Clark had weathered one of the most tumultuous episodes in American business history.[102]

Epilogue

PRODUCT DIVERSIFICATION AND CORPORATE STRATEGY

THE HISTORY OF Kimberly-Clark is a chapter in the rise of the large, diversified, multinational corporations that emerged in the first half of the twentieth century when single-product companies branched out into new product lines. Diversification was triggered by a variety of factors. In many instances companies whose extant product lines approached their growth limits diversified to achieve a higher return on investment. Others sought to supplement their existing business with closely related, high-profit product lines that required preexisting organizational capabilities in manufacturing, research, development, and marketing. Changes in public policy also played a significant role. The Clayton Antitrust Act of 1914, for example, limited the corporation's ability to grow through mergers and acquisitions. DuPont, widely regarded as a pioneer of product diversification among single-product firms, became the target of an antitrust investigation in 1916, precipitating attempts to branch out from gunpowder to chemicals and paints during subsequent years. The Celler-Kefauver Act of 1950, which rendered horizontal and vertical integration more difficult, had similar effects, contributing to a new wave of diversification and the formation of conglomerates.

Changes in tariff policy also encouraged companies to diversify, particularly in industries that found it difficult to compete with inexpensive imports. Like the steel, textile, shoemaking, and other com-modities industries of later decades, the newsprint industry of the early twentieth century was vulnerable to foreign competition as a result of high domestic raw material and labor costs. When the Underwood Tariff Act of 1913 opened U.S. markets to Canadian imports, many U.S. firms branched out into non-newsprint products, including book paper, linerboard, and hydroelectric power. Some U.S. producers also responded to the elimination of the newsprint tariff by building up manufacturing operations in Canada, turning International Paper (IP), Crown-Zellerbach, and Kimberly-Clark into budding multinationals. Canadian operations became a basis for expansion into British markets, which—in Kimberly-Clark's case—became a springboard into Western European markets after World War II.[1]

Like many other diversifiers, Kimberly-Clark developed specialized manufacturing, marketing, and research and development capabilities to compete in new markets. After the passage of the Underwood Tariff Act, the firm quickly phased out its U.S. newsprint to concentrate on magazine and specialty paper. To buttress the latter, Kimberly-Clark established one of the first research and development programs in the U.S. pulp and paper industry, which later served as a launching pad for diversification into consumer nondurables. Highlighting the prominent role of research and development during the 1920s, the company's chief research scientist, Ernst Mahler, joined the company's senior management and became a key figure in the development of both Kotex and Kleenex.

Redeploying some of its existing research, development, and manufacturing capabilities, Kimberly-Clark entered the sanitary napkin market after World War I amidst a seismic shift in U.S. manufacturing from industrial to consumer goods. Facilitated by technological innovations, the rise of professional marketing, changing consumer habits, growing disposable income during the 1920s, installment buying, and a variety of other factors, this development transformed the nation's economic and social structures during the interwar period. In some instances, moves into consumer products were the result of carefully formulated strategies, but one should resist the temptation to over-rationalize these strategies *ex post*. Rational choice theories can perhaps explain product diversification in cases like DuPont, General Electric, and Westinghouse, but some of the most successful attempts to develop new product lines were the result of happenstance. Kimberly-Clark decided to develop the Kotex sanitary napkin in September 1919 because Walter Luecke, a sales professional hired only a few months earlier, persistently argued the case for the new product to reluctant company executives. Without the benefit of either consumer surveys to back up his argument or elaborate proposals to connect the product to Kimberly-Clark's extant capabilities, Luecke based his case on a vague guess that the product was technologically and economically viable. More often than not during this era in American business history, successful product diversification was a leap into the unknown that cannot be explained in terms of rational choice.[2]

Corporate strategy became more deliberate once executives recognized the long-term potential of new product lines. The spectacular financial results of the late 1920s, which were largely attributable to Kotex and Kleenex, convinced Kimberly-Clark's management to launch new research programs, invest heavily into new ad campaigns, and expand the firm's manufacturing operations in consumer nondurables. During the 1930s executives also learned from their mistakes, notably the debilitating price war in sanitary napkins, returning to more financially rewarding attempts to compete on the basis of product quality. These strategies, which turned Kimberly-Clark into one of the nation's most profitable pulp and paper companies, distinguished the firm from the industry mainstream, where large firms engaged in destructive price wars for years, largely ignored the strategic potential of consumer nondurables, and neglected investments into research, development, and advertising. Based on the move into consumer products, Kimberly-Clark differentiated itself from its competitors and established the foundation that would carry the company in subsequent years.

These findings confirm revisionist analyses of interwar economic development. Revisionist historians challenge the orthodox view of the Depression as a failure of internally generated accumulation, recovery from which presumably required external stimuli—foreign market expansion and major increases in federal spending, for example. Revisionists, by contrast, distinguish between technologically mature industries like cotton textiles and steel (we would add newsprint to the list), whose markets yielded marginal returns, and dynamic industries specializing in more profitable consumer services, innovative consumer durables, and nondurable consumer items (disposable handkerchiefs, for example).[3] The interwar U.S. economy was beginning to shift from technologically mature to dynamic industries when the former slumped in the late 1920s. A secular downturn turned into economic collapse because firms (like Kimberly-Clark) that were "located in the dynamic sectors of the economy were simply not present in sufficient numbers to lead a general economic recovery."[4]

A new generation of executives who took control of Kimberly-Clark in the 1940s and 1950 developed more conventional corporate strategies than their predecessors. Convinced that the company's successful line of consumer nondurables required little new research and development, they concentrated on plant networking, industrial products, acquisitions-based product diversification, and multinational expansion. This reflected a widespread trend during the postwar era, when executives in the textile, steel, agricultural machinery, and rubber industries focused primarily on managing growth instead of improving core product lines.

In Kimberly-Clark's case, postwar corporate growth strategies often produced unsatisfactory results. Plant networking, far from producing anticipated efficiency gains, often resulted in higher costs. Heavy investments into industrial products, especially newsprint and magazine paper, failed to generate returns in the 1960s and had to be abandoned in the early1970s. While some acquisitions, notably Schweitzer, produced healthy financial returns, Munising Paper, Blake, Moffitt & Towne, and others were outright failures. Multinational expansion created profitable business in Britain, France, and Mexico but failed to compensate for the increasingly problematic performance of domestic operations. By the end of the 1960s disappointing financial results raised doubts about the long-term viability of conventional growth management.[5]

Slackening investments into core organizational capabilities meanwhile undermined Kimberly-Clark's competitive advantage in consumer nondurables. Inadequate market research capabilities had been an Achilles' heel since the Fibs tampon debacle of the 1930s, when Kimberly-Clark and Lord & Thomas—unwilling or unable to question the company's commitment to sanitary napkins—used flawed market research techniques to determine consumer preferences. Although statistical methods improved in the postwar era, company researchers repeatedly misinterpreted their data. Research and development in sanitary napkins and disposable handkerchiefs meanwhile suffered neglect, enabling more resourceful competitors to make deep inroads into markets that had traditionally been dominated by Kimberly-Clark. This reflected a widespread problem of corporate strategy in the 1960s and 1970s, when leading firms in what Alfred Chandler has categorized as "stable-tech" industries focused on mergers and acquisitions, while neglecting or misallocating investments into organizational capabilities. In the consumer electronics industry, for example, this created strategic opportunities for foreign competitors that eroded the market dominance of U.S. firms with incremental product improvement, better quality, and superior marketing. As Carliss Baldwin and Kim Clark have shown, formal capital budgeting often failed to address the problem of inadequate or misdirected investments. "In many U.S. companies," they argue, "internal systems for profit planning and capital budgeting tended to work against attempts to invest in the organizational capabilities needed for long-term survival. To middle managers proposing such investments, it often appeared that top managers (and the capital markets they claimed to represent) were over-focused on short-term financial results."[6]

Kimberly-Clark's dramatic turnaround was largely the result of the strategic repositioning initiatives implemented in the early 1970s. Keenly aware of the company's structural deficiencies in R&D and market research, Darwin Smith and his team of young executives and middle managers embarked upon a strategic review of past product development and investment initiatives, sometimes reaching back as far as the 1930s to determine what had worked and what had not. Prodded by Smith, product managers conducted detailed reviews of product testing, statistical data, marketing campaigns, and corporate financial data from the 1950s and 1960s. Remarkable for their sheer scope and historical depth, these reviews precipitated the liquidation of most of Kimberly-Clark's magazine paper business and ancillary industrial products, a large-scale reorganization of research and development capabilities, plant reconfigurations, and major departures in marketing and advertising.

Smith's reorganization program, though controversial both within the company and among industry analysts at the time, laid the groundwork for the company's subsequent success in diapers. Deploying product development and marketing strategies that had turned Kotex into a success during the interwar period, Kimberly-Clark positioned Huggies as a design-intensive, premium-priced product that set quality benchmarks for the entire industry.

Smith's strategic repositioning program, precipitated by the severe crisis that befell the company in the late 1960s, turned Kimberly-Clark into one of the most innovative and profitable consumer products companies of the 1970s and 1980s. Longtime competitors—notably International Paper, Johnson & Johnson, and Procter & Gamble—pursued less aggressive departures from past corporate strategies, partly because they survived the 1960s in better financial shape than Kimberly-Clark, rendering repositioning less urgent. Only the prolonged economic crisis of the 1970s and early 1980s convinced executives of the necessity to scale back product diversification, develop new organizational capabilities for their respective core businesses, and launch research and development initiatives along the lines of Smith's "new departure." In more ways than one, the latter foreshadowed the transformation of "stable-tech" industries at the end of the twentieth century.

The 1990s brought a series of new challenges that precipitated a shift in corporate strategy under Wayne Sanders, who succeeded Smith in 1992. Huggies sales grew at a more leisurely pace than in the previous decade, partly because secondary diaper labels started to make inroads against Kimberly-Clark and Procter & Gamble in U.S. markets. Sanders responded by looking for growth opportunities overseas, particularly in Europe, where economic integration reached a new level with the 1992 Common Market reforms which further reduced tariff barriers. Although Kimberly-Clark's Western European presence dated to the postwar era, it lagged far behind that of Procter & Gamble, Scott Paper, and James River Corporation, which dominated the diaper and toilet paper markets. Sanders admitted as much at the beginning of his tenure, stating, "[W]e're playing catch-up in Europe. We've got a big building job to do."[7] The same could be said for Southeast Asia, where Kimberly-Clark had maintained a budding presence since the postwar era with marketing and production operations in Australia, the Philippines, Japan, and Korea that were dwarfed by Scott's and Procter & Gamble's formidable presence in the region.[8]

Sanders, building on initiatives launched during the final years of the Smith administration, pursued two distinct strategies for overseas expansion. First, Kimberly-Clark developed existing capabilities in research, production, and marketing by expanding its established European and Southeast Asian operations. From 1988 to 1991 the company invested $500 million in Western Europe alone. In Germany it teamed up with tissue manufacturer VP-Schickedanz AG to market diapers. In the early 1990s Kimberly-Clark brought a £100 million diaper plant onstream at Barton-upon-Humber, in addition to a consumer products plant in Korea, a tissue mill in Thailand, and a pulp mill in Australia. Predictably, Sanders's spending spree was not well received by competitors. One executive exclaimed, "I'm appalled at the arrogance of Kimberly-Clark, thinking they can come in and put a plant up in the face of all the competition."[9] Expanding the firm's overseas presence indeed proved tougher than anticipated, partly because Kimberly-Clark lacked sufficient country-specific marketing expertise and distribution networks. As a result, Sanders started to eye another option: buying his way into the market through the acquisition of a competitor with extensive experience in European and Asian markets. After contemplating several possible targets, Sanders zoomed in on an old rival. In 1995 Kimberly-Clark acquired Scott Paper for $9.4 billion.

The transaction came none too soon for Scott, which had for years flirted with disaster. CEO Philip Lippincott had initiated a turn-around in the 1980s that was partly based on Scott's strong position in European and Asian markets. Simultaneously, however, he neglected to liquidate the S. D. Warren printing paper business that had been a source of trouble since its acquisition in 1967. At the end of the 1980s S. D. Warren's losses were once again responsible for a down-turn in overall net earnings. A food-service container business acquired at the beginning of the decade also performed poorly, drain-ing profits from the paper towel business which continued to enjoy high operating profitability. Scott continued to slide, reporting a $70 million net loss in 1991 alone. The following year Lippincott finally liquidated the food-service container division but was unable to sell S. D. Warren for lack of a buyer. Sales in 1993 fell 7 percent to $4.7 billion as a result of unfavorable European foreign exchange rates, contributing to a $277 million net loss. The company's restructuring charge (severance packages, shutting down plants, and other costs associated with laying employees off) was $381 million in 1993 after Scott cut 25 percent of its workforce. In 1994 Lippincott was suc-ceeded as CEO by Albert J. Dunlap. True to his nickname "Chainsaw Al," Dunlap immediately cut what he called Scott's "bloated corpo-rate structure," reducing the research and development budget by half, slashing expenses, selling assets, and paring debt. Along the way, Dunlap eliminated more than 11,200 total jobs equaling 35 percent of the Scott payroll. He then sold off S. D. Warren; a Mobile, Alaba-ma, power plant; and the company's corporate headquarters in Philadelphia. Dunlap also began looking for a buyer for the compa-ny. By December 1994 Salomon Brothers had already identified twen-ty-four potential buyers, including Kimberly-Clark.

As a result of the merger, Kimberly-Clark had to undergo a diffi-cult restructuring program in the mid-1990s, including 11,000 layoffs and market share losses among Scott products. Scott had oversold both its manufacturing capabilities and its new product pipeline. Kimberly-Clark found that it had to invest much more time and energy into these areas than anticipated. The long-term efficiencies existed—it would just take longer to get the two companies up to speed, Sanders argued.[10] As a matter of fact, Kimberly-Clark's own lack of expertise in engineering large mergers contributed to the stumble. Throughout its history Kimberly-Clark's leaders chose to grow from within and never aggressively pursued an initiative of buying into market leadership. Unfortunately, the merger also coincided with sharp price drops for consumer goods in the United States and Europe, which affected the overall financial picture. On the positive side, however, Kimberly-Clark used the next several years to improve internal efficiencies and reinvest cash flow from those efforts back into branding campaigns. By late 1999 Kimberly-Clark introduced product improvements to its Scott tissue products and began running the first Scott bath tissue and paper towel TV spots in more than a decade.

While the rest of the world warped through dot-com fever in 2000, the Scott merger began paying off for Kimberly-Clark. The company posted all-time records in sales (nearly $14 billion) and earnings per share ($3.31) for the year. Despite rising raw material and energy costs and declining currencies, revenue grew 7.5 percent, besting all of Kimberly-Clark's competitors in the consumer products industry.

Notes

Notes to Introduction

1. L. Ethan Ellis, *Print Paper Pendulum: Group Pressures and the Price of Newsprint* (New Brunswick, N.J.: Rutgers University Press, 1948); Michael McQuillen and William Garvey, *The Best Known Name in Paper: Hammermill—A History of the Company* (Erie, Pa.: Hammermill Paper Company, 1985); Judith McGaw, *Most Wonderful Machine: Mechanization and Social Change in Berkshire Paper Making, 1801–1885* (Princeton: Princeton University Press, 1987); Norman B. Wilkinson, *Papermaking in America* (Greenville, Del.: Hagley Museum, 1975); David C. Smith, *History of Papermaking in the United States (1691–1969)* (New York: Lockwood, 1970); Avi Cohen, "Technological Change as Historical Process: The Case of the U.S. Pulp and Paper Industry, 1915–1940," *Journal of Economic History* 44 (Autumn 1984): 775–99; Thomas Heinrich, "Product Diversification in the U.S. Pulp and Paper Industry: The Case of International Paper," *Business History Review* 75 (forthcoming, 2004).

2. Eric Taub, *Taurus: The Making of the Car That Saved Ford* (New York: Dutton, 1991).

3. Constantinos C. Markides, *Diversification, Refocusing, and Economic Performance* (Cambridge: MIT Press, 1995); Richard P. Rumelt, *Strategy, Structure, and Economic Performance* (Boston: Harvard Business School Press, 1986); Charles R. Spruill, *Conglomerates and the Evolution of Capitalism* (Carbondale: Southern Illinois University Press, 1982).

4. Alfred D. Chandler, Jr., "The Competitive Performance of U.S. Industrial Enterprise since the Second World War," *Business History Review* 68 (1994), 47–73.

Notes to Chapter 1

1. *Paper Trade Journal*, 12 Dec. 1901 (hereafter cited as *PTJ*); *National Cyclopædia of American Biography*, Vol. 37 (New York: J. T. White Company,

1951), 404; *National Cyclopædia of American Biography, Vol. 52* (New York: J. T. White Company, 1970), 88; *National Cyclopædia of American Biography, Vol. 40* (New York: J. T. White Company, 1955), 108.

2. For an overview of nineteenth-century papermaking and the Pagenstecher episode, see Judith McGaw, *Most Wonderful Machine: Mechanization and Social Change in Berkshire Paper Making, 1801–1885* (Princeton: Princeton University Press, 1987).

3. R. G. Dun & Co., N.Y., vol. 120, 862, R. G. Dun & Co. Collection, Baker Library, Harvard Business School; David C. Smith, *History of Papermaking in the United States (1691–1969)* (New York: Lockwood, 1970); Avi Cohen, "Technological Change as Historical Process: The Case of the U.S. Pulp and Paper Industry, 1915–1940," *Journal of Economic History* 44 (Autumn 1984): 775–99.

4. Hugh Chisholm, *A Man and the Paper Industry: Hugh J. Chisholm (1847–1912)* (New York: Newcomen Society, 1952), 14; R. G. Dun & Co., N.Y., vol. 120, 862, R. G. Dun & Co. Collection, Baker Library, Harvard Business School; *International Paper Monthly* (Dec. 1926), 19; Frank Sensenbrenner, "Kimberly-Clark Corporate History" (1946), 18, RG 8, Subgroup 3, Series 2, Box 8–73, Folder 26, Kimberly-Clark Archives, The History Factory, Chantilly, Va.

5. On the controversies over wood, iron, and steel shipbuilding, see William Thiesen, "From Practical to Theoretical Shipbuilding: The Rationalization of an American Craft," Ph.D. dissertation, University of Delaware, 2000. On the respective advantages of rag- and wood-based pulp, see McGaw, *Most Wonderful Machine*. On the "Völter Combine," see *PTJ*. See also Smith, *History of Papermaking*.

6. On newsprint prices, see Smith, *History of Papermaking*, 139.

7. Sensenbrenner, "Kimberly-Clark Corporate History," 13.

8. Charles N. Glaab and Lawrence H. Larsen, *Factories in the Valley: Neenah-Menasha, 1870–1915* (Madison: State Historical Society of Wisconsin, 1969).

9. Sensenbrenner, "Kimberly-Clark Corporate History," 9–10A; Glaab and Larsen, *Factories in the Valley*.

10. "Meeting of the Stockholders [of Kimberly & Clark], 21 Aug. 1882," and "Meeting of the Stockholders, 8 Jan. 1883," both in: Kimberly & Clark Co., Records 1880–1906, RG 6, Box 1, Folder 1; *Kimberly-Clark Company: 50th Anniversary 1872–1922* (Neenah, Wis.: Kimberly-Clark Company, 1922), 6; McGaw, *Most Wonderful Machine; PTJ*, 24 Sept. 1894.

11. Glaab and Larsen, *Factories in the Valley;* McGaw, *Most Wonderful Machine*.

12. *Neenah Gazette*, 16 Jan. 1875.

13. Kimberly-Clark Company, *50th Anniversary 1872–1922*, 6.

14. Sensenbrenner, "Kimberly-Clark Corporate History"; McGaw, *Most Wonderful Machine*.

15. Hooper represented Kimberly & Clark and its successor organizations in dozens of lawsuits, including numerous cases involving disputes over Fox River water rights, for example, *Kimberly & Clark Company, Respondent, v. Hewitt and Others*, 79 Wis. 334; *Appleton Paper & Pulp Co. v. Kimberly &Clark Co.*, 79 Wis. 334; personal injury suits filed by employees, for example, *Glenesky, Respondent, v. Kimberly & Clark Company*, 140 Wis. 52;

16. Sensenbrenner, "Kimberly-Clark Corporate History," 18; Cohen, "Technological Change as Historical Process," 775–99.

17. Quoted in Sensenbrenner, "Kimberly-Clark Corporate History," 14–15.

18. Quoted in *Four Men and a Machine: Commemorating the Seventy-Fifth Anniversary of Kimberly-Clark Corporation,* 3rd Ed. (Neenah, Wis.: Kimberly-Clark Corporation, 1955), 9–10.

19. "Atlas Mill," *Cooperation,* September 1947, 46; *Four Men and a Machine: Commemorating the Seventy-Fifth Anniversary of Kimberly-Clark Corporation,* 3rd Ed. (Neenah, Wis.: Kimberly-Clark Corporation, 1955), 9–10.

20. "Articles of Association and Incorporation of the Kimberly Clark and Co., of Neenah, Wis., 18 Dec. 1880," Kimberly & Clark Co., Records 1880–1906, RG 6, Box 1, Folder 1; Sensenbrenner, "Kimberly-Clark Corporate History," 16–17.

21. Sensenbrenner, "Kimberly-Clark Corporate History," 17; "Atlas Mill," *Cooperation,* September 1947, 46.

22. "Meeting of the Stockholders, 8 April 1884," Kimberly & Clark Co., Records 1880–1906, RG 6, Box 1, Folder 1; Sensenbrenner, "Kimberly-Clark Corporate History," 19; "Badger-Globe," *Cooperation,* September 1947, 41.

23. Sensenbrenner, "Kimberly-Clark Corporate History," 19.

24. "Meeting of the Stockholders, 8 Aug. 1889," Kimberly & Clark Co., Records 1880–1906, RG 6, Box 1, Folder 1; Sensenbrenner, "Kimberly-Clark Corporate History," 19.

25. *PTJ,* 8 July 1893, 15 July 1893, 22 July 1893; Smith, *History of Papermaking; McGaw, Most Wonderful Machine.*

26. Sensenbrenner, "Kimberly-Clark Corporate History," 21; "Atlas Mill," *Cooperation,* September 1947, 46.

27. Sensenbrenner, "Kimberly-Clark Corporate History," 21–22; "Kimberly Mill," *Cooperation,* September 1947, 52–53.

28. "Meeting of the Stockholders, 8 April 1891," Kimberly & Clark Co., Records 1880–1906, RG 6, Box 1, Folder 1; Sensenbrenner, "Kimberly-Clark Corporate History," 22–23.

29. "Meeting of the Stockholders, 5 Jan. 1881," Kimberly & Clark Co., Records 1880–1906, RG 6, Box 1, Folder 1.

30. "Meeting of the Directors, 27 Dec. 1888," Kimberly & Clark Co., Records 1880–1906, RG 6, Box 1, Folder 1.

31. *PTJ,* 4 Feb. 1893; Sensenbrenner, "Kimberly-Clark Corporate History," 24–25.

32. "Meeting of the Stockholders, 9 Jan. 1894," Kimberly & Clark Co., Records 1880–1906, RG 6, Box 1, Folder 1; *PTJ,* 30 Sept. 1893, 6 Jan. 1894; see also *PTJ,* 19 Aug. 1893.

33. "Meeting of the Stockholders, 13 Jan. 1896," Kimberly & Clark Co., Records 1880–1906, RG 6, Box 1, Folder 1; *PTJ,* 7 July 1894, 5 Jan. 1895, 4 Jan. 1896, 9 Jan. 1897, 30 April 1898, 13 Aug. 1898.

34. "Meeting of the Directors, 8 Nov. 1913," Kimberly & Clark Co. Minute Book, 1907–1921, RG 6, Box 1, Folder 2; Sensenbrenner, "Kimberly-Clark Corporate History," 25B–26B.

35. Ibid., 27, RG 8, Subgroup 3, Series 2, Box 8–73, Folder 26; "Kimberly," *Cooperation,* Sept. 1947, 53.

36. "Meeting of the Directors, 14 May 1904," Kimberly & Clark Co., Records 1880–1906, RG 6, Box 1, Folder 1; "Meeting of the Directors, 8 Nov. 1913," Kimberly & Clark Co. Minute Book, 1907–1921, RG 6, Box 1, Folder 2.

37. "Meeting of the Stockholders, 2 Jan. 1906," Kimberly & Clark Co., Records 1880–1906, RG 6, Box 1, Folder 1; "Meeting of the Stockholders, 2 Jan. 1907," Kimberly & Clark Co. Minute Book, 1907–1921, RG 6, Box 1, Folder 2; "Articles of Association, 2 Jan. 1907," Kimberly & Clark Co. Minute Book, 1907–1921, RG 6, Box 1, Folder 2; *The New York Times,* 23 July 1952.

38. Sensenbrenner, "Kimberly-Clark Corporate History," 40–46

39. "Development of the Technical Department," *Cooperation,* Sept. 1947, 37.

40. Calvin Tomkins, *Printing Paper Trust* (Boston: New England Free Trade League, 1899); John Norris, *The Paper Trust: A Typical Tariff Trust* (Boston: New England Free Trade League, 1901). For a protariff position, see Thomas Marvin, *Protection for Paper Industry, a Great Business Threatened by Free Importations: Reasonable Protection Should Be Granted: Abstract of Brief Filed at Hearing on Schedule M* (Boston: Home Market Club, 1912). For William Howard Taft's position, see *Pulp and News-Print Paper Industry: Message from the President of the United States Transmitting a Report by the Tariff Board Relative to Pulp and News-print Paper Industry* (Washington, D.C.: U.S. Government Printing Office, 1911).

41. Thomas Heinrich, "Product Diversification in the U.S. Pulp and Paper Industry: The Case of International Paper," *Business History Review* 75 (2001), 470–76.

42. "Meeting of the Directors, 1 Aug. 1906," Kimberly & Clark Co., Records 1880–1906, RG 6, Box 1, Folder 1; 60th Congress, House Select Committee on Pulp and Paper, "Pulp and Paper Hearings, vol. 3," 1869, House Documents Vol. 143, No. 1502.

43. "Annual Stockholders' Meeting, 11 Dec. 1912," Kimberly & Clark Co. Minute Book, 1907–1921, RG 6, Box 1, Folder 260th Congress, House Select Committee on Pulp and Paper, "Pulp and Paper Hearings, vol. 3," 1876–77, House Documents Vol. 143, No. 1502; Sensenbrenner, "Kimberly-Clark Corporate History," 46–47; "Woodlands," *Cooperation,* Sept. 1947, 36.

44. G. F. Steele, *Brief for Wisconsin Congressional Delegation, April 5, 1909* (Washington, D.C.: U.S. Government Printing Office, 1909), 1.

45. Ibid.

46. Michael J. McQuillen and William P. Garvey, *The Best Known Name in Paper: Hammermill: A History of the Company.* Erie, Pa.: Hammermill Paper Co., 1985.

47. Kimberly-Clark, "Summary of Proof Required for Hearing before the Federal Trade Commission with Relation to the Use of the Word 'Cellucotton,'" 1–3, RG 9, Subgroup 1, Series 3 Box 9–4, Folder 3.

48. H. M. Cartwright and Robert MacKay, *Rotogravure: A Survey of European and American Methods.* Lyndon, Ky.: MacKay, 1956.

49. "[Minutes of the] Fourth Annual Meeting [of Paper Merchants] of the Kimberly-Clark Company, Drake Hotel, Chicago, Illlinois, Tuesday, June 28, 1921," RG 5, Series 1, Box 5–1, Folder 1.

Notes to Chapter 2

1. *Advertising Age,* 17 June 1974, 106.

2. Ibid. On Lasker's background and early career, see John Morello, "Candi-

dates, Consumers, and Closers: Albert Lasker, Advertising, and Politics," Ph.D. Dissertation, University of Illinois, Chicago, 1998. On Bok and the *Ladies' Home Journal*, see Martha Feldmann, "Never Underestimate Empowerment Consumption: Women and Advertising in the *Ladies' Home Journal* from the 1880's through the 1920's," Ph.D. Dissertation, Memphis State University, 1991, and Bonnie Fox, "Selling the Mechanized Household: 70 Years of Ads in *Ladies' Home Journal*," *Gender and Society* 4 (1990), 25–40. For an insightful analysis of another controversial "first" in consumer advertising, see Herb Kaplan and Rick Houlberg, "Broadcast Condom Advertising: A Case Study," *Journalism Quarterly* 67 (1990), 171–76.

3. Janice Delaney, Mary Lupton, Emily Toth, *The Curse: A Cultural History of Menstruation,* 2nd Ed. (Urbana: University of Illinois Press, 1986), 129–30.

4. See, for example, Stephen Fox, *Mirror Makers: A History of American Advertising and Its Creators* (New York: Morrow, 1985). For a more critical view of marketing professionals, see Pamela Laird, "The Business of Progress: The Transformation of American Advertising," *Business and Economic History* 22 (1993), 13–18. For a useful review of studies in advertising history, see John Staudenmaier and Pamela Laird, "Advertising History," *Technology and Culture* 30 (1989), 1031–36.

5. On bleak market business conditions after the passage of the Underwood Tariff, see "Guy Walo to F. Sensenbrenner, March 8, 1915, Sensenbrenner to Waldo, March 10, 1915," both in RG 13, Series 8, Box 13–19, Folder 12, Kimberly-Clark Archives, The History Factory, Chantilly, Va. On IP, see Thomas Heinrich, "Product Diversification in the U.S. Pulp and Paper Industry: The Case of International Paper," *Business History Review* 75 (2001).

6. For an insightful analysis of the boll weevil's macroeconomic impact, see Kent Osband, "The Boll Weevil vs. King Cotton," *Journal of Economic History* 45 (1985), 627–43; William W. Tomlinson, *The Long Road of Scott Paper Company* (Philadelphia: Scott Paper Company, 1939), 46.

7. "Minutes of the Board of Directors Meeting [of Kimberly-Clark], 10 Oct. 1914" and "Minutes of the Board of Directors Meeting, Nov. 10, 1914," both in RG 6, Series 5, Subgroup 1, Box 6–1, Folder 2; Kimberly-Clark, "Summary of Proof Required for Hearing before the Federal Trade Commission with Relation to the Use of the Word 'Cellucotton,'" 1–2, RG 9, Subgroup 1, Series 3, Box 9–4, Folder 3.

8. Ibid.

9. Ibid., 4; "Annual Directors' Meeting, 22 Dec. 1914," Kimberly & Clark Co. Minute Book, 1907–1921, RG 6, Box 1, Folder 2.

10. Kimberly-Clark, "Summary of Proof," 5; "The Birth of Crepe Wadding," *Cooperation* (1934, Third Quarter), 13.

11. Kimberly-Clark, "Summary of Proof," 3–4; "The Birth of Crepe Wadding," 13.

12. Kimberly-Clark, "Summary of Proof," 4–5; "The Birth of Crepe Wadding," 13; "Minutes of the Board of Directors Meeting [of Kimberly-Clark], May 14, 1918," RG 6, Series 5, Subgroup 1, Box 6–1, Folder 2.

13. Kimberly-Clark, "Summary of Proof," 6–8; "The Birth of Crepe Wadding," 13; "Minutes of the Board of Directors' Meeting, 12 Aug. 1919," RG 6, Series 5, Subgroup 1, Box 6–1, Folder 2.

14. "Minutes of the Board of Directors' Meeting, 14 Oct. 1919," RG 6, Series 5, Subgroup 1, Box 6–1, Folder 2; "[Minutes of the] Fourth Annual Meeting [of Paper Merchants of the] Kimberly Clark Company, Drake Hotel, Chicago, Illinois, Tuesday, June 28, 1921," 14, RG 5, Series 1, Box 5–1, Folder 1.

15. "Proposed Plan of a Pension System for Kimberly-Clark Co., 14 Sept. 1910," RG 6, Series 5, Subgroup 1, Box 6–1, Folder 2; Kimberly-Clark experienced strikes at the Niagara mill during the war, which were settled through wage increases; "Minutes of the Board of Directors Meeting [of Kimberly-Clark], 13 July 1917," RG 6, Series 5, Subgroup 1, Box 6–1, Folder 2. On welfare capitalism at Sears, Roebuck, and Eastman Kodak, see Sanford Jacoby, *Modern Manors: Welfare Capitalism Since the New Deal* (Princeton: Princeton University Press, 1997).

16. "[Minutes of the] Fourth Annual Meeting [of Paper Merchants of the] Kimberly Clark Company, Drake Hotel, Chicago, Illinois, Tuesday, 28 June 1921," 14.

17. "Niagara Falls," *Cooperation*, September 1947, 72–73.

18. In 1914 the board of directors considered selling the obsolete mill for $45,000 but was unable to find a buyer; "Minutes of the Board of Directors Meeting [of Kimberly-Clark], 25 July 1914," RG 6, Series 5, Subgroup 1, Box 6–1, Folder 2. On the Atlas mill reconfiguration program, see "Brains and Wall Paper Rejuvenate the Atlas," *Cooperation* (1933, Second Quarter), 3–5; "The Art of Making Wall Paper," *Cooperation* (1935, First Quarter), 27–28. On technical details of "oatmeal" finishing, see *Harmon Paper Co. v. Kimberly Clark Co.* 289 F. 501; 1922 U.S. Dist., 1–3; see also "Minutes of the Board of Directors Meting [of Kimberly-Clark Co.], 12 July 1927," RG 6, Subgroup 1, Series 1, Box 6–1, Folder 4. On wallpaper, see Lesley Hoskins, Ed., *The Papered Wall: History, Patterns, Technique* (New York: H. N. Abrams, 1994).

19. Walter W. Luecke, "History of Kotex," Subject File 200.2, "Corporate Histories."

20. Ibid.

21. Cellucotton surgical dressings remained a minor product through much of the interwar period. Sales were handled by the Lewis Manufacturing Company of Walpole, Mass., a cotton products jobber; "Agreement between Kimberly-Clark and Lewis Manufacturing Company, July 26, 1919," RG 4, Series 1, Box 4–1, Folder 5.

22. Luecke, "Kotex," 2.

23. Luecke, "Kotex," 3.

24. F. B. Carpenter to Kimberly-Clark, Oct. 9, 1919, RG 9, Subgroup 1, Series 6, Box 9–19, Folder 19.

25. Kimberly-Clark to Walker, Oct. 16, 1919, RG 9, Subgroup 3, Series 7, Box 9–357, Folder 1.

26. Luecke, "Kotex," 3.

27. Jane Farrell-Beck and Laura Kidd, "The Roles of Health Professionals in the Development and Dissemination of Women's Sanitary Products, 1880–1940," *Journal of the History of Medicine and Allied Sciences* 51 (1996), 325–52.

28. Luecke, "Kotex," 3.

29. "Minutes of the Board of Directors Meeting [of Kimberly-Clark], Nov. 16, 1920," RG 6, Series 5, Subgroup 1, Box 6–1, Folder 2. To avoid confusion, this chapter refers to the company by its initial acronym, CPC, even for the post-1927 period, when it was known as International Cellucotton Products Company.

30. Meyer to Luecke, August 18, 1920, RG 9, Subgroup 1, Series 6, Box 9–12, Folder 19.

31. *Kotex Co. v. Clarence McArthur, No. 2527,* 18 C.C.P.A. 787; 45 F.2d 256.

32. [Luecke] to Sensenbrenner, April 24, 1920, RG 9, Subgroup 3, Series 7, Box 9–357, Folder 1.

33. *Dry Goods Economist,* 20 November 1920.

34. Taylor to Luecke, Nov. 11, 1920, RG 15, Subgroup 1, Series 15, Box 15–18, Folder 20.

35. Taylor to Luecke, Dec. 3, 1920, RG 15, Subgroup 1, Series 15, Box 15–18, Folder 20. On 1921 Kotex sales, see "Kotex Sales—Week Ending June 25, 1921" and "Hotel Vending, Philadelphia June 20, 1921," RG 15, Series 1, Subgroup 15, Box 15–19, Folder 29.

36. Taylor to Luecke, Feb. 19, 1921, RG 15, Subgroup 1, Series 15, Box 15–18, Folder 20.

37. Charles F. W. Nichols Co., "To Save Men's Lives Science Discovered Kotex," 21 Aug. 1919, RG 9, Series 2, Box 1, Folder 179.

38. Ibid.

39. Ibid.

40. Ibid.

41. Although Meyer is generally credited with writing the first Kotex ads, it should be noted that one advertising professional later claimed that the first copy was actually written by an unnamed woman. John Heady, an advertising manager for Tupper Corporation and self-proclaimed "scarred, gray and grim veteran of this profession," wrote in 1949: "When Kotex was launched, it was considered necessary that a very delicate approach be made; indeed it was wondered whether ethical publications would even accept the copy. So, a woman was employed to write the copy—an ex–registered nurse. Perhaps she had no flair for writing. In any event the advertising and merchandising and sales flopped until a man was put on the account; I do not recall who he was, but Kotex went over"; *Advertising Age,* 28 February 1949. Heady's account, part of a misogynist diatribe, cannot be corroborated.

42. Nichols Co., "To Save Men's Lives Science Discovered Kotex."

43. Ibid.

44. In discussions of the Kotex symbol, Kimberly-Clark and ICP routinely referred to St. George's cross as the "Geneva cross," indicating its relationship to the International Red Cross symbol adopted at the organization's founding convention in Switzerland. This contradicts the notion proposed in some studies that the marketers intended to evoke Christian symbolism.

45. The depiction of women holding reading materials in product advertisements was one of the many conceptual innovations introduced in interwar advertising; see Megan Benton's insightful "Sizzle and Smoke: Iconography of Books and Reading in Modern American Advertising," *Publishing History* 38 (1995), 77–90.

46. "Cellucotton Products: Corporate Records, 1920–1931," Record Group 15, Series (number unknown), Box 15–12, Folder 1, KCA.

47. "Story of ICP," *Cooperation,* September 1947, 27.

48. "Minutes of the Special Meeting of the Board of Directors of the Cellucotton Products Co, November (date unknown), 1922, RG 15, Subgroup 1, Series 9, Box 15–12, Folder 1.

49. Quoted in Kimberly-Clark to H. A. Jost, April 29, 1921, RG 15, Subgroup 1, Series 15, Box 15–18, Folder 20.

50. Ibid.

51. "Every Woman Wants Kotex," Trade Advertisement, 1924, RG 9, Series 2, Box 5, Folder 2 (oversize).

52. "Kotex Trade Advertisement," 27 July 1926," RG 9, Subgroup 2, Series 5, Folder 3 (oversize); Mike Freeman, "Clarence Saunders: The Piggly Wiggly Man," *Tennessee Historical Quarterly* 51 (1992), 161–69.

53. *Advertising Age*, 15 December 1952, 63.

54. Meyer Papers, 21 September 1960.

55. *International Cellucotton Products Co. v. Sterilek Co., Inc.*, 94 F.2d 10; 1938 U.S. App.

56. "Minutes of the Board of Directors Meeting [of Kimberly-Clark], 21 July 1921," and "Minutes of the Board of Directors Meeting [of Kimberly-Clark], 23 June 1924," both RG 6, Series 5, Subgroup 1, Box 6–1, Folder 3; "Minutes of the Board of Directors Meeting [of Kimberly-Clark], 14 Aug. 1923," "Minutes of the Board of Directors Meeting [of Kimberly-Clark], 5 Nov. 1923," "Minutes of the Board of Directors [of Kimberly-Clark Co.], Meeting, 22 Nov. 1927," RG 6, Subgroup 1, Series 1, Box 6–1, Folder 4; "First Kotex Machine Celebrates 10th Birthday," *Cooperation* (1934, Fourth Quarter), 16.

57. George Weiss to Kimberly-Clark, 9 July 1920; Cyrill Soanes to Luecke, 24 Sept. 1923, both in RG 4, Series 1, Box 4–1, Folder 6; see also "Exclusive Sales Agreement," RG 4, Series 1, Box 4–1, Folder 11.

58. *Cellucotton Products Co. v. Wilson,* cited in United States Tariff Commission, "Reports of the United States Tariff Commission to the President of the United States. Findings and Recommendations in the Matter of Alleged Unfair Methods of Competition in the Importation and Sale of Revolvers, Sanitary Napkins, and Brierwood Pipes" (Washington, D.C., 1927), 52.

59. Ibid.

60. George Williamson, "Hygiene of Menstruation" (1929), 5, RG 9, Subgroup 1, Series 3, Box 9–4, Folder 3, Exhibit 50. To his credit, Williamson did not discourage women from physical exercise during menstruation, unlike other interwar commentators who claimed that such activity could result in a prolapsed uterus; see Delaney et al., *The Curse*, 108.

61. *Good Housekeeping*, March 1926.

62. Shelley Park, "From Sanitation to Liberation? The Modern and Postmodern Marketing of Menstrual Products," *Journal of Popular Culture* 30 (1996), 149–68; for an interesting analysis of medical themes in advertising of nonmedical products, see Rima Apple, "'They Need it Now': Science, Advertising, and Vitamins," *Journal of Popular Culture* 22 (1988), 65–83. On Buckland, see "Agreement between Kotex Company and Ellen J. Buckland, 3 July 1930," RG 4, Subgroup 1, Box 4–1, Folder 12. On deodorant, see *Rotex Surgical Appliance Co. v. Kotex Co., No. 2531*, 18 C.C.P.A. 746; 44 F.2d 879.

63. Cited in Kimberly-Clark, "Summary of Proof," 12.

64. "Meeting of the Board of Directors of the International Cellucotton Products Company, 8 May 1928," "Meeting of the Board of Directors of the International Cellucotton Products Company, 23 Oct. 1928," RG 15, Subgroup 1, Box 15–16, Folder 1.

65. Lillian Gilbreth, "Report to the Johnson & Johnson Company, 1 January 1927," Special Collections, Purdue University, West Lafayette, Ind., Gilbreth Collection, Box (number unknown), Folder (number unknown). See also Vern Bullough, "Merchandizing the Sanitary Napkin: Lillian Gilbreth's 1927 Survey," *Signs* 10 (1985), 615–27.

66. Gilbreth, "Report to the Johnson & Johnson Company."

67. Ibid.

68. All quotes ibid.

69. "Development of the Technical Department," *Cooperation* (September 1947), 37.

70. Miller was first depicted in a Kotex ad a year earlier, published in the *Delineator*, July 1928.

71. Jane Livingston, *Lee Miller, Photographer* (New York: Thames and Hudson, 1989).

72. Elspeth Brown, "Rationalizing Consumption: LeJaren A. Hiller and the Origins of American Advertising Photography," *Enterprise and Society* 1 (2000), 715–38.

73. "Annual Meeting of the Board of Directors [of Kimberly-Clark Co.], 1 April 1926," RG 6, Subgroup 1, Series 1, Box 6–1, Folder 4.

74. On Mahler's bonuses, see "Minutes of the Board of Directors Meeting [of Kimberly-Clark], 26 Jan. 1925," RG 6, Series 5, Subgroup 1, Box 6–1, Folder 4. On Lasker and Pearce, see "Minutes of the Special Meeting of the Stockholders of the International Cellucotton Products Company, 28 Jan. 1927," RG 15, Subgroup 1, Box 15–16, Folder 1. On CPC's 1928 and 1929 operating results, see "International Cellucotton Products Company and Subsidiary Companies . . . Accumulated Consolidated Profit and Loss Statement for the Period Ended December 31, 1928," and "International Cellucotton Products Company and Subsidiary Companies . . . Accumulated Consolidated Profit and Loss Statement for the Period Ended December 31, 1929," Record Group 15, Series 15, Box 15–16, Folder 1.

75. "Marketing Milestones in the History of Kleenex Tissues," RG 9, Subgroup 1, Series 5, Box 9–8, Folder 15.

76. Vincent Vinikas, *Soft Soap, Hard Sell: American Hygiene in an Age of Advertisement* (Ames: Iowa State University Press, 1992), 57; see also Paula Fass, *The Damned and the Beautiful: American Youth in the 1920s* (New York: Oxford University Press, 1977), 283–84.

77. Vinikas, *Soft Soap*, 59.

78. *Trade Marks Journal*, 15 July 1925, 1545.

79. *Advertising Age*, 15 December 1952, 63.

80. "Marketing Milestones in the History of Kleenex Tissues," RG 9, Subgroup 1, Series 5, Box 9–8, Folder 15.

81. Lawrence Davis to Raymond Kelly, Feb. 12, 1923, and Raymond Kelly to Lawrence Davis, 20 Feb. 1923, both in RG 4, Series 1, Box 4–1, Folder 5; "Minutes of the Board of Directors [of Kimberly-Clark Co.], Meeting 28 November 1927," RG 6, Subgroup 1, Series 1, Box 6–1, Folder 4; see also Raymond Kelly to Terminal Barber Shops, April 3, 1926, RG 4, Series 1, Box 4–1, Folder 10.

82. "Badger-Globe," *Cooperation*, Sept. 1947, 42.

83. "Minutes of the Board of Directors Meeting [of Kimberly-Clark], 13 July 1923," RG 6, Series 5, Subgroup 1, Box 6–1, Folder 4.

84. "[Minutes of the] Fourth Annual Meeting [of Paper Merchants of the] Kimberly Clark Company, Drake Hotel, Chicago, Illinois, Tuesday, June 28, 1921," 29.

85. Heinrich, "Product Diversification," 480–81.

86. "Resolution of the Board of Directors, 5 June 1920," RG 6, Series 5, Subgroup 1, Box 6–1, Folder 2; "Minutes of the Board of Directors Meeting [of Kimberly-Clark], 26 Jan. 1925," "Minutes of the Special Meeting of the Board of Directors, 8 Sept. 1925," "Annual Meeting of the Board of Directors [of Kimberly-Clark Co.], 1 April 1926," all RG 6, Subgroup 1, Series 1, Box 6–1, Folder 4; "Kimberly-Clark and *New York Times* Join in Big Canadian Enterprise," *Cooperation* (May 1926), 2.

87. "Minutes of a Special Meeting of the Board of Directors of the International Cellucotton Products Company, 11 April 1927," RG 15, Subgroup 1, Box 15–16, Folder 1.

88. "Reorganization Plan of Kimberly-Clark Company, 10 July 1928," "Minutes of the Board of Directors Meeting, 20 July 1928," "First Meeting of Trustees in Liquidation of Kimberly-Clark Company, 10 Aug. 1928," all in RG 6, Series 5, Subgroup 1, Box 6–1, Folder 3; "New Kimberly-Clark Plan," *The New York Times*, 5 July 1928, 30; "New Stock Issues," *The New York Times*, 10 July 1928, 31; on Hancock, see *National Cyclopedia of American Biography, vol. 46* (New York, 1963), 507.

89. *Financial Statement of Kimberly-Clark Corporation* (Neenah, Wis.: Kimberly-Clark Corporation, 1929); *Financial Statement of Kimberly-Clark Corporation* (Neenah, Wis.: Kimberly-Clark Corporation, 1930); [Frank Sensenbrenner, Harry Price, Ernst Mahler] "Report [on Kotex and Kleenex Manufacturing], 6 Aug. 1928," RG 15, Subgroup 1, Box 15–16, Folder 1; International Paper Company, *32nd Annual Report* (New York: International Paper Co., 1929); George S. Armstrong, *Crown Zellerbach Corporation: A Survey* (San Francisco, Calif.: n.p., 1937), 34–35.

90. "Thirsty Fibre: His Biography" (1921), RG 15, Subgroup 3, Series 7, Box 4416, Folder 67; see also Scott Paper Company, *Annual Report to the Stockholders [for 1924]*, [n.d.], Scott Paper Company, *Treasurer's Annual Report Year 1926* (Chester, Pa., 1927), both in RG 13, Subgroup 3, Series 3, Subdivision 4, Box 3–11, Folder 1.

Notes to Chapter 3

1. *Financial Statement of Kimberly-Clark Corporation [for Year Ended Dec. 31, 1930]* (Neenah, Wis.: Kimberly-Clark Corporation, 1931).

2. *Financial Statement of Kimberly-Clark Corporation [for Year Ended Dec. 31, 1931]* (Neenah, Wis.: Kimberly-Clark Corporation, 1932).

3. Thomas Heinrich, *Ships for the Seven Seas: Philadelphia Shipbuilding in the Age of Industrial Capitalism* (Baltimore: Johns Hopkins University Press, 1997), 196–217.

4. Arthur Kuhn, *GM Passes Ford, 1918–1938: Designing the General Motors Performance-Control System* (University Park: Pennsylvania State University Press, 1986).

5. Michael Bernstein, *The Great Depression: Delayed Recovery and Econom-*

ic Change in America, 1929–1939 (New York: Cambridge University Press, 1988); Michael Bernstein, "Why the Great Depression Was Great: Toward a New Understanding of the Interwar Economic Crisis in the United States," in *The Rise and Fall of the New Deal Order, 1930–1980*, eds. Steve Fraser and Gary Gerstle (Princeton: Princeton University Press, 1980); see also *Understanding American Economic Decline*, eds. Michael A. Bernstein, David E. Adler (New York: Cambridge University Press, 1994).

6. Thomas McGaw, "The New Deal and the Mixed Economy," in *Fifty Years Later: The New Deal Evaluated*. Ed. Harvard Sitkoff. (Philadelphia: Temple University Press, 1985), 43.

7. Christina Romer, "The Great Crash and the Onset of the Great Depression," *Quarterly Journal of Economics* 105 (1999), 597–624; Martha Olney, "Demand for Consumer Durable Goods in 20th Century America," in *Explorations in Economic History* 27 (1990), 322–49; Martha Olney, "Consumer Durables in the Interwar Years: New Estimates, New Patterns," *Research in Economic History* 12 (1989), 119–50.

8. "History of Kotex, 1929–1930–1931," RG 9, Subgroup 1, Series 6, Box 9–11, Folder 14, Kimberly-Clark Archives, The History Factory, Chantilly, Va.

9. John R. Kimberly, "Better to Use, Cheap Enough to Throw Away: The Disposable Paper Product," *Business Decisions That Changed Our Lives*, eds. Sidney Furst and Milton Sherman (New York: Random House, 1964), 162; see also "Marketing Milestones in the History of Kleenex Tissues, 1930," RG 9, Subgroup 1, Series 5, Box 9–8, Folder 15.

10. "[Kleenex] Marketing Milestones, 1932," RG 9, Subgroup 1, Series 5, Box 9–8, Folder 15.

11. "Minutes of the Special meeting of the Board of Directors of the International Cellucotton Products Company, March 24, 1931," RG 15, Subgroup 1, Series 15, Box 15–16, Folder 1; "[Kleenex] Marketing Milestones, 1934," RG 9, Subgroup 1, Series 5, Box 9–8, Folder 15.

12. "[Kleenex] Marketing Milestones, 1935," RG 9, Subgroup 1, Series 5, Box 9–8, Folder 15.

13. "[Kleenex] Marketing Milestones, 1936," RG 9, Subgroup 1, Series 5, Box 9–8, Folder 15.

14. "[Kleenex] Marketing Milestones, 1939," RG 9, Subgroup 1, Series 5, Box 9–8, Folder 15; "Minutes of the Board of Directors Meetings of the International Cellucotton Products Company, Nov. 5, 1935," RG 15, Subgroup 1, Series 15, Box 15–16, Folder 2; see also Elizabeth Fones-Wolf, "Creating a Favorable Business Climate: Corporations and Radio Broadcasting, 1934 to 1954," *Business History Review* 73 (1999), 221–55; Kathleen Newman, "Critical Mass: Advertising, Audiences and Consumer Activism in the Age of Radio," Ph.D. dissertation, Yale University, 1997. For the earlier period, see Susan Smulyan, "'And Now a Word from Our Sponsors . . .'": Commercialization of American Broadcast Radio, 1920–1934," Ph.D. Dissertation, Yale University, 1986.

15. "[Kleenex] Marketing Milestones, 1938," RG 9, Subgroup 1, Series 5, Box 9–8, Folder 15.

16. "Minutes of the Special Meeting of the Board of Directors of the International Cellucotton Products Company, May 13, 1931," RG 15, Subgroup 1, Series 15, Box 15–16, Folder 1.

17. Ibid.; see also "History of Kotex, 1932," RG 9, Subgroup 1, Series 6, Box 9–11, Folder 14.

18. *Financial Statement of Kimberly-Clark Corporation [for Year Ended Dec. 31, 1932]* (Neenah, Wis.: Kimberly-Clark Corporation, 1933).

19. Walter W. Luecke, "History of Kotex," Subject File 200.2, "Corporate Histories," KCA.

20. *Annual Report of International Cellucotton Products Company and Subsidiaries for the Calendar Year 1933* (Neenah, Wis.: International Cellucotton Products Company, 1934), RG 15, Subgroup 1, Series 15, Box 15–16, Folder 1; Kimberly-Clark Corporation, *Financial Statement, Dec. 31, 1933* (Neenah, Wis.: Kimberly-Clark Corporation, 1934).

21. "Minutes of the Special Meeting of the Board of Directors of the International Cellucotton Products Company, Nov. 1, 1933," RG 15, Subgroup 1, Series 15, Box 15–16, Folder 1; "Minutes of the Board of Directors Meetings of the International Cellucotton Products Company, Nov. 5, 1935," RG 15, Subgroup 1, Series 15, Box 15–16, Folder 2. Walter W. Luecke, "History of Kotex," Subject File 200.2, "Corporate Histories," KCA; see also "History of Kotex, 1934," RG 9, Subgroup 1, Series 6, Box 9–11, Folder 14.

22. Frank Sensenbrenner, "Kimberly-Clark Corporate History," 44–45, RG 8, Subgroup 3, Series 2, Box 8–73, Folder 26; *Financial Statement of Kimberly-Clark Corporation, Dec. 31, 1929* (Neenah, Wis.: Kimberly-Clark Corporation, 1930); Kimberly-Clark Corporation, *Financial Statement, Dec. 31, 1937* (Neenah, Wis.: Kimberly-Clark Corporation, 1938); "Lakeview," *Cooperation* (September 1947), 79–80.

23. *Annual Report of International Cellucotton Products Company and Subsidiaries for the Calendar Year 1934* (Neenah, Wis.: International Cellucotton Products Company, 1935) and *Annual Report of International Cellucotton Products Company and Subsidiaries for the Calendar Year 1935* (Neenah, Wis.: International Cellucotton Products Company, 1936), both in RG 15, Subgroup 1, Series 15, Box 15–16, Folder 1; Kimberly-Clark Corporation, *Financial Statement, Dec. 31, 1934* (Neenah, Wis.: Kimberly-Clark Corporation, 1935) and Kimberly-Clark Corporation, *Financial Statement, Dec. 31, 1935* (Neenah, Wis.: Kimberly-Clark Corporation, 1936); see also "Minutes of the Board of Directors Meetings of the International Cellucotton Products Company, Nov. 5, 1935," RG 15, Subgroup 1, Series 15, Box 15–16, Folder 2.

24. The American edition was probably based on a pamphlet issued by ICPC in 1928 in Australia.

25. Quoted in Joan Brumberg, *The Body Project: An Intimate History of American Girls* (New York: Random House, 1997), 43; see also Corrine Krause, *Grandmothers, Mothers, and Daughters: An Oral History of Ethnicity, Mental Health and Continuity of Three Generations of Jewish, Italian, and Slavic Women* (Boston: Twayne Publishers, 1991).

26. Brumberg, *The Body Project*, 40; see also Jürgen Habermas, *Theorie des kommnikativen Handelns, II* (Frankfurt, Germany: Suhrkamp, 1988), 489–547.

27. Brumberg, *The Body Project*, 47.

28. "History of Kotex, 1933," RG 9, Subgroup 1, Series 6, Box 9–11, Folder 14.

29. "How K-C Researchers Blaze the Trail for the Rest of Us," *Cooperation* (January 1940), 6.

30. Ibid.

31. "Kimberly-Clark Names Agency," *The New York Times*, 29 Dec. 1939, 32; "Badger-Globe," *Cooperation* (September 1947), 44.

32. L. C. Fleck, "Wipeable [*sic*] Wall Paper Versus Varnished Tile," *Cooperation* (1933, Second Quarter), 6.

33. Arthur Pond, "Wood, Water and Brains: Modern Paper Making and Merchandising As Revealed by the Rise of Kimberly-Clark Corporation," *Atlantic Monthly*, Sept. 1935, 381.

34. Kimberly-Clark Corporation, *Financial Statement [for Year Ended December 31, 1932]* (Neenah, Wis.: Kimberly-Clark Corporation, 1933); Frank Sensenbrenner, "Kimberly-Clark Corporate History," 44, RG 8, Subgroup 3, Series 2, Box 8–73, Folder 26.

35. Kimberly-Clark Corporation, *Financial Statement [for Year Ended December 31, 1933]* (Neenah, Wis.: Kimberly-Clark Corporation, 1934); Kimberly-Clark Corporation, *Financial Statement [for Year Ended December 31, 1934]* (Neenah, Wis.: Kimberly-Clark Corporation, 1935); F. S. Seaborne, "Kleerfect," *Cooperation* (1933, First Quarter), 3–4, 6; *Discoveries and Inventions Thru the Ages That Have Made Today's Fine Printing Possible* (Neenah, Wis.: Kimberly-Clark Corporation, 1935).

36. For a detailed description of Tampax production methods and brand name issues, see *Tampax, Inc. et al. v. Personal Products Corporation et al., No. 58,* 123 F.2d 722; 1941 U.S. App., and *Breeze v. Tampax Sales Corporation No. 4079,* 26 C.C.P.A. 994; 102 F.2d 808. For interesting conceptual suggestions for the analysis of businesswomen like Tenderich, see Kathy Peiss, "'Vital Industry' and Women's Ventures: Conceptualizing Gender in Twentieth Century Business History," *Business History Review* 72 (1998), 219–41.

37. Quoted in "Tampon Review" [n.d.], RG 9, Subgroup 1, Series 6, Box 9–16, Folder 78.

38. Quoted in "Tampon Review" [n.d.], RG 9, Subgroup 1, Series 6, Box 9–16, Folder 78.

39. "Respondent O 116, Preliminary Report [on Fibs], April 1935," RG 9, Subgroup 3, Series 7, Subseries 1, Box 9–357, Folder 4.

40. "Respondent P 183, Preliminary Report [on Fibs], April 1935," RG 9, Subgroup 3, Series 7, Subseries 1, Box 9–357, Folder 4.

41. "Tampon Review" [n.d.], RG 9, Subgroup 1, Series 6, Box 9–16, Folder 78.

42. "Laboratory Observations, 1934," Record Group 9, Subgroup 3, Series 7, Subseries 11, Box 9–357, Folder 3.

43. Nadja Buckley to [person unknown], November 5, 1934, quoted in Lawrence Meyer to Charles Fourness, November 9, 1934, RG 9, Subgroup 3, Series 7, Subseries 11, Box 9–357, Folder 3.

44. "Tampax—Girl 505 [1934]," Record Group 9, Subgroup 3, Series 7, Subseries 11, Box 9–357, Folder 3.

45. "Tampax—Girl 83 [1934]," Record Group 9, Subgroup 3, Series 7, Subseries 11, Box 9–357, Folder 3.

46. "Fibs—Girl 505 [1934]," Record Group 9, Subgroup 3, Series 7, Subseries 11, Box 9–357, Folder 3.

47. "Respondent O 058, Preliminary Report [on Fibs], April 1935," RG 9, Subgroup 3, Series 7, Subseries 1, Box 9–357, Folder 4.

48. "Respondent S 161, Preliminary Report [on Fibs], April 1935," RG 9, Subgroup 3, Series 7, Subseries 1, Box 9–357, Folder 4. The episode casts an interesting light on interwar firms' abilities to use consumer surveys effectively; for examples of more successful uses of early surveys, see Sally Clark, "Consumer Negotiations," *Business and Economic History* 26 (1997), 101–22.

49. [Fibs] Production Standard, March 27, 1936, RG 13, Series 1, Box 13–1, Folder 6.

50. Lawrence Meyer to Mrs. Bruce, Mrs. Maxfield, and Miss Daly, July 18, 1935, RG 9, Subgroup 3, Series 7, Subseries 8, Box 9–357, Folder 2.

51. C. Rickard to Lawrence Meyer, Aug. 28, 1935, RG 9, Subgroup 3, Series 7, Subseries 8, Box 9–357, Folder 2.

52. Memo to Kotex Consultants, September 21, 1935, RG 9, Subgroup 3, Series 7, Subseries 8, Box 9–357, Folder 2; emphasis in the original.

53. Quoted in "Tampon Review" [n.d], RG 9, Subgroup 1, Series 6, Box 9–16, Folder 78.

54. Ibid.

55. "Respondent H 143, Preliminary Report [on Fibs], April 1935," RG 9, Subgroup 3, Series 7, Subseries 1, Box 9–357, Folder 4.

56. "Respondent B 136, Preliminary Report [on Fibs], April 1935," RG 9, Subgroup 3, Series 7, Subseries 1, Box 9–357, Folder 4.

57. "Respondent C 132, Preliminary Report [on Fibs], April 1935," RG 9, Subgroup 3, Series 7, Subseries 1, Box 9–357, Folder 4.

58. Ibid.

59. Thomas Heinrich, "Product Diversification in the U.S. Pulp and Paper Industry: The Case of International Paper," *Business History Review* 75 (forthcoming, 2004).

60. Ibid.

61. Scott Paper Company, *Annual Report to Stockholders for Year Ended Dec. 31, 1931* (Philadelphia, Pa: Scott Paper Company, 1932) through *Annual Report to Stockholders for Year Ended Dec. 31, 1939* (Philadelphia, Pa.: Scott Paper Company, 1940), all RG 13, Subgroup 3, Series 3, Subdivision 4, Box 3–11, Folder 1.

62. Sanford Jacoby, *Modern Manors: Welfare Capitalism Since the New Deal* (Princeton: Princeton University Press, 1997), 40.

63. "Opening of Sensenbrenner Hospital," *Cooperation* (July 1929), 16–17.

64. Robert H. Zieger, *Rebuilding the Pulp and Paper Workers' Union, 1933–1944.* (Knoxville: University of Tennessee Press, 1984), 75.

65. Quoted in Kimberly-Clark Corporation, *Financial Statement [for Year Ended December 31, 1935]* (Neenah, Wis.: Kimberly-Clark Corporation, 1936).

66. Kimberly-Clark Corporation, *Financial Statement [for Year Ended December 31, 1935]* (Neenah, Wis.: Kimberly-Clark Corporation,, 1936); see also *Cooperation* (September 1947), 35.

67. "Kimberly-Clark Considers 7-A an Asset," *Cooperation* (1934, Fourth Quarter), 5, emphasis in the original.

68. Robert H. Zieger, *Rebuilding the Pulp and Paper Workers' Union*, 85.

69. *Paper Trade Journal*, 2 Sept. 1937, 16 Sept. 1937, 7 Oct. 1937.

70. *Paper Trade Journal*, 4 Nov. 1937.

71. Ibid.

72. *Appleton Post-Crescent*, 6 December 1937.

73. "What Can You and I Do to Rebuild Our Democracy?" *Cooperation* (1938, First Quarter), 5.

74. "Employee Representation under the National Labor Relations Act," *Cooperation* (1935, Fourth Quarter), 3.

75. Thomas Foristall, "The Inquiring Investor: Kimberly-Clark Corp," *The Wall Street Journal*, 21 April 1938, 7.

Notes to Chapter 4

1. Quoted in Cynthia F. Mitchell, "Paper Tiger: How Kimberly-Clark Wraps Its Bottom Line in Disposable Huggies," *The Wall Street Journal*, 23 July 1987, 1.

2. Alfred D. Chandler, Jr., "The Competitive Performance of U.S. Industrial Enterprise since the Second World War," *Business History Review* 68 (1994), 47–73. See also Peter G. Klein, "Conglomerate Organization and Economic Performance: Evidence from the 1960s," Ph.D. Dissertation, University of California, Berkley, 1995; Richard P. Rumelt, *Strategy, Structure, and Economic Performance* (Boston: Harvard Business School Press, 1986); Charles R. Spruill, *Conglomerates and the Evolution of Capitalism* (Carbondale: Southern Illinois University Press, 1982).

3. "Retires as the Chairman of Kimberly-Clark Board," *The New York Times*, 7 Jan. 1945, 23; "Kimberly-Clark Names C. G. Parker Chairman," *The Wall Street Journal*, 20 Aug. 1953, 6; "Cola Parker Retiring," *The New York Times*, 1 July 1955, 27.

4. Kimberly-Clark Corporation, *Annual Report [for Year Ended April 30, 1955]* (Neenah, Wis.: Kimberly-Clark Corporation, 1955), 5–6.

5. Kimberly-Clark Corporation, *Annual Report [for Year Ended Dec. 31, 1948]* (Neenah, Wis.: Kimberly-Clark Corporation, 1949), 17; "Kimberly-Clark Proceeds with Financing Plan," *Paper Trade Journal*, 28 November 1946, 14; "Kimberly-Clark Plans $45,700,000 Expansion," *Paper Trade Journal*, 3 July 1947, 7; "Product Switch Proves Profit Booster," *Business Week*, 24 Dec. 1949, 26.

6. "K-C's Memphis Mill: Modern Material Handling," *Pulp and Paper* 23 (1950), 53–56; "Kimberly-Clark Buys Government Plant," *Paper Trade Journal*, March 21, 1946, 20.

7. "Memphis Kleenex Plant to Use Alabama Pulp," *Paper Trade Journal*, 15 Jan. 1948, 34; "Veteran K-C Men to Manage Coosa Mill," *Paper Mill News*, 10 July 1948, 7; Kimberly-Clark Corporation, *Annual Report [for the Year Ended Dec. 31, 1948]* (Neenah, Wis.: Kimberly-Clark Corporation, 1949), 14; Kimberly-Clark Corporation, *Annual Report [for Year Ended April 30, 1950]* (Neenah, Wis.: Kimberly-Clark Corporation, 1950), 6.

8. "Kimberly-Clark Plans $5,000,000 Expansion," *The New York Times*, 15 Oct. 1945, 30; Kimberly-Clark Corporation, *Annual Report [for the Year Ended April 30, 1955]* (Neenah, Wis.: Kimberly-Clark Corporation, 1955), 18.

9. Kimberly-Clark Corporation, *Annual Report [for Year Ended Dec. 31, 1946]* (Neenah, Wis.: Kimberly-Clark Corporation, 1947), 4; "Minutes of the Board of Directors," 15 April 1958, 3–4, RG 6, Subgroup 1, Series 1, Box 6–1, Folder 5, Kimberly-Clark Archives, The History Factory, Chantilly, Va.; "New Kimberly-Clark Plant," *The New York Times*, 20 July 1956, 32.

10. Kimberly-Clark Corporation, *Annual Report [for Year Ended April 30, 1953]* (Neenah, Wis.: Kimberly-Clark Corporation, 1953), 2–3.

11. Kimberly-Clark Corporation, *Annual Report [for Year Ended April 30, 1953]* (Neenah, Wis.: Kimberly-Clark Corporation, 1953), 18 (quote); see also Kimberly-Clark Corporation, *Annual Report [for Year Ended April 30, 1952]* (Neenah, Wis.: Kimberly-Clark Corporation, 1952), 5; Kimberly-Clark Corporation, *Annual Report [for Year Ended April 30, 1955]* (Neenah, Wis.: Kimberly-Clark Corporation, 1955), 18.

12. "Kimberly-Clark Expands," *The New York Times*, 12 Dec. 1951, 70; "Minutes of the Board of Directors," 29 August 1961, 4.

13. John R. Kimberly, "Comments on Kimberly-Clark Corporation to the New York Society of Security Analysts," 26 Jan. 1960, 1–2, Record Group 2, Series 3, Box 6, Folder 2; "International Cellucotton Slated to Merge with Kimberly-Clark," *The New York Times*, 23 June 1955, 41; "Cellucotton Company, Kimberly-Clark Plan Complete Integration," *The Wall Street Journal*, 23 June 1955; "Cola Parker Retiring," *The New York Times*,1 July 1955, 27; "International Cellucotton Merger," *The Wall Street Journal*, 4 Aug. 1955, 6.

14. "I Didn't Know It Was So Simple! to use Tampax," *Parents' Magazine*, 1942.

15. *As One Girl to Another* (Chicago: Kotex, 1940), 2.

16. Ibid., 3.

17. Ibid., 7.

18. Ibid., 13.

19. Ibid., 16; emphasis in original.

20. Ibid., 16.

21. Ibid.

22. Robert L. Dickinson, "Tampons as Menstrual Guards," *Journal of the American Medical Association* (16 June 1945), 490–94.

23. Leah L. Anderson, "The subject was most delicate, but careful planning produced a good P.R. film" [n.d.], 46, Record Group 9, Subgroup 4, Series 1, Box 3, Folder 13.

24. Walt Disney Productions, "'The Story of Menstruation'—International Cellucotton Products Company—Final Narration, June 15, 1945," 19, Record Group 9, Subgroup 1, Series 1, Box 3, Folder 1.

25. Ibid., 20.

26. Ibid., 23.

27. Leah L. Anderson, "The subject was most delicate," 46.

28. All quotes ibid., 46.

29. Marion Jones, "Teaching Guide—Menstrual Education" [n.d.], 13, Record Group 9, Subgroup 1, Series 1, Box 3, Folder 9.

30. Ibid., 14.

31. Leah L. Anderson, "The subject was most delicate," 46.

32. Marion Jones, "Teaching Guide—Menstrual Education," 13.

33. Joan Jacobs Brumberg, *The Body Project: An Intimate History of American Girls* (New York: Vintage Books, 1997), 47.

34. "History of Kotex Feminine Napkins, 1914–1965" (1965), 51–53, Record Group 9, Series 1, Box 6, Folder 17.

35. L. E. Meyer to Don Belding, 18 October 1949, Record Group 9, Series 4, Subgroup 2, Box 1, Folder 2.

36. Ibid.; "Kleenex Educational Program," 26 September 1960, 1–3, Record

Group 9, Series 4, Subgroup 2, Box 1, Folder 1; Carl Nater to Marion Jones, 1 November 1963, Record Group 9, Series 4, Subgroup 2, Box 1, Folder 2.

37. "How to Catch a Cold," *Film News* 11 (October 1951), 8.

38. "How to Catch an Audience," *Public Relations Journal*, Dec. 1962, 25; see also Loren Hoch, "The Use of Sponsored Films in Teaching Biology," *Science Teacher*, September 1955, 179–81.

39. "Kleenex Educational Program," 26 September 1960, 2–3, Record Group 9, Series 4, Subgroup 2, Box 1, Folder 1.

40. John R. Kimberly, "Comments on Kimberly-Clark Corporation to the New York Society of Security Analysts," 26 Jan. 1960, 11, Record Group 2, Series 3, Box 6, Folder 2.

41. Kimberly-Clark Corporation, *Annual Report [for Year Ended April 30, 1957]* (Neenah, Wis.: Kimberly-Clark Corporation, 1957), 8–12; "Kimberly-Clark Buys Munising Paper Co.," *The Wall Street Journal*, 12 Dec. 1951, 14.

42. Kimberly, "Comments on Kimberly-Clark Corporation to the New York Society of Security Analysts," 2–3; "Minutes of the Board of Directors," 21 Oct. 1958, 2; "Kimberly-Clark Agrees to Acquire All Stock of Schweitzer Concern," *The Wall Street Journal*, 15 February 1957, 5.

43. "Minutes of the Board of Directors," 15 April 1958, 3.

44. Kimberly-Clark Corporation, *Annual Report [for Year Ended April 30, 1955]* (Neenah, Wis.: Kimberly-Clark Corporation, 1955), 8; "Minutes of the Board of Directors," October 21, 1958, 6–7; "Minutes of the Board of Directors," 30 Aug. 1960, 11.

45. "Minutes of the Board of Directors," 13 Feb. 1961, 2.

46. Kimberly, "Comments on Kimberly-Clark Corporation to the New York Society of Security Analysts," 10–11. "Minutes of the Board of Directors," 29 Aug. 1959, 4; "Minutes of the Board of Directors," 13 Feb. 1961, 2–3.

47. "Minutes of the Board of Directors," 17 June 1958, 2–3.

48. "Minutes of the Board of Directors," 21 Oct. 1958, 7.

49. Ibid., 7–8; "Minutes of the Board of Directors," 17 Feb. 1959, 3; "Minutes of the Board of Directors," 25 Aug. 1959.

50. Kimberly, "Comments on Kimberly-Clark Corporation to the New York Society of Security Analysts," 3; "Kimberly-Clark Sales Rise But Net Dips; 35% Interest in Pulp Maker Acquired," *The New York Times*, 22 Nov. 1957, 48.

51. On Berkley, "Minutes of the Board of Directors," 25 Feb. 1963, 3; Kimberly, "Comments on Kimberly-Clark Corporation to the New York Society of Security Analysts," 2–3; "Minutes of the Board of Directors," 21 April 1959, 2–3.

52. On Smith Lumber, "Minutes of the Board of Directors," 17 April 1961, 4; "Minutes of the Board of Directors," 12 Oct. 1961; on BMT, "Minutes of the Board of Directors," 17 April 1961, 5; "Minutes of the Board of Directors," 19 June 1961, 3; "Minutes of the Board of Directors," 21 Feb. 1967, 3; "Minutes of the Board of Directors," 25 April 1967, 1–2; "Kimberly-Clark Acquisition," *The Wall Street Journal*, 27 April 1961, 3; "Kimberly-Clark Sued on Antitrust Charge, Asked to Divest Firm," *The Wall Street Journal*, 16 Feb. 1962, 16; "Kimberly-Clark Is Ordered to Divest Itself of West Coast Wholesaler Acquired in '61," *The Wall Street Journal*, 20 February 1967, 9.

53. Guy M. Minard, "Kimberly-Clark Corporation: A Study in Management Technique," February 5, 1968, Record Group 2, Series 5, Box 6, Folder 1.

54. Ibid.

55. M. J. Schulenberg to Albert Wilson, 19 March 1947; M. J. Schulenberg to John Cornell, 17 September 1947; [unknown person] to Albert Wilson, 30 Oct. 1950; J. J. Shipman, "Presentation to Enginner's [sic] Club," 19 September 1962, all in Record Group 12, Series 1, Box 3, Folder 1; "Minutes of the Board of Directors," 21 Dec. 1959, 2; Kimberly-Clark Corporation, *Annual Report [for Year Ended Dec. 31, 1946]* (Neenah, Wis.: Kimberly-Clark Corporation, 1947), 6–7; "Building Paper Laboratory," *The New York Times*, 27 Aug. 1945, 26.

56. J. J. Shipman, "Kimberly-Clark's Research and Development Operations," 19 September 1962, Record Group 12, Series 1, Box 3, Folder 1; on American Envelope, see "Minutes of the Board of Directors," 21 Oct. 1958, 5–6 and *The Wall Street Journal*, 31 December 1958, 6.

57. "Sanitary Protection Story, 1950–1958" [n.d.], 6, Record Group 9, Series 1, Box 6, Folder 26.

58. "Sanitary Protection Story," 4 Oct. 1957, 1, Record Group 9, Series 1, Box 6, Folder 26.

59. Ibid.; see also April S. Dougal, "Kotex," *Encyclopedia of Consumer Brands, Vol. 2: Personal Products*, ed. Janice Jorgensen (Detroit: St. James Press, 1994), 318.

60. "Sanitary Protection Story," 4.

61. Ibid.

62. "Minutes of the Board of Directors," 18 April 1960, 3; see also Dougal, "Kotex," 318.

63. "Sanitary Protection Story, 1950–1958," 2.

64. Ibid., 3.

65. "History of Kotex Feminine Napkins: 1962," 2–3, Record Group 9, Series 1, Box 6, Folder 17.

66. David Smith, "History of Fems: Fiscal 1961–62," 1962, 12, Record Group 9, Series 1, Box 6, Folder 1.

67. Ibid.

68. "History of Fems, May 1968–December 1969," 1969, Record Group 9, Series 1, Box 6, Folder 1.

69. "Historical Personnel Turnover—Tampons—Draft," 2, [n.d.] Record Group 9, Series 1, Box 6, Folder 79.

70. On Tampax's postwar history, see April S. Dougal, "Tampax," *Encyclopedia of Consumer Brands, Vol. 2: Personal Products*, ed. Janice Jorgensen (Detroit: St. James Press, 1994), 535.

71. C. K. Clarke, "Rough Draft—History of Tampon Process and Product Development," 4 June 1975, 5, Record Group 9, Series 1, Box 6, Folder 79.

72. Ibid., 3.

73. "Tampon Review Project: Competitive Tampons: Modess, Carefree, Playtex, and Rely," June 11, 1975, 3, Record Group 9, Series 1, Box 6, Folder 79.

74. Quoted in ibid.

75. Ibid., 5.

76. Clarke, "Rough Draft—History of Tampon Process and Product Development," 7.

77. Ibid., 5.

78. Ibid.

79. David L. Smith, "History of Kotams Tampons," June 13, 1962, 8, Record Group 9, Series 1, Box 6, Folder 76.

80. Ibid., 18.

81. "History of Kotams Tampons," 1966–67, 1–10, Record Group 9, Series 1, Box 6, Folder 76.

82. "Draft—Historical Personnel Turnover—Tampons," n.d. [1975?], 5, Record Group 9, Series 1, Box 6, Folder 79.

83. "Company in a Quandary," *Time*, 24 December 1965.

84. Quoted in Oscar Schisgall, *Eyes on Tomorrow: The Evolution of Procter & Gamble* (Chicago: J. G. Ferguson Publishing, 1981), 213.

85. Ibid., 212–14.

86. Quoted in "P&G vs. Scott: Battle of the Century," *Forbes*, 15 June 1963, 15.

87. "Minutes of the Board of Directors," 18 April 1960, 2.

88. "Minutes of the Board of Directors," 19 December 1960, 2.

89. "Chronological History of Kleenex Tissues," 5, Record Group 9, Series 1, Box 5, Folder 4.

90. "Minutes of the Board of Directors," April 17, 1961, 2.

91. "Minutes of the Board of Directors," November 9, 1961, 2.

92. "Minutes of the Board of Directors," February 13, 1961, 2.

93. "History of Boutique Facial Tissues" [n.d.], 1–2, Record Group 9, Series 1, Box 5, Folder 33.

94. Ibid., 4.

95. "Kleenex Boutique Tissues: Creative Strategy" [n.d.], Record Group 9, Series 1, Box 5, Folder 33.

96. "History of Boutique Facial Tissues," 5.

97. Ibid., 4.

98. Ibid., 12.

99. Quoted in Schisgall, *Eyes on Tomorrow*.

100. Susan W. Brown, "Pampers," *Encyclopedia of Consumer Brands, Vol. 2: Personal Products*, ed. Janice Jorgensen (Detroit: St. James Press, 1994), 405.

101. Ibid.

102. Thomas Heinrich, "Product Diversification in the U.S. Pulp and Paper Industry: The Case of International Paper," *Business History Review* 75 (2001): 500–503.

103. "How Financial Community Leaders View Our Industry and Companies," *Paper Trade Journal*, 10 May 1971, 53.

104. "International Paper Net Fell to $5.46 a Share," *The Wall Street Journal*, 13 March 1959, 7; "International Paper Unit to Cut Plywood Output at 2 Plants as Orders Dip," *The Wall Street Journal* 4 June 1959, 10; "International Paper 1st Period Net Rose; Holders Berate Management on Dividends," *The Wall Street Journal*, 12 May 1960, 28; "International Paper," *The Wall Street Journal*, 12 May 1966, 33; "International Paper to Enter U.S. Market for Paper Towels, Napkins and Tissue Items," *The Wall Street Journal*, 23 October 1968, 34; "International Paper Sees Lag in 3-Month Net," *The Wall Street Journal*, 11 September 1970, 20; "Paul Gorman to Head International Paper; Operating Net Plunged in 4th Period, Year," *The Wall Street Journal*, 10 February 1971, 16; "International Paper, Kimberly-Clark Report Profit Dropped Sharply," *The Wall Street Journal*, 14 April 1971, 31. The Federal Trade Commission unsuccessfully challenged the Long-Bell acquisition

under the Clayton Act; see *Federal Trade Commission v. International Paper Company*, United States Court of Appeals Second Circuit, 241 F.2d 372.

105. "Paper Giant Gets Itch for the East," *Business Week*, 1 March 1958; "Catching Up with the Times," *Forbes*, 15 July 1969, 43; "Crown-Zellerbach, Time Plan $25 Million Expansion of Paper Mill," *The Wall Street Journal*, 3 July 1961, 4; "Crown-Zellerbach Unit Proposes to Construct Mill in British Columbia," *The Wall Street Journal*, 30 August 1965.

106. Johnson & Johnson, *Annual Report [for Year Ending Dec. 31, 1964]* (New Brunswick, N.J.: Johnson & Johnson, 1965).

107. On good performance of trademarked products in the early 1960s, see "Scott Paper President Optimistic for Future Because of '59 Results," *The Wall Street Journal*, 18 February 1960, 20. On S. D. Warren, "Scott Paper Board Votes Plan to Merge with S. D. Warren," *The Wall Street Journal*, 15 March 1967, 3. On crisis in the early 1970s, see "Scott Paper's Decision to Drop Diaper Line Cost Firm $12.8 Million," *The Wall Street Journal*, 15 July 1971, 19.

108. James W. Davant, "Wall Street Looks at the Pulp and Paper Industry," *Paper Trade Journal*, 14 February 1966, 46.

109. Ibid.

110. "Why Is the Financial Community Viewing Us More Optimistically?" *Paper Trade Journal*, 17 March 1969, 38. Scott Paper's chairman Harrison Dunning voiced similar criticisms, attributing his company's poor financial performance to "a penchant [among paper makers] to keep their machines running; [they are] apt to cut prices to do it." "Scott Paper Attempting to Adjust Its Spending to Match Slower Sales," *The Wall Street Journal*, 31 July 1971.

111. "Minutes of the Board of Directors," 19 June 1961, 2.

112. On Kellett's background, "Biographical Summary—William Kellett, April 1973," Record Group 2, Series 4, Box 2, Folder 1. On postwar capital budgeting, see Carliss Y. Baldwin and Kim B. Clark, "Capital Budgeting Systems and Capabilities Investment in U.S. Companies after the Second World War," *Business History Review* 68 (1994), 73–109.

113. "Minutes of the Board of Directors," 19 June 1961, 2.

114. "Minutes of the Board of Directors," 29 August 1961, 5.

115. "Minutes of the Board of Directors," 25 June 1968, 3; "Minutes of the Board of Directors," 27 August 1968, 3; "Minutes of the Board of Directors," 25 October 1966, 2.

116. "Minutes of the Board of Directors," 23 October 1962, 4.

117. "Minutes of the Board of Directors," 25 June 1963, 2.

118. Kimberly-Clark Corporation, *Kimberly-Clark Report for Year Ended December 31, 1964* (Neenah, Wis.: Kimberly-Clark Corporation, 1965).

119. "Minutes of the Board of Directors," 25 October 1966, 2.

120. "Minutes of the Board of Directors," 25 June 1968, 3; "Minutes of the Board of Directors," 27 August 1968, 3; "Minutes of the Board of Directors," 25 October 1966, 2.

121. Kimberly quoted in "Delicately Balanced Equation," *Forbes*, 1 June 1967, 62; see also "Kimberly-Clark Plans to Buy Its Associated Coosa Newsprint Firm," *The Wall Street Journal*, 13 February 1962, 19.

122. "Delicately Balanced Equation," *Forbes*, 1 June 1967, 63.

123. Ibid.

124. Kimberly-Clark Corporation, *Kimberly-Clark Report for Year Ended December 31, 1969* (Neenah, Wis.: Kimberly-Clark Corporation, 1970), 1; on Coosa River, see also "Kimberly-Clark to Lift Paper Plant's Capacity by 55% for $35 Million," *The Wall Street Journal,* 23 December 1964, 5.

125. "Minutes of the Board of Directors," 21 December 1959, 2.

126. Kimberly-Clark Corporation, *Kimberly-Clark Report for Year Ended December 31, 1969* (Neenah, Wis.: Kimberly-Clark Corporation, 1970), 1.

127. "How Financial Community Leaders View Our Industry and Companies," *Paper Trade Journal,* 10 May 1971, 54.

128. Kimberly-Clark Corporation, *Kimberly-Clark Report for Year Ended December 31, 1970* (Neenah, Wis.: Kimberly-Clark Corporation, 1971), 3.

129. On Minard's background, see *Investor's Reader,* 3 July 1968, 19–20; "Kimberly-Clark Elects G. M. Minard President, J. R. Kimberly Chairman," *The Wall Street Journal,* 30 August 1967, 18.

130. "Kimberly-Clark Names Guy Minard Chief Officer," *The Wall Street Journal,* 12 April 1967, 14; "Five Kimberly-Clark Mills Are Closed by Two Striking Unions," *The Wall Street Journal,* 22 Aug. 1968, 6; "Kimberly-Clark, Union Locals Settle Strikes at 3 Plants," *The Wall Street Journal,* 30 Aug. 1968, 6; "Kimberly-Clark Appoints Guy Minard Chairman, Darwin Smith President," *The Wall Street Journal,* 29 April 1970, 16.

131. Kimberly-Clark Corporation, *Kimberly-Clark Report for Year Ended December 31, 1970* (Neenah, Wis.: Kimberly-Clark Corporation, 1971), 1.

132. Ibid., 2.

133. Ibid., 3.

134. Kimberly-Clark Corporation, *Kimberly-Clark Report for Year Ended December 31, 1970* (Neenah, Wis.: Kimberly-Clark Corporation, 1971), 1; "Kimberly-Clark Corp. Plant at Memphis Closed by Strike," *The Wall Street Journal,* 8 September 1970, 4; "Kimberly-Clark Stops Operations at 2 Plants in a Contract Dispute," *The Wall Street Journal,* 11 September 1970, 9; "Six-Week Strike Is Ended at Kimberly-Clark Facility," *The Wall Street Journal,* 27 October 1970, 40; "Kimberly-Clark Says Part Ends Strike by Two Unions," *The Wall Street Journal,* 7 December 1970, 21.

135. "How Financial Community Leaders View Our Industry and Companies," *Paper Trade Journal,* 10 May 1971, 53

136. Kimberly-Clark Corporation, *Kimberly-Clark Report for Year Ended December 31, 1971* (Neenah, Wis.: Kimberly-Clark Corporation, 1972).

137. Kimberly-Clark Corporation, *Kimberly-Clark Report for Year Ended December 31, 1971* (Neenah, Wis.: Kimberly-Clark Corporation, 1972).

Notes to Chapter 5

1. Cynthia Mitchell, "Paper Tiger," *The Wall Street Journal,* 23 July 1987, 1.

2. Ibid.

3. Kevin Kelly, "Darwin Smith May Have Done Too Good a Job," *Business Week,* 1 Aug. 1988, 52.

4. Jim Collins, *Good to Great: Why Some Companies Make the Leap . . . and Others Don't* (New York: Harper Business, 2001), 17–18.

5. Ibid., 20.

6. Board of Directors Minutes, 2 Aug. 1971, 2, Record Group 6, Series 1, Box 5, Folder 2, Kimberly-Clark Archives, The History Factory, Chantilly, Va.

7. Kimberly-Clark Corporation, Annual Report for 1971 (Neenah, Wis.: Kimberly-Clark Corporation, 1972).

8. Ibid.

9. "The Last Hurrah," *Forbes*, 15 Oct.1971, 24.

10. Board of Directors Minutes, 2 Aug. 1971, 2–3, Record Group 6, Series 1, Box 5, Folder 2.

11. Ibid.

12. Ibid.; "Kimberly-Clark and St. Regis Paper Plan to Sell or Close Down Four Paper Mills," *The New York Times*, 3 Aug. 1971, 40.

13. "Minard Retiring as Chief of Kimberly-Clark Corp., 3rd Quarter Net Sagged," *The Wall Street Journal*, 27 Oct. 1971, 65; "Sale of Plants Set by Kimberly-Clark," *The New York Times*, 31 Dec. 1971, 27.

14. Kimberly-Clark Corporation, Annual Report for 1971 (Neenah, Wis.: Kimberly-Clark Corporation, 1972).

15. "Kimberly-Clark Corp.," *The New York Times*, 4 Feb. 1972, 41; "Kimberly-Clark Expects Rise in Sales, Earnings to Continue to Year-End," *The Wall Street Journal*, 4 Oct. 1973, 10.

16. Kimberly-Clark Corporation, *Annual Report [for Year Ended 31 Dec. 1974]*, (Neenah, Wis.: Kimberly-Clark Corporation, 1975).

17. Board of Directors Minutes, 25 Feb. 1975, 7, Record Group 6, Series 1, Box 5, Folder 2.

18. *Chemical Week*, 11 Aug. 1976, 16. Other paper companies banked on labor-management cooperation to resolve similar problems; see Jill Kriesky and Edwin Brown, "The Union Role in Labor-Management Cooperation: A Case Study at the Boise Cascade Company's Jackson Mill," *Labor Studies Journal* 18 (1993), 17–32.

19. On Pentair's Niagara Falls investment, see "Pentair to Expand Wisconsin Mill," *The Wall Street Journal*, 25 Oct. 1979. On mill investments and market trends, "Publishers Are Scratching for Coated Paper," *Business Week*, 20 Aug. 1984, 33. On Repap, Robert Gibbens, "Repap Optimistic on Outlook," *Financial Times*, 4 June 1992, 32; Jan Ravensbergen, "Repap in 'Positive cash position after interest,' Petty says," *The Gazette* (Montreal), 19 June 1993, D3; Christopher Chipello, "Repap Out of the Woods," *The Wall Street Journal*, 1 June 1995, B4.

20. Quoted in "Hardly a Paper Tiger," *The New York Times*, 20 May 1973.

21. "Kimberly-Clark Closes Plant at Elizabeth, N.J.," *The Wall Street Journal*, 7 Jan. 1976, 16.

22. Gary Jacobson, "A Teamwork Ultimatum Puts Kimberly-Clark's Mill Back on the Map," *Management Review*, July 1989, 29.

23. "The Shrinking Press," *Newsweek*, 21 July 1975; "Kimberly-Clark Corp. to Spend $92 Million at Mill Over 3 Years," *The Wall Street Journal*, 2 May 1974; "Kimberly-Clark to Boost Newsprint Price $25 a Ton," *The Wall Street Journal*, 19 Nov. 1974, 40; "More Paper Workers Walk Out in Canada over Contract Issues," *The Wall Street Journal*, 15 Sept. 1975; "Kimberly-Clark Says Sales Set Record, Net Was Close in 1st Period," *The Wall Street Journal*, 12 April 1977; "Kimberly-Clark Lifts Price on Newsprint by $25 a Ton," *The New York Times*, 31 Jan. 1976. On Coosa Pines, "Kimberly-Clark Buys Plant to Power Newsprint Mill," *The Wall Street Journal*, 12 Aug. 1977, 5. On Kapuskasing, see Kimberly-Clark Corporation,

Annual Report [for Year Ended 31 Dec. 1979] (Neenah, Wis.: Kimberly-Clark Corporation, 1980), 7; Sept. 1975, 12 April 1977; Kimberly-Clark Corporation, *Annual Report [for Year Ended 31 Dec. 1985]* (Dallas: Kimberly-Clark Corporation, 1986), 4; see also Brett S. McMurran, "The Evolution of Market Structure in the North American Newsprint Paper Industry, 1870 to 1970," Ph.D. Dissertation, University of California, Riverside, 1988.

24. "Newsprint's Big Migration to the Sunbelt," *Business Week*, 2 Oct. 1978, 94; "Thermo-mechanical Pulping Gets Boost for Southeast," *Chemical Week*, 1 Sept. 1976, 40.

25. Kimberly-Clark Corporation, Annual *Report [for Year Ending 31 Dec. 1979]*, (Neenah, Wis.: Kimberly-Clark Corporation, 1980), 3.

26. "Lumber Is Finally Booming," *Business Week*, 18 Oct. 1976, 63; "Company News," *The New York Times*, 16 March 1979, Section 4, 4; "Kimberly-Clark Sells California Assets," 18 Sept. 1979, Section 4, 4; "Kimberly-Clark Moves toward a Possible Sale of West Coast Division," *The Wall Street Journal*, 11 July 1979, 33.

27. W. H. Drew, "Kimberly-Clark Corporation Involvement in the U.S. Feminine Hygiene Business (1970 through May 1987)," 1 July 1987, Record Group 9, Series 1, Subseries 6, Box 42 (oversize).

28. Quoted in "No Test for TV Ban," *The New York Times*, 24 Jan. 1972, 62.

29. W. H. Drew, "Kimberly-Clark Corporation Involvement in the U.S. Feminine Hygiene Business (1970 through May 1987)," 1 July 1987, Record Group 9, Series 1, Subseries 6, Box 42 (oversize); "Advertising: Tampax Turns to TV Commericals," *The New York Times*, 10 Jan. 1978, 54.

30. "Kotex Invents the Dry Napkin" [Product Advertisement], enclosed with "Kimberly-Clark–Kelly, Nason: Feminine Care Products Orientation Meeting," July 1974, RG 9, Series 3, Box 357, Folder 9.

31. Ibid.

32. Board of Directors Minutes, 26 Feb. 1974, 5, Record Group 6, Series 1, Box 5, Folder 2.

33. Cited in Jean A. Briggs, "The Paper Chase," *Forbes*, 10 Nov. 1980, 40.

34. Drew, "Kimberly-Clark Corporation Involvement."

35. Ibid.

36. New Freedom" [Product Advertisement], enclosed with "Kimberly-Clark–Kelly, Nason: Feminine Care Products Orientation Meeting," July 1974, Record Group 9, Series 3, Box 357, Folder 9.

37. Ibid.

38. Foote, Cone & Belding, "Four Girls," 16 June 1975, enclosed with "Kimberly-Clark–Kelly, Nason: Feminine Care Products Orientation Meeting," July 1974, Record Group 9, Series 3, Box 357, Folder 9.

39. Quoted in "Advertising: Dallas's Loss Is Needham's Gain," *The New York Times*, 6 Oct. 1975, 43.

40. W. H. Drew, "Kimberly-Clark Corporation Involvement in the U.S. Feminine Hygiene Business (1970 through May 1987)," 1 July 1987, 83, Record Group 9, Series 1, Subseries 6, Box 42 (oversize).

41. Quoted in "Tampon Brand Tied to Shock Syndrome," *The New York Times*, 18 September 1980, C3.

42. *Marketing*, 8 June 1995.

43. Janice Delany et al., *The Curse: A Cultural History of Menstruation,* Rev. Ed. (Urbana, Ill.: University of Illinois Press, 1988).

44. Briggs, "The Paper Chase," 40.

45. Quoted in Gregg Fields, "P&G Aims at 20-Percent Market Share with 'Always' Rollout," *Adweek* 14 May 1984.

46. Mark Potts, "P&G to Test-Market Feminine Hygiene Line," *Washington Post,* 8 Feb. 1983, D7.

47. W. H. Drew, "Kimberly-Clark Corporation Involvement in the U.S. Feminine Hygiene Business (1970 through May 1987)," 1 July 1987, 77, Record Group 9, Series 1, Subseries 6, Box 42 (oversize).

48. Ibid.

49. Ibid.

50. John H. Allan, "Pampers and Profits at P.&G.," *The New York Times,* 25 Feb. 1973, Section 3, 1.

51. Liz Armstrong and Adrienne Scott, *Whitewash: Exposing the Health and Environmental Dangers of Women's Sanitary Products and Disposable Diapers: What You Can Do about It* (Toronto: Harper Perennial, 1992).

52. United States Patent Office, Patent Number 3,196,874, Filed 27 July 1965; "Chart of Significant Events and Concurrent Assignments—K-C Disposable Diaper History, 1966–1975," (1975) [no pagination], Record Group 9, Series 1, Box 4, Folder 2 (oversize).

53. United States Patent Office, Patent Number 3,196,874, Filed 27 July 1965.

54. "Chart of Significant Events and Concurrent Assignments—K-C Disposable Diaper History, 1966–1975" (1975) [no pagination], Record Group 9, Series 1, Box 4, Folder 2 (oversize).

55. Ibid.

56. Board of Directors Minutes, 29 June 1971, 3; 27 Feb. 1973, 7, Record Group 6, Series 1, Box 5, Folder 2. "Chart of Significant Events and Concurrent Assignments—K-C Disposable Diaper History, 1966–1975" (1975) [no pagination], Record Group 9, Series 1, Box 4, Folder 2 (oversize).

57. "Chart of Significant Events and Concurrent Assignments—K-C Disposable Diaper History, 1966–1975" (1975) [no pagination], Record Group 9, Series 1, Box 4, Folder 2 (oversize).

58. Ibid.; Gary Jacobson, "K-C Never Gets Too Large for Smith's Personal Style," *Post-Crescent* (Wisconsin), 8 March 1987, D4.

59. Susan Windisch Brown, "Huggies," in *Encyclopedia of Consumer Brands,* vol. 2, Janice Jorgensen, ed. (Detroit: St. James Press, 1994), 271; Evelyn S. Dorman, "Pampers," in *Encyclopedia of Consumer Brands,* vol. 2, Janice Jorgensen, ed. (Detroit: St. James Press, 1994), 404; Larry Edwards, "Premium Diapers Gear for Eastern Clash," *Advertising Age,* 25 Sept. 1978, 136.

60. "Chart of Significant Events and Concurrent Assignments—K-C Disposable Diaper History, 1966–1975" (1975) [no pagination], Record Group 9, Series 1, Box 4, Folder 2 (oversize).

61. United States Patent Office, Patent Number 4,050,462, Filed 29 March July 1977.

62. Ibid.

63. "Huggies—The Philadelphia Plan," Record Group 9, Series 3, Box 4, Folder 15.

64. David Ogilvy, *Blood, Brain, and Beer: An Autobiography* (New York: Wiley, 1997).

65. "Huggies—The Diaper That Stops Leaks" [Product Advertisement], enclosed with "Huggies—The Philadelphia Plan," Record Group 9, Series 3, Box 4, Folder 15.

66. "Here's Great News" [Product Promotion], enclosed with "Huggies—The Philadelphia Plan," Record Group 9, Series 3, Box 4, Folder 15.

67. Anonymous from Brownsville, Ill., to Kimberly Clark Corp., 6 Feb. 1978, enclosed with "Huggies—The Philadelphia Plan," Record Group 9, Series 3, Box 4, Folder 15.

68. Ibid.

69. "Diaper Rash at Johnson & Johnson," *Business Week*, 16 June 1980, 63.

70. Ibid.

71. Kenneth Noble, "Johnson to Phase Out U.S. Diaper Business," *The New York Times*, 12 Feb. 1981, D5.

72. Larry Edwards, "Luvs Beats Huggies across U.S.," *Advertising Age*, 16 June 1980, 3; Zachary Schiller and Amy Dunkin, "P&G's Rusty Marketing Machine," *Business Week*, 21 Oct. 1985, 111.

73. Quoted in Larry Edwards, "Luvs Beats Huggies across U.S.," *Advertising Age*, 16 June 1980, 3.

74. Brown, "Huggies," 271.

75. "The Procter & Gamble Company, Plaintiff, v. Kimberly-Clark Corporation, Defendant," Civil Action No. 2:87-0047-1, 740 F. Supp. 1177, 8.

76. Ibid.; Zachary Schiller and Jerome Zukosky, "Procter & Gamble Banks on a New Baby: Ultra Pampers," *Business Week*, 24 Feb. 1986, 36; Zachary Schiller, "At Home, P&G Is Bouncing Back," *Business Week*, 13 Oct. 1986, 74.

77. "Kimberly-Clark Wins in Suit against Procter & Gamble," *Adweek*, 27 July 1987; Martin Friedman, "Baby Tech: His-and-Hers Diapers, Crumb-Proof Bibs," *Adweek*, 21 Nov. 1988.

78. Fara Warner, "'Pull-Ups' Are a Hit, But Where's P&G?" *Brandweek*, 5 Aug. 1991, 10.

79. Ibid.

80. Stephanie Anderson Forest, "Kimberly-Clark's European Paper Chase," *Business Week*, 16 March 1992, 94; Robert McMath, "Marketers Seek Ways to Shed the 'Me-Too' Tag," *Adweek*, 8 Jan. 1990, 17; Hanna Liebman, "Drypers Training Pants: In Pursuit of Pull-Ups," *Adweek*, 7 Sept. 1992.

81. Quoted in Dorman, "Pampers," 406.

82. Schiller and Dunkin, "P&G's Rusty Marketing Machine," 111; "Luvs on the Rocks," *Brandweek*, 4 April 1994, 1.

83. Quoted in Gary Jacobson, "K-C Never Gets Too Large for Smith's Personal Style," *Post-Crescent* (Wisconsin), 8 March 1987, D4.

84. Alfred D. Chandler, Jr., "The Competitive Performance of U.S. Industrial Enterprise Since the Second World War," *Business History Review* 68 (1994), 47–73.

85. Ibid.; Allen Kaufman and Ernest J. Englander, "Kohlberg Kravis Roberts & Co. and the Restructuring of American Capitalism," *Business History Review* 67 (1993), 52–97; George Baker and George Smith, *The New Financial Capitalists: Kohlberg Kravis Roberts and the Creation of Corporate Value* (New York: Cambridge University Press, 1998); Bennett Harrison, *Lean and Mean: The Changing*

Landscape of Corporate Power in the Age of Flexibility (New York: Berz Books, 1994).

86. David G. Santry, "Analysts scowl at International Paper," *Business Week*, 13 Nov. 1978, 148 (quote); International Paper Company, *Annual Report [for Year Ending Dec. 31, 1971]* (New York: International Paper Company, 1972); International Paper Company, *Annual Report [for Year Ended Dec. 31, 1975]* (New York: International Paper Company, 1976); International Paper Company, *Annual Report [for Year Ended Dec. 31, 1978]* (New York: International Paper Company, 1978); International Paper Company, *Annual Report [for Year Ended Dec. 31, 1979]* (New York, 1979); "Paper: Toughening Out a Slump in Demand," *Business Week,* 9 Jan. 1978, 52–53; "International Paper Lands a Water Expert," *Business Week*, 30 Jan. 1978, 25; Jack P. Oden, "Development of the Southern Pulp and Paper Industry, 1900–1970," Ph. D. Dissertation, Mississippi State University, 1973.

87. Cited in Gene Marcial, "What Weighs International Paper Down," *Business Week*, 14 March 1984, 167.

88. "International Paper Spins Off to Grow," *Business Week*, 19 March 1979, 34; "International Paper Intends to Place Timberland in New Limited Partnership," *Wall Street Journal*, 20 Dec. 1984, 2; "Business Briefs," *Wall Street Journal*, 23 Dec. 1985, 10; Bruce Nussbaum and Judith H. Dobrzynski, "The Battle for Corporate Control," *Business Week*, 18 May 1987, 102; Christopher Power and Vicky Cahan, "Shareholders Aren't Just Rolling Over Anymore," *Business Week*, 27 April 1987, 32.

89. "Now an Outsider Will Run Scott Paper," *Business Week* 23 April 1979, 39.

90. "'Mistakes' at Scott Paper," *Business Week*, 1 Dec. 1981.

91. Scott Paper Company, *Annual Report [for Year Ended Dec. 31, 1969]*, (Philadelphia: Scott Paper Company, 1970), 2–3, 12–13; Scott Paper Company, *Annual Report [for Year Ended Dec. 31, 1975]* (Philadelphia: Scott Paper Company, 1976), 2; Scott Paper Company, *Annual Report [for Year Ended Dec. 31, 1980]* (Philadelphia, 1981), 2–3; Jim Hyatt and John E. Cooney, "How Procter & Gamble Put the Big Squeeze on Scott Paper Co.," *The Wall Street Journal*, 20 October 1971, 1; "Brascan's Bigger Share," *Business Week*, 6 April 1981, 40; "Scott's Crafty Capital Spending Push," *Business Week*, 8 March 1982, 91; Terry Byland, "Major Scott Paper Sales Show New Group Strategy," *Financial Times*, 24 Aug. 1983, 11; Judith H. Dorbrzynski, "Scott Paper Ends a Takeover Threat."

92. "Crown-Zellerbach: Sir James Arrives with his Axe," *Economist* (London), 3 Aug. 1985, 64.

93. Kaufman and Englander, "Kohlberg Kravis Roberts," 52–97; Baker and Smith, *New Financial Capitalists* (New York: Cambridge University Press, 1998). For a more pessimistic view, see George Anders, *Merchants of Debt: KKR and the Mortgaging of American Business* (New York: Berz Books, 1992); Bennett Harrison, *Lean and Mean: The Changing Landscape of Corporate Power in the Age of Flexibility* (1994); Max Hollander, *When the Machine Stopped: A Cautionary Tale from Industrial America* (Boston: Harvard Business School Press, 1989). On hostile takeovers in the paper and consumer industries, "Grand Union: Jimmy Goldsmith's Maverick Plan to Restore Profitability," *Business Week*, 14 May 1984, 188–90; Jonathan B. Levine and Judith H. Dobrzynski, "Crown Digs in against Sir Jimmy," *Business Week*, 15 April 1985, 45; "A Setback for a Black Knight," *Maclean's*, 6 May 1985, 46; "International Paper Pays a Fancy Price for a Fancy Paper Maker,"

Business Week, 1 Sept. 1986, 69.

94. Kimberly-Clark Corporation, *Annual Report [for Year Ended Dec. 31, 1978]* (Neenah, Wis.: Kimberly-Clark Corporation, 1979), 2.

95. "Earnings That Go Up and Up," *U.S. News & World Report*, 8 Nov. 1982, 70.

96. For an overview of multinational operations, see Kimberly-Clark, *Annual Report [for Year Ended Dec. 31, 1981]—Supplemental Data* (Neenah, Wis.: Kimberly-Clark Corporation, 1982); on Mexican crisis, Kimberly-Clark, *Annual Report [for Year Ended Dec. 31, 1982]* (Neenah, Wis.: Kimberly-Clark Corporation, 1983), 6–8; "Company Briefs," *The New York Times*, 24 June 1980, D1.

97. Kimberly-Clark Corporation, *Annual Report [for Year Ended Dec. 31, 1984]* (Neenah, Wis.: Kimberly-Clark Corporation, 1985), 6.

98. "Huggable Shares," *Forbes*, 29 May 1989.

99. Jean A. Briggs, "The Paper Chase," *Forbes*, 10 Nov. 1980, 40.

100. Quoted in "Corporate Critics Confidential: Forest Products/Paper Industry," *Wall Street Transcript*, 1990; see also "Earnings That Go Up and Up," *U.S. News & World Report*, 8 Nov. 1982, 70.

101. Quoted in Kevin Kelly, "Darwin Smith May Have Done Too Good a Job," *Business Week*, 1 Aug. 1988, 52.

102. Alison Leigh Cowan, "The Lure of Stock Buybacks," *The New York Times*, 5 March 1987, D1; Kevin Kelly, "Darwin Smith May Have Done Too Good a Job," *Business Week*, 1 Aug. 1988, 52.

Notes to Epilogue

1. Richard P. Rumelt, *Strategy, Structure, and Economic Performance* (Boston, Mass., 1986); Alfred D. Chandler, Jr., *Scale and Scope: The Dynamics of Industrial Capitalism* (Boston: Harvard Business School Press, 1990).

2. For a different analytical approach, see Constantinos C. Markides, *Diversification, Refocusing, and Economic Performance* (Cambridge: Cambridge University Press, 1995).

3. Michael Bernstein, *The Great Depression: Delayed Recovery and Economic Change in America, 1929–1939* (Cambridge: Cambridge University Press, 1987), 30.

4. Michael Bernstein, "Why the Great Depression Was Great: Toward a New Understanding of the Interwar Economic Crisis in the United States," *The Rise and Fall of the New Deal Order, 1930–1980*, eds. Steve Fraser and Gary Gerstle (Princeton: Princeton University Press, 1980), 34–35.

5. Alfred D. Chandler, Jr., "The Competitive Performance of U.S. Industrial Enterprises since the Second World War," *Business History Review* 68 (1994), 1–72; for an interesting case study of overdiversification, see Gordon Donaldson, "Voluntary Restructuring: The Case of General Mills," *Journal of Financial Economics* 27 (1990), 117–41.

6. Carliss Y. Baldwin and Kim B. Clark, "Capital Budgeting Systems and Capabilities Investments in U.S. Companies after the Second World War," *Business History Review* 68 (1994), 79; see also Chandler, "Competitive Performance," 43–57; and Coleman H. Wells, "Remapping America: Market Research and American Society, 1900–1940," Ph.D. Dissertation (University of Virginia, 1999).

7. Quoted in Stephanie Anderson Forest, "Kimberly-Clark's European Paper Chase," *Business Week*, 16 March 1992, 94.

8. Alan Mitchell, "Huggies to Wage War on Pampers: Nappies," *Marketing*, 25 Feb. 1993.

9. Quoted in Stephanie Anderson Forest, "Kimberly-Clark's European Paper Chase," *Business Week*, 16 March 1992, 94.

10. Jack Neff, "Kimberly-Clark Finally Reaps Boon from Scott," *Advertising Age*, 8 Nov. 1999, 24.

Bibliography

Books

Eleanor Amigo and Mark Neuffer, *Beyond the Adirondacks: The Story of the St. Regis Paper Company* (Westport, Conn.: Greenwood Press, 1980).

George Baker and George Smith, *The New Financial Capitalists: Kohlberg Kravis Roberts and the Creation of Corporate Value* (Cambridge: Cambridge University Press, 1998).

Richard Bartlett, *Troubled Waters: Champion International and the Pigeon River Controversy* (Knoxville: University of Tennessee Press, 1995).

Susan Porter Benson, *Counter Cultures: Saleswomen, Managers, and Customers in American Department Stores, 1890–1940* (Champaign: University of Illinois Press, 1986).

Michael Bernstein, *The Great Depression: Delayed Recovery and Economic Change in America, 1929–1939* (Cambridge: Cambridge University Press, 1987).

Joan Brumberg, *The Body Project: An Intimate History of American Girls* (New York: Vintage Books, 1997).

Alfred Chandler, Jr., *Pierre S. DuPont and the Making of the Modern Corporation* (New York: Harper & Row, 1971).

Alfred Chandler, Jr., *The Visible Hand: The Managerial Revolution in American Business* (Weatogue, Conn.: Belknap Press, 1977).

Alfred Chandler, Jr., *Scale and Scope: The Dynamics of Industrial Capitalism* (Weatogue, Conn.: Belknap Press, 1995).

Hugh Chisholm, *A Man and the Paper Industry: Hugh J. Chisholm (1847–1912)* (Exton, Pa.: Newcomen Society in North America, 1952).

Encyclopedia of Consumer Brands, Vol. 2: Personal Products, ed. Janice Jorgensen (Detroit: St. James Press, 1994).

Paula Fass, *The Damned and the Beautiful: American Youth in the 1920s* (New York: Oxford University Press, 1977).

Charles N. Glaab and Lawrence H. Larsen, *Factories in the Valley: Neenah-Menasha, 1870–1915* (Madison: State Historical Society of Wisconsin, 1969).

Jürgen Habermas, *Theorie des kommnikativen Handelns, II* (Frankfurt, Germany: Suhrkamp, 1988).

Bennett Harrison, *Lean and Mean: The Changing Landscape of Corporate Power in the Age of Flexibility* (New York: Basic Books, 1994).

Thomas Heinrich, *Ships for the Seven Seas: Philadelphia Shipbuilding in the Age of Industrial Capitalism* (Baltimore: Johns Hopkins University Press, 1997).

Richard S. Hodgson, *In Quiet Ways: George H. Mead, The Man and the Company* (Dayton, Ohio: Mead Corporation, 1970).

John Hoerr, *And the Wolf Finally Came: The Decline of the American Steel Industry* (Pittsburgh: University of Pittsburgh Press, 1988).

Max Hollander, *When the Machine Stopped: A Cautionary Tale from Industrial America* (Boston: Harvard Business School Press, 1989).

Morton Horwitz, *The Transformation of American Law, 1870–1960: The Crisis of Legal Orthodoxy* (Cambridge: Oxford University Press, 1992).

David Hounshell, *From the American System to Mass Production, 1800–1932: The Development of Manufacturing Technology in the United States* (Baltimore: Johns Hopkins University Press, 1984).

David Hounshell, *Science and Corporate Strategy: DuPont R&D, 1902–1980* (Cambridge: Cambridge University Press, 1988).

Sanford Jacoby, *Modern Manors: Welfare Capitalism since the New Deal* (Princeton: Princeton University Press, 1997).

Corrine Krause, *Grandmothers, Mothers, and Daughters: An Oral History of Ethnicity, Mental Health and Continuity of Three Generations of Jewish, Italian, and Slavic Women* (Boston: Twayne Publishers, 1991).

Arthur Kuhn, *GM Passes Ford, 1918–1938: Designing the General Motors Performance-Control System* (University Park: Pennsylvania State University Press, 1986).

Pamela W. Laird, *Advertising Progress: American Business and the Rise of Consumer Marketing* (Baltimore: Johns Hopkins University Press, 1998).

Gary Bryan Magee, *Productivity and Performance in the Paper Industry: Labour, Capital, and Technology in Britain and America, 1860–1914* (Cambridge: Cambridge University Press, 1997).

Roland Marchand, *Advertising the American Dream: Making Way for Modernity, 1920–1940* (Berkeley: University of California Press, 1985).

Judith McGaw, *Most Wonderful Machine: Mechanization and Social Change in Berkshire Paper Making, 1801–1885* (Princeton: Princeton University Press, 1987).

Daniel Nelson, *Managers and Workers: Origins of the Twentieth-Century Factory System in the United States, 1880–1920* (Madison: University of Wisconsin Press, 1995).

Nancy Kane Ohanian, *The American Pulp and Paper Industry, 1900–1940: Mill Survival, Firm Structure, and Industry Relocation* (Westport, Conn.: Greenwood Press, 1993).

The Rise and Fall of the New Deal Order, 1930–1980, eds. Steve Fraser and Gary Gerstle (Princeton: Princeton University Press, 1980).

Richard P. Rumelt, *Strategy, Structure, and Economic Performance* (Boston: Harvard Business School Press, 1986).

Oscar Schisgall, *Eyes on Tomorrow: The Evolution of Procter & Gamble* (Chicago: J. G. Ferguson, 1981).

Philip Scranton, *Proprietary Capitalism: The Textile Manufacture at Philadelphia, 1800–1885* (Cambridge: Cambridge University Press, 1983).

Philip Scranton, *Endless Novelty: Specialty Production and American Industrialization, 1865–1925* (1997).

David C. Smith, *History of Papermaking in the United States (1691–1969)* (New York: Lockwood, 1970).

Charles R. Spruill, *Conglomerates and the Evolution of Capitalism* (Carbondale: Southern Illinois University Press, 1982).

Vincent Vinikas, *Soft Soap, Hard Sell: American Hygiene in an Age of Advertisement* (Ames: Iowa State University Press, 1992).

Robert H. Zieger, *Rebuilding the Pulp and Paper Workers' Union, 1933–1941* (Knoxville: University of Tennessee Press, 1984).

Articles and Dissertations

Philip Sayre Adkins, "The Impact of Government and Technology on Business and Labor in the Pulp and Paper Industry: A Case Study of the Pensacola Paper Firms, 1940–1985," Ph.D. Dissertation, Florida State University, 1999.

Rima Apple, "'They Need it Now': Science, Advertising, and Vitamins," *Journal of Popular Culture* 22 (1988), 65–83.

Carliss Y. Baldwin and Kim B. Clark, "Capital Budgeting Systems and Capabilities Investment in U.S. Companies after the Second World War," *Business History Review* 68 (1994), 73–109.

Megan Benton, "Sizzle and Smoke: Iconography of Books and Reading in Modern American Advertising," *Publishing History* 38 (1995), 77–90.

Barry E. C. Boothman, "High Finance/Low Strategy: Corporate Collapse in the Canadian Pulp and Paper Industry, 1919–1932," *Business History Review* 74 (2000), 611–56.

Elspeth Brown, "Rationalizing Consumption: LeJaren A. Hiller and the Origins of American Advertising Photography," *Enterprise and Society* 1 (2000), 715–38.

Stephen Cernek, "Beyond the Return to Normalcy: The Decline of Organized Paperworkers, 1921–26," Ph.D. Dissertation, Ball State University, 1978.

John H. Church, "Determinants of the Performance and Development of the Canadian Newsprint Industry, 1920 to 1970," Ph.D. Dissertation, University of Western Ontario, 1978.

Avi Cohen, "The Economic Determination of Technological Change: A Theoretical Framework and a Case Study of the U.S. Pulp and Paper Industry, 1915–1940," Ph.D. Dissertation, Stanford University, 1993

Avi Cohen, Technological Change as Historical Process: The Case of the U.S. Pulp and Paper Industry, 1915–1940," *Journal of Economic History* 44 (Autumn 1984): 775–99.

Susan E. Dick and Mandi D. Johnson, "The Smell of Money: The Pulp and Paper-Making Industry in Savannah, 1931–1947," *Georgia Historical Quarterly*.

Trevor Dick, "Canadian Newsprint, 1913–1930: National Policies and the North American Economy," *Journal of Economic History* 42 (1982), 659–87.

Jane Farrell-Beck and Laura Kidd, "The Roles of Health Professionals in the Development and Dissemination of Women's Sanitary Products, 1880–1940," *Journal of the History of Medicine and Allied Sciences* 51 (1996), 325–52.

Martha Feldmann, "Never Underestimate Empowerment Consumption: Women and Advertising in the *Ladies' Home Journal* from the 1880's through the 1920's," Ph.D. Dissertation, Memphis State University, 1991.

Elizabeth Fones-Wolf, "Creating a Favorable Business Climate: Corporations and Radio Broadcasting, 1934 to 1954," *Business History Review* 73 (1999), 221–55.

Bonnie Fox, "Selling the Mechanized Household: 70 Years of Ads in *Ladies' Home Journal*," *Gender and Society* 4 (1990), 25–40.

Mike Freeman, "Clarence Saunders: The Piggly Wiggly Man," *Tennessee Historical Quarterly* 51 (1992), 161–69.

Charles N. Glaab and Lawrence H. Larsen, "Neenah-Menasha in the 1870s: The Development of Flour Milling and Papermaking," *Wisconsin Magazine of History* 52 (1968), 19–34.

Jill Kriesky and Edwin Brown, "The Union Role in Labor-Management Cooperation: A Case Study at the Boise Cascade Company's Jackson Mill," *Labor Studies Journal* 18 (1993), 17–32.

Thomas Heinrich, "Product Diversification in the U.S. Pulp and Paper Industry: The Case of International Paper," *Business History Review* 75 (2001), 467–505.

James P. Hull, "Strictly by the Book: Textbooks and the Control of Production in the North American Pulp and Paper Industry," *History of Education* 27 (1998), 85–95.

Herb Kaplan and Rick Houlberg, "Broadcast Condom Advertising: A Case Study," *Journalism Quarterly* 67 (1990), 171–76.

John R. Kimberly, "Better to Use, Cheap Enough to Throw Away: The Disposable Paper Product," *Business Decisions That Changed Our Lives*, eds. Sidney Furst and Milton Sherman (New York, 1964), 162.

Mark Kuhlberg, "We Have 'Sold' Forestry to the Management of the Company: Abitibi Power & Paper Company's Forestry Initiatives in Ontario, 1919–1929," *Journal of Canadian Studies* 34 (1999), 187–209.

Gary Bryan Magee, "Technological Divergence in a Continuous Flow Production Industry: American and British Papermaking in the Late Victorian and Edwardian Era," *Business History* 39 (1997), 21–46.

Brett S. McMurran, "The Evolution of Market Structure in the North American Newsprint Paper Industry, 1870 to 1970," Ph.D. Dissertation, University of California, Riverside, 1988.

John Morello, "Candidates, Consumers, and Closers: Albert Lasker, Advertising, and Politics," Ph.D. Dissertation, University of Illinois, Chicago, 1998.

Jack P. Oden, "Development of the Southern Pulp and Paper Industry, 1900–1970," Ph.D. Dissertation, Mississippi State University, 1973.

Jack P. Oden, "Origins of the Southern Kraft Paper Industry, 1903–1930," *Mississippi Quarterly* 30 (1977), 565–84.

Martha Olney, "Consumer Durables in the Interwar Years: New Estimates, New Patterns," *Research in Economic History* 12 (1989), 119–50.

Martha Olney, "Demand for Consumer Durable Goods in 20th Century America," *Explorations in Economic History* 27 (1990), 322–49.

Kent Osband, "The Boll Weevil vs. King Cotton," *Journal of Economic History* 45 (1985), 627–43.

Bill Parentau, "The Woods Transformed: The Emergence of the Pulp and Paper Industry in New Brunswick, 1918–1931," *Acadiensis* 22 (1992), 5–43.

Christina Romer, "The Great Crash and the Onset of the Great Depression," *Quarterly Journal of Economics* 105 (1999), 597–624.

John Staudenmaier and Pamela Laird, "Advertising History," *Technology and Culture* 30 (1989).

Susan Smulyan, "'And Now a Word from Our Sponsors . . . ': Commercialization of American Broadcast Radio, 1920–1934," Ph.D Dissertation, Yale University, 1986.

Thomas W. Steele, "Capacity Expansion and Strategic Behavior in the Canadian–United States Newsprint Industry," Ph.D. Dissertation, University of Wisconsin, Madison, 1995.

Robert H. Zieger, "The Limits of Militancy: Organizing Paper Workers, 1933–1935," *Journal of American History* 33 (1976), 638–57.

Index

HISTORICAL PERSPECTIVES ON BUSINESS ENTERPRISE
Mansel G. Blackford and K. Austin Kerr, Series Editors

The scope of this series includes scholarly interest in the history of the firm, the history of government-business relations, and the relationship between business and culture, both in the United States and abroad. Included are histories of individual companies and biographies of business people.